SHOTS IN THE MIRROR

SHOTS IN THE MIRROR
Crime Films and Society
Second Edition

Nicole Rafter

UNIVERSITY PRESS

2006

OXFORD
UNIVERSITY PRESS

Oxford University Press, Inc., publishes works that further
Oxford University's objective of excellence
in research, scholarship, and education.

Oxford   New York
Auckland   Cape Town   Dar es Salaam   Hong Kong   Karachi
Kuala Lumpur   Madrid   Melbourne   Mexico City   Nairobi
New Delhi   Shanghai   Taipei   Toronto

With offices in
Argentina   Austria   Brazil   Chile   Czech Republic   France   Greece
Guatemala   Hungary   Italy   Japan   Poland   Portugal   Singapore
South Korea   Switzerland   Thailand   Turkey   Ukraine   Vietnam

Published by Oxford University Press, Inc.
198 Madison Avenue, New York, New York 10016

www.oup.com

Oxford is a registered trademark of Oxford University Press

Library of Congress Cataloging-in-Publication Data
Rafter, Nicole Hahn, 1939–
  Shots in the mirror : crime films and society / Nicole Rafter.—2nd ed.
    p.   cm.
  Includes bibliographical references and index.
  ISBN-13 978-0-19-517505-9; 978-0-19-517506-6 (pbk.)
    1. Gangster films—History and criticism.   2. Police films—History and
criticism.   3. Prison films—History and criticism.   4. Justice, Administration
of, in motion pictures.   5. Motion pictures—Social aspects—United States.
I. Title.
PN1995.9.G3R34 2005
791.43'6556—dc22   2005015262

9 8 7 6 5 4 3 2

Printed in the United States of America
on acid-free paper

ONCE AGAIN,
FOR ALEX HAHN

Preface to the Second Edition

When I told a colleague I was writing a book on crime films, he said, "Oh, I don't like that stuff—children shouldn't be exposed to so much blood and gore." In a sense, this book is my response. Crime films are one of the world's most effective means of debating issues of crime and justice. Creating a common language familiar the world over, they invite us to participate in global examinations of social problems while keeping us entertained. Crime films, in truth, are not a problem but a response to problems, a way of posing questions and evaluating solutions. They are also, significantly, a great source of shared pleasure, for adults and children alike.

Happily, the favorable response to the first edition of this book suggests that many readers agree with me. Thus, I am delighted to be introducing this second edition, both because working on it has persuaded me more than ever of the importance of a critical study of crime films and because I now have another opportunity to identify and discuss changes occurring in this field. Although I continue to define crime films as a category that includes movies of any type in which crime or its consequences play central roles, genre transformations, which have dated some of the generalizations I offered just a few years ago, call for a rethinking of categories and reframing of theory.

Specifically, this new edition of *Shots in the Mirror* gives me an opportunity to address four issues that have been on my mind since the book was first published. The first is the meaning of the recent spate of serial killer movies—films such as *American Psycho, Dahmer, Gacy, Hannibal,* and *Red Dragon*—whose flat, vampire-like characters and episodic plots contrast markedly with the carefully crafted psychological studies of earlier repeat-killer movies (*The Boston Strangler,* for example, or *Psycho*). What roles do these new superpredator films play in debates about crime? Do their images of violent, repetitive victimization relate to current U.S. policies for the containment of dangerous criminals? What is their genealogical relationship to the movies they resemble most closely: teen horror flicks of the *Friday the 13th* variety? These questions led me to include a new chapter in which I discuss serial killer, slasher, and psycho films as different types of cinematic discourse, each with a distinctive history, audience, and message about social order.

Second, the new edition has given me an opportunity to explore one of the most intriguing phenomena in recent cinema, the appearance of films that insist on moral uncertainty. Earlier crime movies usually assumed a social consensus about right and wrong, guilt and punishment; and so do many of today's crime films—those that stick to tradition. But others—those that I call alternative-tradition or critical crime films—assume a world of moral ambiguity, and they are being released in increasing numbers. Some have no hero at all while others feature a hero who is searching for an elusive moral clarity. *Mystic River* (2003), one of the best-known examples, makes no attempt to reconcile its central clash between the values of an insular community and those of the formal justice system. In *Collateral* (2004), the cab-driver victim survives and even saves the beautiful young woman, but the movie ends with him heading off into an uncertain future and the dead shooter circling an empty city in an empty train. *Capturing the Friedmans,* the 2003 documentary, puts viewers in the position of searchers, forcing us to quest for clarity in a world that denies final truths. This second edition includes a full chapter on recent films of moral ambiguity, concentrating in particular on a subset concerned with sex crime and sexual deviation.

Third, I have used the new edition to track changes in traditional crime film genres and discover how these developments affect what movies tell us about crime, law, and social control. The familiar genres— cop films, courtroom dramas, prison movies—are in a state of flux, with new forms emerging as the older genres recombine and mutate. The most significant change, and the one to which I here give the most attention, is the evolution of the old courtroom drama into a new type of law film that meditates on the nature of criminal law without recourse to courtroom scenes and even, in some cases, without characters who are lawyers.

Fourth, I have used this edition as an opportunity to address a basic epistemological issue raised by both my title and central thesis: If crime films and society are indeed engaged in a feedback loop of endless, mirrorlike reflections, then how might this work on the individual level? What do viewers learn from crime films? What is our relationship to the phenomenon called popular culture, and to what extent is that a participatory relationship that can be mediated by movies? Drawing on work in psychology and the sociology of culture, in the introduction I propose a model of movies as a source of cultural information, some of which feeds into our ideologies and other mental constructs. In chapter 2, I draw on this model to explain why movies themselves can never be a direct cause of crime. Movies can affect behavior, but only indirectly, through contributing to our tool kits of narratives and beliefs.

This new edition omits the first edition's final chapter on the future of crime films. (Many of my predictions came to pass, and some—such as the casting of people of color in central, heroic roles in mainstream movies—more quickly than I'd expected.) I have replaced it with the two new chapters on recent films of moral ambiguity and on serial killer, slasher, and psycho movies. I have revised and updated the other chapters to include recent films and identify trends. While my emphasis remains on Hollywood films, this new edition expands the focus to include movies made outside of the United States, including those such as *Breathless, The Bicycle Thief, M,* and *Rashomon* which are among the acknowledged classics of the field.

This edition, like the last, has relied on the help of Drew Todd, a film instructor at Suffolk University, specialist in movie history, and author of the chapter on the history of crime films. I am also grateful to students in my crime films courses, who introduced me to movies I might otherwise have missed and helped me grasp what *crime films* means to those whose cinema life did not seriously start until the late 1990s. My editors at Oxford University Press, Shannon McLachlan and Elissa Morris, have been efficient and tactful guides. I have also benefited from conversations with Dedi Felman, Oxford's law books editor. Susette Talarico of the University of Georgia, instructor of one of the first crime films courses in the country, enabled me to meet with her students and pick their brains about my approach; she also gave me detailed feedback on chapters 5 and 8 and, more generally, strongly supported this project from the start. Cecil Greek of the Florida State University School of Criminology and Criminal Justice forwarded his students' comments on the first edition, a great help as I revised; in addition, he and his colleague Caroline Joan (Kay) Picart generously shared unpublished materials on crime films. Similarly, Russell Campbell of the University of Victoria, Wellington, kindly shared chapters from his forthcoming *Marked Women: Prostitutes and Prostitution in the Cinema* (University of Wisconsin Press). Others who contributed to this second edition are Gwen Booth of Oxford University Press,

England; Ros Burnett of Oxford University's Centre for Criminological Research; Steve Chermak and Michelle Brown of Indiana University; Laura Frader and Simon Singer of Northeastern University; Michael Freeman of University College, London; Elizabeth Horan of Arizona State University; Rebecca A. Singer of Brookline, Massachusetts; Giovanni Tiso of the University of Victoria, Wellingon; Suzanne and Tony Whedon of East Berkshire, Vermont; and Oxford's anonymous reviewers of my proposal for the new edition. I owe my greatest debt to the usual suspects—my favorite viewing companions and indefatigable editors, Alex Hahn, Robert Hahn, and Sarah Hahn.

Preface to the First Edition

Some will say I wrote this book so I could spend a couple of years watching movies. While there may be some truth to that, I prefer to think that the book grew out of my misgivings about the way my colleagues and I were teaching criminology courses. Ignoring almost every other source of information on crime and criminals, we concentrated on the sociological literature. Although I slipped in bits of history from time to time and assigned an occasional short story or film to stimulate discussions, I knew I was not satisfying my students' hunger (one I discovered almost daily during office hours) to talk about criminological issues raised by movies. Films were clearly one of the wellheads of their ideas about legality and illegality, the volume of various types of crime, and the motives of lawbreakers. Uneasy about this gap between the classroom and daily life, I designed a course called "Crime Films and Society."

I soon found, however, that there was only one book on the subject and that it in fact mainly discussed gangster movies, whereas I wanted to cover cop, trial, and prison films as well. Since then a few studies on crime and the media have appeared, but none deals exclusively with movies. (Indeed, most of them concentrate on news media and television.) I needed a book that would take the messages of crime films seriously and uncover not inaccuracies in their depiction of crime but their central themes and ideologies. I wanted to know what crime films say about law, why they so often turn criminals into heroes, and why audiences of all ages and genders find them deeply enjoyable. So I wrote this book.

Movies have become the central vehicle for the dissemination of popular culture in the United States. Due to the globalization of film markets, movies also play a major role internationally in the dispersion of images, myths, and values. For many of us, they are a significant source—perhaps the most significant source—of ideas about crime and criminals. Thus, it seems important for ordinary moviegoers to know something about the history of crime films, how they interrelate with society, what they say about the causes of crime, and the moral valences of their criminal heroes. I have written this book for general readers as well as students in courses on criminology and film, and I have sentenced scholarly debates to solitary confinement in the footnotes. Everyone watches crime movies, and I would like the text to be as accessible as movies themselves, one of our most democratic forms of entertainment.

The American Film Institute's 1998 list of the hundred top movies names nineteen crime films, including *The Godfather* (no. 3 on the list), *Sunset Boulevard* (no. 12), *Psycho* (no. 18), *Chinatown* (no. 19), *The Maltese Falcon* (no. 23), *Bonnie and Clyde* (no. 27), *Treasure of the Sierra Madre* (no. 30), *The Godfather, Part 2* (no. 32), and *To Kill a Mockingbird* (no. 34). A composite list that I compiled by pestering friends, colleagues, students, and total strangers on airplanes for their top ten crime films includes those nine movies but also outliers such as *Trainspotting, The Untouchables, The Usual Suspects,* and *White Heat.* My own list changes all the time, but on it *The Godfather, Psycho,* and *Taxi Driver* usually compete for first place; *Reservoir Dogs, Goodfellas, Rear Window,* and *The Grifters* also place in the top ten.

Drew Todd, who is completing his doctorate in film studies at Indiana University, wrote chapter 1, and although I have made many revisions, it is still essentially his work. Charles Alexander Hahn ("my son the lawyer") wrote the first two drafts of the chapter on courtroom films, and although this chapter, too, is greatly changed, it retains key elements of the original. To Alex I am also grateful for his enthusiastic support of this project from its inception, close readings of several chapters, and some astute film analyses. In recognition of his role, I have dedicated this book to him.

I owe thanks as well to many other people, including Lisa Cuklanz of Boston College for helping in the initial stages of this project; Gary Edgerton and Lucien X. Lombardo for inviting me to participate in their film festival at Old Dominion University; James Burton Hahn for sharing his vast knowledge of movies; Sarah Rachel Hahn for her sensitive readings of films and for urging me to see the stunning, sad *Eye of God;* Jeroen G. W. Kok and Peter J. Lepeska for their ideas about the future of crime films; Stefan Machura and Stefan Ulbrich for their work on law in the movies; Michael Shively and Courtney Allen [now Graceson] of Northeastern University for film suggestions; Debra Stanley of Central Connecticut State University for carrying the burden of a joint writing project while I worked on this book; and Judith Yarnall for the talks on film violence. Others who contributed include T. Susan Chang; Susan Erony; Jacque Friedman; Joseph Ferrara, Daniel Towner, Kit Cooke, and the library staff of Johnson State College in Vermont; Valerie Jenness; Gary Marx; Dario Melossi; Theodore Sasson; Alexandra Todd; and Friend Weiler. Robert Hahn was, as always, my staunchest support, in this case fixing the VCRs, editing every chapter (some more than once), and sitting through a number of movies that he would have preferred to skip. These friends and colleagues are the good guys; insofar as there are problems with this book, I am the bad guy.

Contents

Note on Use of Dates

I give the date of release whenever a movie is first mentioned in a chapter. An appendix lists all crime films referenced in this book and their release dates, so readers who want to look up a date in midchapter can find it there.

SHOTS IN THE MIRROR

Introduction

CRIME FILMS AND SOCIETY

> John Dillinger, . . . obsessed with movies, was shot by agents
> after seeing *Manhattan Melodrama,* which featured Clark
> Gable playing a character a lot like John Dillinger.
> —Mark Costello

Crime films reflect our ideas about fundamental social, economic, and political issues while, at the same time, they shape the ways we think about these issues. When we look at the relationship between crime films and society, we see a dynamic interplay of art and life. This book examines that interplay from the multiple perspectives of film history and technique, social history, criminal justice, and criminology.

Within this broad analytical framework, *Shots in the Mirror* argues that crime movies, whether they portray cops, private eyes, courts, prisons, or crime itself, have traditionally made two arguments at once. On the one hand, they criticize some aspect of society—police brutality, prison violence, legal barriers to justice, or the menace of crime, often by encouraging viewers to identify with a "good" bad guy who challenges the system. On the other hand, they enable us to identify with a character who restores order at the end, even if that means the punishment or death of the bad-guy hero. Thus, crime films offer contradictory sorts of satisfaction: pride in our ability to think critically and root for the character who challenges authority, exposes injustice, champions the underdog; and pride in our maturity for backing the restoration of the moral order, an overhaul that makes further rebellion unnecessary. Most crime films from the earliest days of cinema have offered this dual satisfaction, enabling us to dwell, if only for an hour or two, in a state of happy hypocrisy.

This double movement characterized most crime films made before 1970. Since the 1970s, however, an alternative tradition has been developing that refuses the easy solutions of the past. Bleak and stern, this alternative tradition of critical crime films rejects heroic fantasies and happy endings to show us the confirmed delinquent's delight in violence (*A Clockwork Orange* [1971]); the tawdriness that drives lives in crime (*Mean Streets* [1973]); the circumstances that engender vigi-

3

lantism (*Mystic River* [2003]); the threats that make it difficult for women to move freely in a city (*In the Cut* [2003]); and other failures of fairness and justice. No one is saved in these critical crime films; indeed, there may be no hero at all, or the apparent hero may be almost indistinguishable from the villain. While the perspective of this alternative tradition is unlikely to replace the easy satisfactions of more familiar crime films, it will continue to pose sharp challenges across the spectrum of crime film genres, probing deeply into the social realities of crime.

Even though film plays a central role in generating representations and understandings of crime, criminologists have traditionally ignored it, clinging to a narrow social science perspective that pays little attention to the interactions of crime and culture.[1] No one—within any field—has tried to explain the ongoing attraction of crime films, which have engrossed audiences since the earliest days of silent film, or to analyze the ways in which crime films construct our worlds, ideals, and norms of acceptable behavior. This book aims at understanding how crime films contribute to and reflect our ideas of crime and justice, good and evil, and at identifying the nature of their attraction. It also traces the history of crime films and identifies thematic undercurrents that have pulsed through them over time.

When this book first appeared, it stood alone as an attempt to analytically embrace the entire gamut of crime films; but now it has been joined by a second effort, Thomas Leitch's *Crime Films*.[2] As part of a series on genres in American cinema, Leitch's volume naturally emphasizes film studies, whereas *Shots in the Mirror* emphasizes what films say about crime, criminals, and criminal law. But Leitch, too, recognizes the double movement that enables viewers to identify first with the transgressor and then the avenger. Writing of this "contradictory double project," Leitch explains that "the central function of the crime film" is "to allow viewers to experience the vicarious thrills of criminal behavior while leaving them free to condemn this behavior, whoever is practicing it, as immoral."[3] He, too, concludes that one cannot perceive the double movement by focusing simply on one subtype such as the gangster or cop or prison film; only if one has a sense of the entire range of crime films will this pattern emerge.

While the overall topic of crime films was neglected until recently, the same was not true of its most popular subdivisions. There is now a significant body of commentary on cop, detective, gangster, and lawyer films, together with studies of film noir and the femme fatale.[4]

Moreover, a body of literature is emerging on psycho films, and Russell Campbell's *Marked Women* offers a thorough analysis of prostitutes and prostitution in cinema.[5] But if some subtypes of crime films have received considerable attention, others have gone almost unnoticed, leaving the field wide open to those interested in analyzing movies about criminal insanity, domestic violence, drug abuse and the drug trade, heists, political crime, sex crimes, stalking, surveillance, terrorism, vigilantism, and women in prison. As crime films come into their own as topics of study, and as scholars in various disciplines turn their attention in this direction, these and other understudied topics will become the focus of new books and articles.

The gap between film studies and criminology may eventually be bridged by cultural criminology, a new area of inquiry that aims at understanding how social groups perceive and create knowledge about crime.[6] Taking into consideration creative productions and emotional affects as well as illegal behaviors, cultural criminology approaches crime as a resource, one that generates media images of crime causation and control. Cultural criminology, in the words of two advocates, "attempts to make sense of a world in which the street scripts the screen and the screen scripts the street."[7] Cultural criminology also emphasizes the attractions of transgression, the pleasures of the forbidden. In all these respects, it promises to expand and reinvigorate the territory of traditional criminology; but it is not yet well developed, and its advocates have as yet paid little attention to film. Should this situation change, cultural criminology is well positioned to encourage exchanges of ideas between film specialists and criminologists, fulfilling its promise to open up the study of "not only images but images of images, an infinite hall of mediated mirrors."[8] We might discover an entire Versailles of possibilities in which crime films and daily life endlessly reflect one another, framing sequences, receding into copies of one another, revealing ways in which our selves and movies interpenetrate. We would be better able to watch ourselves seeing—a purpose of this book as well.

Scholars' traditional reluctance to examine the topic of crime films in its entirety has no doubt stemmed from the sprawling and complex nature of the topic. Thousands of movies might be classified as crime films. How is one to get an analytical handle on this vast, amorphous material? Should we include films such as the *Beverly Hills Cop* series (1984, 1987, 1994), Alfred Hitchcock's *Frenzy* (1972), the *Naked Gun* series (1988, 1991, 1994), *Ocean's Eleven* (2001), and

Ocean's Twelve (2004) that pivot around crime but are predominantly comedies? What about *Shock Corridor* (1963), director Sam Fuller's story of a journalist hunting for the killer of a mental hospital patient, which is concerned more with madness than with crime (at the end, the journalist himself, disabled by electric shock treatments, goes crazy)? Should we toss the net so broadly as to include Quentin Tarantino's *Kill Bill* films (2003, 2004), even though their characters are closer to comic book superheroes than to the human protagonists of most crime films? These examples, which could be multiplied almost endlessly, illustrate a few of the conceptual problems in defining crime films.

Defining Crime Films

The best way to skirt these conceptual pitfalls is to define crime movies as *films that focus primarily on crime and its consequences.* Crime films do not constitute a genre (a group of films with similar themes, settings, and characters) as Westerns and war films do. Rather, they constitute a *category* that encompasses a number of genres—caper films, detective movies, gangster films, cop and prison movies, courtroom dramas, and the many offerings for which there may be no better generic label than, simply, *crime stories*. Like the labels *dramas* and *romances, crime films* is an umbrella term that covers several smaller and more coherent groupings.

It can be useful to think of movie analysis in terms of variously sized boxes. The smallest boxes hold individual movies while the next size up holds series (such as Dirty Harry films or all movies directed by Alfred Hitchcock), and the next, works that share a subject (vigilante films, sex crime movies) or a recurrent character (the corrupt cop, the innocent on death row). Big boxes hold genres, such as Westerns or courtroom films. The biggest boxes of all hold thematic groupings of related genres; one of these is the "crime films" category, which at a minimum includes films about cops and detectives, types of crime (for example, heists) and types of criminals (for example, gangsters), criminal trials, and prisons.[9] But while these distinctions among series, genres, and thematic groupings can clarify relationships, what is ultimately important is not definitional labels but rather understanding the complex relations between film and society—the ways they reflect and influence one another. In the long run, then, how the boxes are labeled is less important than what the analytical process reveals about film, culture, law, and society, and the boxes must remain open so that we can shift films around, juxtaposing and regrouping them to identify trends, detect previously unnoticed concerns, and discover new meanings. In chapter 3, for example, I shift a number of films into a genre-sized box labeled *psycho films* in order to see what that exercise reveals about the stock characters and legal themes of such movies. In other chapters I point to the growing fluidity of the traditional crime film genres (cop, courtroom, and prison movies), which are subdividing, recombining, and evolving to produce new configurations such as the *law film,* an outgrowth of the traditional courtroom drama.

Using the Internet Movie Database (http://www.imdb.com), I calculated the number of crime films in existence (excluding those made for television), ending up with a figure of more than ten thousand. The sobering realization that I would need to watch four movies a day for seven years to see all of the world's crime films (by which time, of course, more would have appeared) forced me to impose limits on the subject matter of this book. After chapter 1, I usually steer clear of crime film comedies; throughout, I avoid courtroom films that deal with civil rather than criminal cases and films whose main goal is historical, even when that history involves crimes and punishments (the 1996 version of *The Crucible,* for example). I also keep my distance from Westerns (nearly all of which could also be classified as crime films, but only by muddying the conceptual waters), war movies, and sci-fis. With a few exceptions, I ignore crime films made for television on the grounds that made-for-TV films are shaped by different considerations of audience, artistic aspiration, duration, and financing than feature movies. While the boundaries that historically have divided film and television are crumbling, running the two together makes it impossible to discover what is distinctive about the meanings and social roles of feature-length crime movies.[10]

Within my self-imposed constraints, I developed four criteria for choosing which crime films, among the thousands of remaining possibilities, to emphasize in this book. First, I weighed critical reputation and audience reception. Second, I considered the degree to which a film says something significant about the relationship between crime and society or has shaped understandings of that relationship. For example, I treat the big-three gangster movies of the early 1930s (*Little Caesar* [1931], *Public Enemy* [1931], and *Scarface* [1932]) as well as *The Godfather* (1972) and *Natural Born Killers* (1994)—all films that take a cogent and forceful stand on the social origins of crime—and also *The Bad Seed* (1956), a movie that, in contrast, claims that criminality is hereditary and hence impervious to social influences. Third, I assessed a film's significance to film history (either in technical, critical, or filmic terms, or in terms of subject, script, and sensibility), which led me to include D. W. Griffith's *The Musketeers of Pig Alley* (1912), one of the earliest gangster movies, and *Dirty Harry* (1971), one of the first highly successful cop films and the trigger for a national controversy about police brutality. Considerations of significance also led me to include, in this edition, films made outside of the United States that have strongly influenced the direction of American crime films. Fourth and finally, I chose movies that provide useful points of entry for discussing crime films' implications for the politics of everyday life, particularly for constructions of human value on the basis of gender, ethnicity, race, and sexuality.

These criteria enable me to discuss the best and most substantive crime films and avoid the worst and most trivial, the endless stream of ephemera about cop buddies and babes in prison. However, because I have an interest in breadth as well as depth of coverage, I include lesser films in my lists of examples.[11] Overall, I deal in one way or another with well over four hundred crime movies, discussing about a third of them in some depth.

Crime Films, Ideology, and Culture

While some scholars have taken a positivist approach, investigating whether movie representations of crime and justice processes are accurate,[12] my approach is different. Instead of comparing crime films to social realities and measuring the gap between them, I conceive their relationship as dialectical, a two-way street: Crime films draw from and in turn shape social thought about crime and its players. My approach is less concerned with the realism of representations than with their ideological messages, by which I mean the assumptions about the nature of reality embedded in film narratives and imagery.

As an illustration, consider the imagery of *Thelma and Louise* (1991) after the two women embark on their crime spree. Time and again director Ridley Scott frames the women against huge expanses of blue sky, mountain ranges, and open country. Filling the screen and dominating these magnificent backdrops, Thelma and Louise gain an aura of significance and elemental power. Moreover, because moviegoers associate this type of framing with the traditional Western (in which an admiring camera looks up at the horse and rider, framing them against wide-open spaces) and with the male buddy film, the two women take on associations of perfect friendship, independence, purity, and force. These meanings, deriving from the nature of film and our responses to it, form some of the ideological messages of *Thelma and Louise,* messages that are buried deeply in the imagery and narrative line and cannot be disengaged from them.[13]

My view of ideology is close to that of film theorist Ann Kaplan, who uses the term *ideology* to refer not to the "beliefs people consciously hold but to the myths that a society lives by, as if these myths referred to some natural, unproblematic 'reality.'"[14] *Myths* in this context is not pejorative but merely a descriptive term for the fundamental notions that people hold (usually without much conscious thought) about how the world is structured, what is valuable and unworthy, who is good and who is bad, and which kinds of actions are wrong or right. We cannot negotiate the world or get through a day without drawing on the myths, attitudes, beliefs, convictions, and assumptions that constitute ideology.[15] *Thelma and Louise* explicitly illustrates this meaning of ideology by showing how Thelma (played by Geena Davis) abandons traditional notions about ideal womanhood (act harebrained, stand by your man) in favor of the convictions that Louise (played by Susan Sarandon) holds about the value of freedom and independence. As this example also illustrates, ideology is in a constant state of flux. In the process of encountering the world, we absorb new narratives and mental pictures that may encourage shifts in our fundamental myths and assumptions. Much as Thelma goes through encounters with men that encourage her to change her attitudes toward heterosexual romance, so too (albeit with less drama) do moviegoers experience cinematic narratives and imagery that may challenge their attitudes about crime and criminals.

Ideology relates to power. The myths, attitudes, and assumptions that we live by influence what can be said and what modes of expression can be used. What is not said is easily as important, ideologically, as what is said. Before films began portraying African American police officers, it was more difficult to picture them, and so long as African American cops were portrayed as compliant second fiddles (as they are, for instance, in *Magnum Force* [1973], one of the Dirty Harry movies), it was difficult to picture them as heroes. Not until we began to find black leads such as Morgan Freeman in *Seven* (1995) and Denzel Washington in *Devil in a Blue Dress* (1995) and *The Bone Collector* (1999) did African American men achieve full Eastwoodian stature as heroic sleuths.[16] Earlier, through absence or marginalization, they were denied access to a form of power. Thus, movies mold ideology by what they fail to show as well as by the narratives they do present, and part of my aim in this book is to point out the ideological significance of missing representations and silences. This is a way of examining how movies reflect and produce power.

The relationship of crime films to ideology, to other aspects of thought, and to actual behavior is illuminated by work in the sociology of culture.[17] In the mid-1980s, sociologists began rejecting the traditional view of culture as a body of beliefs, customs, goals, values, and institutions accepted fairly uniformly by all members of a group, instead adopting a view of culture as a repository or "tool kit," what sociologist Paul DiMaggio terms "a grab-bag of odds and ends: a pastiche of mediated representations, a repertoire of techniques."[18] This new view anticipates that individuals and groups will interpret movies differently, that interpretations will vary over time, and that viewers will carry away from films different bits of cultural information. (The view fits well with actual reactions to films: One person may love the Al Pacino remake of *Scarface* [1983] for its operatic extravagance and another hate it for its violence while a second-generation audience, attuned to hip-hop and drug cultures, turns it into a cult favorite.) Although the new sociology of culture does not discuss films directly, it implies that movies provide fragments of culture and that culture is to be found both in individual viewers' heads and in the larger collective consciousness. It further suggests that we use these cultural fragments selectively, picking out some to construct what sociologist Ann Swidler calls "strategies of action."[19] (It is in these strategies of action that we find the link between culture and behavior; I return to this link in chapter 2, when I discuss the much-debated issue of whether movies cause crime.) Relying on Swidler and others who work in the area, we can, then, conclude that crime films are a cultural resource available to all of us, including criminals who derive from them information about "being" criminal. We can understand why gangster John Dillinger was obsessed with gangster movies.

Sociologists and psychologists have studied how people organize the bits of culture in their heads. Much of this work is speculative, but according to the evidence currently available, it seems that the fragments of cultural information in our minds form themselves into schemata or templates that we then draw on in the form of assumptions, social norms, principles, and so on, using them as handy guides to behavior so we do not have to think through every action from the start every time. Schemata then aggregate into even larger mental structures—ideologies (including assumptions about the nature of heroes), paradigms, logics, and narratives of the self (perhaps including the self as bank robber). In sum, movies are a source of cultural information, most of which simply rattles around in our heads waiting to be called upon, but some of which feeds into our ideologies and other mental schemata. The schemata in turn interact with the external world, where we encounter new cultural phenomena (including new movies) that then feed back into our schemata, usually reinforcing but sometimes disconfirming them.

Crime Films and Pleasure

Their serious implications notwithstanding, crime films have a nearly endless capacity to confer pleasure. Aside from the subset of critical, countertraditional movies, crime films provide escapes from daily life, opportunities to solve mysteries, chances to identify with powerful and competent heroes, and occasions to ponder moral choices without in fact having to make them. Their predictable plots and stock characters, far from disappointing audiences, deliver the pleasure of variations on the familiar. They enable us to identify with the bad guys and be cooler than cool without paying a price. In addition, most mainstream crime films reassure us that our society and system of criminal justice are salvageable despite their many failings.

Most movies offer the joy of escape; crime films offer the ancillary joy of watching others suffer. "People just love seeing other people in jeopardy," actor Pierce Brosnan observes. "It is the same fascination as driving by road accidents. You swear you are not going to be one of those people who look, but you look anyway."[20] (One of my students made the same point by explaining that she enjoys crime movies because "for two hours I can watch someone else struggle.") Moreover, crime films are often inspirational in their portrayal of underdog characters who triumph against all odds. They offer access to places few of us visit in person, such as drug factories, the inner sanctums of mafia chieftains, and the tops of hurtling trains. Good crime films evoke these worlds in terms so vivid, gripping, and emotionally compelling that we identify with their characters even when

Figure 1. Alfred Hitchcock's *Psycho* (1960) carries viewers into the minds of the victim and the killer simultaneously, even while chiding us for our sado-masochism. Photo used by permission of Photofest.

we know that the stories are in large part fantasies. Opening a window on exotica, crime films enable viewers to become voyeurs, secret ob-servers of the personal and even intimate lives of characters very dif-ferent from themselves. That the shower scene in *Psycho* (1960) is the most famous single scene in crime film history probably has something to do with what it shows: a naked woman being stabbed to death.[21]

Crime films also offer opportunities to participate virtuously in the pursuit of justice, often at the side of a charismatic and capable hero. Not only can we decipher baffling clues; we can also identify with someone who is unusually intelligent, self-possessed, and successful. Characters such as Mike Hammer (*Kiss Me Deadly* [1955]), Clarice Starling (*Silence of the Lambs* [1991]), and William Somerset (*Seven*) are determined and effective in their tasks, pursuing difficult goals without hesitation—and with astounding success. Viewers enjoy identifying with such protagonists and with the attractive stars who portray them. They also enjoy identifying with less heroic characters such as J.D., the sleazy seducer played by Brad Pitt in *Thelma and Louise,* who so gratifyingly torments Thelma's boorish husband, and with the adept young con artist played by Leonardo Di Caprio in *Catch Me If You Can* (2002), who eludes the FBI for years.

A key source of crime films' enduring attraction (and again, for the moment I am setting aside critical crime films) lies in the way they provide a cultural space for the expression of resistance to authority. While most people support social control of some sort, crime films have carved out a piece of emotional territory where it is acceptable to entertain antagonism toward the criminal justice system, the state, and other institutions of power and to feel, for ninety minutes or so, like a heroic rebel. Crime films' antiauthority messages, however, are conveyed through moral, narrative, and cinematic frameworks that constrain or even counter the critique. Thus, while crime films are often subversive, they also promote systems of social control by making these seem normal, unproblematic, or even useful. Crime films condemn institutions of power such as prisons but at the same time reinforce them. As cultural theorist bell hooks notes, a "film may have incredibly revolutionary standpoints merged with conservative ones. This mingling of standpoints is often what makes it hard for audiences to critically 'read' the overall filmic narrative."[22] Simultaneously radical and conservative, crime films can appeal to nearly everyone. They enable us to regress to the level of two-year-olds, identifying with characters who defy authorities, and at the next moment to recognize, with a touch of self-congratulation for our maturity, the need for discipline.

Escape from Alcatraz, a 1979 film starring Clint Eastwood, provides an example of this double movement. Through various rhetorical devices, the movie encourages us to sympathize with the prisoners and hope that their escape plot succeeds. An evil warden and associate warden reinforce this sympathy on the level of character and narrative, and camera work that dwells on miles of cells, pipes, and other apparatus of containment visually reinforces viewer antagonism toward social control.

At the same time, however, *Escape from Alcatraz* offers no criticism of the prison system as a whole. There is nothing extremist here that might offend or incite. The prisoners' pain is blamed on specific, sadistic officials, not incarceration itself. (In fact, *Escape from Alcatraz* includes a couple of "good" officers to show that the system is not all bad.) No class differences divide the convicts, whose camaraderie is disturbed only by Wolf, the stock prison rapist. Nor are there profound problems in race relations at this Alcatraz, where few people of color are imprisoned in any case and the black leader almost immediately bonds with Eastwood's character. The film reduces racial tensions to banter in which the central white and black prisoners call each other "boy"—affectionately. Pleasure here includes escape into a world of simple morality and intense friendship. It also includes the cost-free thrill of identifying with a revolt against authority that frees the good guys, embarrasses the nasty warden, and leaves the status quo undisturbed.

Finally, crime films are pleasurable because they provide unfamiliar and challenging material for "self-talk": our inner conversations with our selves, imagined others, and even generalized others.[23] Nearly everyone conducts such inner dialogues—evaluating experiences, projecting plans, formulating ideals, and telling annoying people how to improve. Self-talk enables us to interpret the world and develop our meaning systems; it plays a crucial role in the construction of personal identity and in bridging the gap between our selves and our social situations. Yet many of us find little fresh material for self-talk in our daily routines; wearying of our usual conversations, we sometimes turn to movies. Crime films in particular offer stimulating materials—ethical dilemmas, dubious role models, opportunities to debate tempting but illegal courses of action. Also pleasurable is the speed with which that material arrives: At the start of an unfamiliar film, everything is new and must be decoded from scratch. Our self-talk goes into overdrive as we hurry to figure out who the hero is and where danger lies, experiencing exhilaration without the slightest exertion.

Critical Crime Films and the Alternative Tradition

In recent decades, some innovative filmmakers have broken with crime films' tradition of safe critique and sanitized rebellion, developing a critical alternative of alienated, angry (or at least cynical) movies that subject viewers to harsh realities and refuse to flatter either their characters or their audiences. For instance, the same year that *Escape from Alcatraz* was released, there appeared another prison movie, *On the Yard* (1979), that flew in the face of prison film tradition. The most appealing character is killed in the middle of the movie—for a cigarette debt—and forgotten. Although inmates team up for mutual support, there are no heroic friendships between buddies, and prisoner factions openly war for control of the yard. More recently, *American Me* (1992), a movie about the Mexican Mafia, again broke with prison film formulas. Made by Hispanic director Edward James Olmos, *American Me* paints an unrelievedly bleak picture of Hispanic culture disintegrating under the twin pressures of American mores and the Mexican Mafia's criminal activities. Children commit murder, personal relationships founder, and the leader dies ignominiously in his cell.

Retrospectively, we can identify the progenitors of this line of critical crime films. One of the first was Fritz Lang's *M* (1931), the story of a child sex murderer; although "M" is captured in the end, Lang leaves open the question of whether a man so mentally ill and so driven by his obsessions should be brought to justice. *M* has no hero, and its ending, while resolving the story on the level of plot, offers no resolution to the movie's legal or moral dilemmas. The roots of critical crime films also lie in the tradition of films noirs, the brooding mysteries and urban crime movies of the 1940s and 1950s that take corruption for granted, assuming that brutality and criminality are part of the human condition.[24] More specifically, critical crime films can trace their ancestry to director Joseph H. Lewis's noir classic *Gun Crazy* (1949), a tragic, haunting tale of a very-much-in-love couple who aspire to little more than bourgeois comfort but are brought down by their fixation with firearms—and willingness to use them. The critical success of Akira Kurosawa's *Rashomon* (1950), describing a rape and murder from four different points of view, encouraged other filmmakers to think more deeply about the ambiguities and complexities of crime, and to reach for, instead of slick endings, the indeterminacy of daily life. Jean-Luc Godard's *Breathless* (1960), too, has protagonists but no heroes, and its ending raises more questions than it answers. Yet another progenitor of the critical strain within crime films was Sam Peckinpah's *The Wild Bunch* (1969), which, its syrupy interludes notwithstanding, insists on the evil in human nature and demonstrates an unashamed fascination with torn flesh and spraying blood.

Figure 2. Jean-Luc Godard's *Breathless* (1960) shows a young gangster
(Jean-Paul Belmondo) scripting his own life with material he has picked up
from movies. Its disinterest in moralizing about crime marked a radical
break with Hollywood's traditions. Photo used by permission of Photofest.

The critical tradition took shape with the appearance of such films
as Martin Scorsese's *Mean Streets,* an iconoclastic probe of the harsh-
ness of criminal life; Roman Polanski's *Chinatown* (1974), in which
the detective hero is stymied by the incestuous bad guy; Scorsese's
Taxi Driver (1976), in which the main character may be a Christ figure
or a crazy assassin (or both, or neither); and Sidney Lumet's *The Offence*
(1973), a little-known but powerful study of similarities between a
worn-down police detective and the sex criminal he is hunting. Director Stephen Frears made another of these dark crime films, *The
Grifters* (1990), a movie that again uses incest to mark the corruption
of the criminal heart. In one of director Abel Ferrara's contributions
to the line, *Bad Lieutenant* (1992), the lead character (played by Harvey Keitel) is a cop who has spiraled so far downward into a filthy
world of alcoholism and drug addiction that he is even rude to Jesus,
who comes down from the cross to save him. Other films of this type
include *The Asphalt Jungle* (1950), *The Conversation* (1974), *Blow Out*

(1981), *State of Grace* (1990), *American Buffalo* (1995), *Kids* (1995), *Normal Life* (1996), *Trainspotting* (1996), *Thin Blue Line* (1988), *Open Doors* (1990), *Let Him Have It* (1991), *Capturing the Friedmans* (2003), and *Mystic River*.

Critical crime films have none of the high spirits or good humor we find in movies such as *Goodfellas* (1990), *Natural Born Killers*, *Pulp Fiction* (1994), and *Fargo* (1996). Sardonic and even grim in tone, many of them are suffused with bitterness. They are not defined by their lack of happy endings, for crime films since silent film days have killed off or otherwise punished their protagonists. Instead, the crucial differences lie in their lack of a traditional, admirable hero and in their recognition of the inevitability of confusion, crime, and suffering. The bad lieutenant may be saved by Jesus, but neither he himself nor anyone else can rescue him from depravity. Michael Douglas's D-Fens, the lead character in *Falling Down* (1993), can never do anything but fall under the weight of his rage against a world in which middle-class, white-male earnestness reaps no rewards. In *Ghost Dog* (1999), director Jim Jarmusch's philosophical meditation on the inevitability of death, a contract killer (Forest Whitaker) who has adopted the ancient rules for Samurai warriors dances toward his fate.

These critical movies comprise but a small minority of all crime films, and given their scorn for comforting messages, they are likely to remain a minority. Nonetheless, their refusals to pander to popular taste do pose sharp ideological challenges to crime film traditions. While mainstream crime films continue to offer the pleasure of rebellion within safe constraints, this subgroup insists on the impossibility of heroism and the certainty of injustice.

This book's chapters are organized around themes and genres that have been pivotal in the development of crime films and have conveyed particular sets of ideas relating to crime and society. Chapter 1 deals specifically with the history of crime films and the emergence of various genres. It is less concerned with ideology than with how, over time, movies have interacted with the social contexts in which they were produced. Chapter 2 examines what crime films have to say, sociologically and ideologically, about the causes of crime. It also examines the much-debated issue of whether media representations of violence cause crime, arguing that crime films do not lead to crime but rather make available narratives about crime and criminality that viewers then incorporate into their beliefs about how the world works.

Chapter 3, which is entirely new to this edition, examines types of violent crime films, drawing distinctions among slashers, serial killer movies, and psycho cinema and arguing that works in the latter category carry a strong conservative subtext about the need for law.

The next three chapters deal with specific genres within the crime films category. Chapter 4 concentrates on cop and detective films, tracing their evolution, discussing their obsessive preoccupation with ideal masculinity, and examining new directions in which they are heading. Chapter 5, on lawyer and law films, argues that of all traditional crime film genres, the courtroom drama has been least successful in addressing current concerns. As a result, courtroom dramas, with their lawyer heroes, are being supplanted by a new type of film that is deeply concerned with law but ignores lawyers and courtrooms. Chapter 6 investigates key themes in traditional prison films and discusses the critical prison movies, recent documentaries, and self-reflexive films that are trying to turn this genre in new directions, albeit with mixed success. Chapter 7 focuses on crime films' tendency to portray criminals as heroes, proposing answers to questions about why crime films valorize criminals, how they make criminals seem heroic, and how they reconcile their message of criminal heroism with cultural assumptions about the wrongness of crime. The book concludes with another entirely new chapter, chapter 8, which discusses a subset of critical crime films: recent films of moral ambiguity, particularly those that deal with sex crimes.

Notes

1. For an exception to this rule and example of the kind of work I have in mind, see Tzanelli, Yar, and O'Brien 2005. These authors write:

   Popular crime discourses and the "re-dramatization" of crime are real in their effects and effective in their circulation of frameworks for making sense of crime and deviance. But, much more than this, they are effective in situating criminal activity at the intersection of wider discourses on family, gender, success and failure, role-legitimacy, morality and much more. Specific dramatizations . . . certainly draw upon popular ideologies and understandings about crime and criminals, but they also provide specific contextual inflections of those frameworks. (114)

   I hope for more work that, like this study, will open up both criminology and cinema studies to explorations of the ways in which crime and culture interpenetrate.

2. Leitch 2002.

3. Leitch 2002: 16, 306.
4. For example: Chase 2002; Clarens 1997; Doane 1991; Hannsberry 1998; Kaplan 1998; King 1999; Krutnik 1991; Mason 2003; McCarty 1993a, 2004; Munby 1999; Naremore 1995–96; and Telotte 1989. Many other examples appear in the notes to the following chapters.
5. Campbell (forthcoming). For the literature on psycho movies, see chapter 3.
6. On cultural criminology, see Ferrell and Sanders 1995, Presdee 2000, and Ferrell, Hayward, Morrison, and Presdee 2004. Law-and-film scholars have gone further in theorizing and bridging the gap between legal studies and film studies than have cultural criminologists in making connections between criminology and cinema studies; see, especially, Robson 2005 and the examples cited in chapter 5, this volume.
7. Hayward and Young 2004: 259.
8. Ferrell and Sanders 1995:14, as quoted and cited in Hayward and Young 2004: 268.
9. Readers who prefer more sophisticated terminology should think of my "boxes" as "frames." On the concepts of frames and frame analysis, and ways in which these concepts relate to media constructions of reality, see Gamson, Croteau, Hoynes, and Sasson 1992.
10. There is a separate literature on television crime dramas; see, for example, Doyle 2003, Rapping 2003, and Sumser 1996.
11. Indeed, I have a strong interest in breadth of coverage, for methodological reasons. Like others with a sociological background, I prefer either to study every example of a phenomenon or to sample systematically from all the examples. One of the best genre studies in the crime films area, Neal King's *Heroes in Hard Times* (1999), is admirable for its saturation coverage. King bases his conclusions on every one of the 193 cop action films produced in the United States and released internationally, in theaters, between 1980 and 1997; as a result, we can be confident that his conclusions are not based on anomalous selections. Generic film studies often proceed more selectively, examining a few outstanding examples, a method that enables authors to avoid boring films but also means that their conclusions are not generalizable.

For this book, I surveyed the genres and subgenres of crimes films by viewing all the well-known films in each category and also some peripherals to determine the category's parameters (typical characters and action, standard meaning, and significant variations). Thus, my generalizations are based on a range of examples. In no case are they based on an entire universe of relevant films—an undertaking that would have been impossible due to the great number of possibilities. However, my generalizations are testable, and I did test them—by viewing new examples (either recent releases or older films that I had not previously seen) to determine whether my generalizations held up. I am confident that over the next few years, as more dissertations appear on crime films, an agreed-upon methodology will evolve for systematically studying such works.
12. See, for example, Bergman and Asimow 1996, Gutterman 2002, and Harding 2005. In contrast, and for examples of the constructionist approach that

I adopt here, see Dyer 1997, 2002; Surette 1998; and Ruth 1996, the latter a study of the "invention" of the gangster that is "concerned with the meanings rather than the facts of crime" (1).

13. For more on the ideological meanings of *Thelma and Louise,* see Spelman and Minow 1992.

14. Kaplan 1983: 12–13.

15. See Silbey 1998.

16. For earlier approximations, see Richard Roundtree's popular *Shaft* films (*Shaft* [1971], *Shaft's Big Score* [1972], *Shaft in Africa* [1973]), about the adventures of a black private eye.

17. This paragraph and the next are based mainly on DiMaggio 1997 and Swidler 1986. Also see Callero 1994, Morgan and Schwalbe 1990, and Swidler and Arditi 1994.

18. Swidler 1986 (the article that contributed the term "tool kit"); DiMaggio 1997: 267.

19. Swidler 1986.

20. Koltnow 1997: D8.

21. Lyng's 2004 work on risk-taking and the erotics of crime does not deal directly with film but is certainly relevant to the type of pleasure some people take in scenes of violence, especially violence against women. Also relevant is a remark attributed to director Quentin Tarantino, who, when asked about sadomasochism in films, is said to have explained, "I'm the 'S,' you [the viewer] are the 'M.'"

22. hooks 1996: 3.

23. On inner conversations, see Archer 2003, Lawrence and Valsiner 2003.

24. In fact, what I call the alternative tradition of critical crime films is close to what Telotte, in *Voices in the Dark,* calls "the *noir* spirit" (3), noting that "*film noir* can designate a field of deviation that mirrors the problems of modern America in particular and modern man in general" (1989: 12, emphasis original). Telotte contrasts the dark voice of noir with the "classical film narrative" or "conventional voice," "characterized by a seemingly objective point of view, adherence to a cause-effect logic, use of goal-oriented characters to direct our attention and elicit our sympathies, and a progression toward narrative closure" (3). I use the terms *Hollywood movies* and *traditional crime films* to indicate the body of work that critical crime films react against. A contrast similar to the one I am drawing here can also be found in Robert Altman's film *The Player* (1992), which revolves around the tension between "happy endings" and "reality." Altman resolves the tension with an ironic happy ending.

1 The History of Crime Films

DREW TODD

I always wanted to use the Mafia as a metaphor for America.
—Francis Ford Coppola

Crime films feed our apparently insatiable hunger for stories about crimes, investigations, trials, and punishments. From almost the first moment of moviemaking, film writers and directors realized that nothing pleases audiences more than deception, mayhem, and underdog characters who refuse to be trampled by institutions and laws. The plots of crime films may draw on actual historic events, reproducing celebrated cases while simultaneously fashioning out of the past new heroes for the present. More frequently, crime film plots are fictions that draw on widespread attitudes toward crime, victims, law, and punishment prevalent at the time of the films' making. Whatever the basis of their stories, crime films reflect the power relations of the context in which they are made—attitudes toward gender, ethnicity, race, and class relations, opinions about fairness and justice, and beliefs about the optimal relationship of the state to individuals. Examining the history of crime films helps explain why different types of crime films flourish at different points in time. By locating movies at some distance, in the social and political contexts in which they were produced, film history enables us to see more clearly movies' underlying assumptions about the nature of American society.

This chapter provides an overview of the origins and evolution of crime films, focusing on their thematic history. Its goal is twofold: to establish a chronology of major crime films and genre developments, and to show how crime film history reflects more fundamental social and cultural currents. This emphasis on the social-historical contexts in which crime films evolved will lay a foundation for the more detailed examinations of specific genres and issues in later chapters. (Later chapters also develop the distinction, emphasized in the introduction, between mainstream and alternative-tradition or critical crime films.) The chapter proceeds chronologically, first discussing crime films of the silent film era (the late nineteenth century until the late 1920s) and then the emergence during the 1930s of two enduring genres, gangster films and prison movies. Next, covering World War II and its aftermath, it spotlights the development of film noir, the movie style that for nearly two decades defined crime films. The late 1950s and 1960s became a transitional period for crime films in America as the aesthetics and values of film noir grew less relevant and as social changes encouraged the popularity of youth-marketed vehicles, spy thrillers, trial movies, and heist films. The penultimate section examines a relatively fertile period, 1967–80, showing how new themes emerged and older genres revived, and the chapter closes with remarks on recent changes in crime films.

The Silent Film Era, ca. 1897–1927

Movies first appeared in the last years of the nineteenth century, the result of a series of technological innovations that made it possible to create the illusion of movement on film. The earliest movies lasted only a few minutes; they were too brief to develop characters or complex plots, but they delighted audiences with their ability to re-create events and conjure up magical illusions. Some of the first movies were shown in vaudeville theaters, between live entertainment acts; by the early twentieth century, movies were more likely to be shown in their own nickelodeons, theaters where patrons paid a nickel to see the films. Nickelodeons, as Peter Roffman and Jim Purdy point out, were a working-class form of entertainment, and silent films often reflected "sympathy for the common man and the prevailing criticism of the corrupt and wealthy."[1] However, it was not yet clear what movies would or could be, or what place they would have in American life and culture. Would they depict real-life events? Fictional tales? True or invented crime stories? How would movies relate to newspapers, theater, vaudeville, and the visual arts? Under what circumstances would people view them? Who would comprise their primary audience? Such questions were asked—and at least partially answered—during the silent film period.

In the United States, movies emerged during the so-called Progressive Era (roughly 1890–1920), a time of intense social reform, though one in which white, middle-class reformers felt there was a great deal of work to do. One major concern was social unrest and street crime. Cities were expanding rapidly and filling with immigrants and the poor, creating an ideal climate for organized crime. "White slavery" or forced prostitution was another pervasive concern. The police, a third important target of Progressive reforms, were in many cases uneducated, corrupt, and brutal. The Progressive period drew to a close with Prohibition, the enactment of the antialcohol Eighteenth Amendment, but this law backfired, encouraging bootlegging and organized crime—new causes for alarm. The silent film era, then, was one during which Americans became seriously worried about the manifestations of crime. For the first time, large numbers of ordinary citizens began to think about both the sources of criminality and ways to improve social control.

Few early movies have survived. "By some estimates," John McCarty writes, "as much as 80 percent of the entire output of the silent film era has been lost to us forever" due to stock deterioration or deliberate destruction.[2] Insofar as one can tell from the fragmentary evidence, Edwin S. Porter's *The Great Train Robbery* (1903) may have been the first crime film. Although today it is often classified as a Western, early-twentieth-century viewers may well have considered *The Great Train Robbery* a movie about crime, an argument with which Richard Maltby concurs in his work on genre recognition: "Contemporary audiences recognized *The Great Train Robbery* as a melodramatic example of one or more of the 'chase films,' the 'railway genre,' and the 'crime film.'"[3] This early narrative film is also notably violent: Innocents are shot by the criminals, and one man is viciously bludgeoned to death with a rock before being thrown off the moving train. From the very beginning, then, the crime film promised its viewers explicit violence.

The first enduring type of crime film was the gangster movie, and one of the most innovative of the early gangster films was director D. W. Griffith's *The Musketeers of Pig Alley* (1912). A one-reeler of less than fifteen minutes, *The Musketeers* tells the story of an impoverished but virtuous young woman (played by Lillian Gish) hounded by the Snapper Kid, a mobster and seducer. Outdoor scenes were shot in the gangland territory of New York's Lower East Side, and the "extras" were said to include actual gang members. *The Musketeers* establishes early precedents for the gangster genre by focusing on urban problems, portraying them naturalistically, and featuring dapper thugs, corrupt policemen, helpless female victims, and gang violence.[4]

Regeneration (1915), directed by Griffith's colleague Raoul Walsh, may have been the first feature-length gangster film.[5] Based on an autobiography, it tells how a gangster was saved from a life of crime ("regenerated") by a social worker. *Regeneration* influenced later gangster films through its development of a new screen type, the criminal antihero in whom base and virtuous impulses coexist.[6] Walsh realized that the most interesting characters are complex and paradoxical. His decision to concentrate on a character who combines good with bad struck a chord with viewers, who may have become bored by predictable tales of villainy and virtue. In his essay "The Gangster as Tragic Hero," Robert Warshow discusses this responsiveness in slightly different terms: "The real city . . . produces only criminals; the imaginary city produces the gangster: he is what we want to be and are afraid we might become."[7] Walsh's antihero was an immediate success, and nearly every subsequent gangster film followed this early example.

With Prohibition in place, speakeasies numerous, and organized crime flourishing, Hollywood churned out gangster films during the 1920s. American crime films in fact largely evolved out of the gangster genre, whose grimy cities and themes of corruption anticipated the bleak moral universe of film noir during the 1940s. Concomitantly, the horror film emerged as a popular genre during the silent period. One director specializing in horror and crime films was Tod Browning, who, in addition to making more traditional horror pictures such as *Dracula* (1931), made highly unconventional, sordid crime films (e.g., *The Unholy Three* [1925], *The Unknown* [1927]), and, after the industry-wide transition to synchronized sound, *Freaks* [1932]); these included seedy carnival atmospheres, disguised, desperate criminals, and gruesome amputations. These characteristics meant that Browning's films had more in common with European than American productions of the same time.

European films of the silent era featured the serial killers and convoluted psychotics that help define crime movies as we know them today. More gothic in style and tone, more philosophical, aberrant, and psychological in their interests, European silent films reflected post–World War I continental culture. Still recovering from the divisive war, Europeans tended to create darker and more plaintive art. Of equal importance, Freudian analysis was taking root in European culture, which had long been receptive to notions of inborn and acquired psychopathology. Europeans were readier than Americans to accept the notion that a villain resides in each of us and that dysfunction often inheres in families and other social institutions.

In addition, Europe had long been fertile ground for gothic, even morbid, narrative and art. Painting, music, and literature (from *Grimm's Fairy Tales,* Bram Stoker's *Dracula,* and Charles-Pierre Baudelaire's *Flowers of Evil* to works by Pieter Brueghel, Fyodor Dostoevsky, and, in his later years, Beethoven) reflected this fascination with the perverse and disturbed. The gothic and symbolist traditions encouraged European filmmakers to explore mental pathologies and murderous impulses. Directors such as Robert Wiene, F. W. Murnau, and Fritz Lang made pictures featuring mad criminals and monstrous crimes. Now considered quintessential crime films, these works made a strong case not only for their eloquent German expressionistic style (marked by chiaroscuro lighting, complex setting, and sharply angled camera work) but also for the crime film itself.

In Robert Wiene's *The Cabinet of Dr. Caligari* (1919), for instance, a magician uses hypnosis to commit his heinous crimes. Murnau's silent classic *Sunrise* (1927) deals with a city woman who disrupts a quiet, rural community and persuades a farmer to kill his devoted wife. Although made in America, *Sunrise* was an anomaly when it opened in 1927, displaying a psychological and moral cynicism unusual in American art and entertainment of the time. Its shadowy, expressionistic style further marked it as European. Not surprisingly, the German-born Murnau had arrived in Hollywood only the year before he made *Sunrise.* Americans showed their admiration by awarding Janet Gaynor, the film's lead, the 1928 Academy Award for best actress.

After releasing several important silent crime films (for example, *Dr. Mabuse* [1922])—and anticipating his later classics (for example, the noirish *Fury* [1936] and *Scarlet Street* [1945])—Fritz Lang directed his grisly *M* (1931). In this seminal film, Peter Lorre plays a pedophiliac serial killer who lures children with candy in order to violate and eventually murder them. In the end we understand that "M" is helpless and sick, unable to control his lust to kill. This film was a very early talkie, but it proceeds much like a silent movie, an effect heightened for Americans by subtitles translating the German original. With one foot in the silent film era and the other in the new world of sound, *M* bridges one of the great divides in film history.

The 1930s

Sound movies made their debut in 1927, an event that inaugurated the richest decade in crime film history, one in which two classic genres, the gangster film and the prison film, came of age. "Seemingly overnight the silent film era ended," writes Douglas Gomery.

> Hollywood switched completely to talkies. In 1925 silent filmmaking was the standard; a mere five years later Hollywood produced *only* films with sound. The speed of the transition surprised almost everyone. Within thirty-six months, formerly perplexing technical problems were resolved . . . and fifteen thousand theaters were wired for sound.[8]

While sound intensified the demand for movies of all types, crime itself helped make the 1930s a golden decade for the crime film. Prohibition ended in 1933, but organized crime did not. J. Edgar Hoover, crusading on behalf of his Federal Bureau of Investigation, popularized not only the heroic efforts of "G-men" (for "government men") but also the exploits of what he called "flag-bearers of lawlessness," such as John Dillinger, "Pretty Boy" Floyd, "Baby Face" Nelson, and Wilbur ("The Tri-State Terror") Underhill.[9] At the same time, the famous Wickersham Report of 1931 and numerous state follow-ups condemned criminal justice agencies for ineffectiveness and corruption. Criminals and officials alike stimulated a public appetite for movies about crime and punishment.

The three most vivid of the early gangster films—*Little Caesar* (1930), *Public Enemy* (1931), and *Scarface* (1932)—appeared at the start of the decade, setting the pattern for the many imitations that followed. In this pattern, an ambitious, ruthless criminal rises to the top only to die violently. He and his cronies sport double-breasted suits, fedoras, and Tommy guns; they talk tough, scorn dames, and are infinitely more interesting than the bland G-men who gun them down. Two of the three stars of these vehicles—Edward G. Robinson from *Little Caesar* and James Cagney from *Public Enemy*—became tough-guy icons. (Paul Muni, the lead in *Scarface,* went on to more varied roles.)

To deflect charges that they were sympathetic to criminals, the big-three gangster films of the 1930s tried to fashion an anticrime image. *Scarface* begins with a text announcing, "This picture is an indictment of gang rule in America and of the callous indifference of the government to this constantly increasing menace to our safety and our liberty. . . . And the purpose of this picture is to demand of the government: 'What are you going to do about it?'" Similarly, *Public Enemy* starts by claiming, "it is the ambition of the authors . . . to honestly depict an environment that exists today in a certain strata of American life, rather than glorify the hoodlum or the criminal." But the movies fail to live up to their admonitions. They portray gangsters as desperate men in a desperate hour, victims of a society that stresses wealth and status while failing to provide working-class men with the means to achieve these ends. Despite their proclamations of anticriminal intent, 1930s gangster films turned criminals into heroes.

No matter how violent and unlawful the movie gangsters, many Americans identified with them, sharing their economic disadvantages and dreams of wealth during hard times. The stock market crashed in 1929, shortly before the big-three gangster films appeared. These movies echoed the financial predicaments of many ordinary Americans during the Great Depression and, in so doing, influenced the genre thereafter, associating criminality with economic hardship and portraying gangsters as underdogs. Walking a populist tightrope, these films spoke to Americans struggling to make ends meet while simultaneously attacking crime and the government's ability to control it.

Public Enemy, organized around chapters in the life of gangster Tom Powers, opens with his childhood in a working-class immigrant family. Tom is uninterested in a life of virtuous poverty. Watching his family work strenuous hours just to break even, he concludes that crime does indeed pay. Although Tom grows into a tough-talking, barbaric character, seemingly meant to be hated, it is difficult not to root for him. He is far more appealing than his tepid, straight-as-an-arrow brother, and his lines are smart, honest, and authentic. What he lacks in charm (and Tom is the character who rubs a grapefruit in Mae Clark's face) is counterbalanced by his chutzpah and determination to succeed. Even after we have seen him destroy everything in his path, Tom can disarm us with his modesty: Gunned down, stumbling in a gutter, he mutters, "I guess I'm not that tough after all." When his mangled body is dropped off on his family's doorstep, we are left feeling that Tom is as much a victim as he is a villain.

Like the gangster genre, prison movies had roots in silent film, and they too became popular in the 1930s. Even more so than gangster movies, prison films leave viewers cheering for the "wrong" side. These movies naturally emphasize the most dramatic aspect of prison life: inmates' deprivations, the electric chair just down the hall, and intricate plans for escape. Due to this perspective (we rarely see prison life from the warden's angle), the viewer has little choice but to recognize the good in convicts and rally behind their against-all-odds escape efforts. The past is seldom mentioned, and when it does come up, we often learn that the convicts were framed. This pattern was established early, beginning with *The Big House* (1930), and it has remained integral to the prison genre ever since.

Few prison films fail to indict the state and its authorities, casting them as brutal oppressors. Much as we learn to sympathize with the convicts, we learn to despise the officials who torment them. This antistate perspective is best exemplified by the melodramatic exposé *I Am a Fugitive from a Chain Gang* (1932). Based on a true story, it features Paul Muni as James Allen, a World War I veteran who, having inadvertently become an accomplice to a holdup, is sent south to toil on a chain gang. Becoming spiteful and bitter, Allen berates the criminal justice system for jailing the wrong man: "The state's promise didn't mean anything. It was all lies! . . . Why, their crimes are worse than mine! Worse than anybody here! They're the ones that should be in chains, not we!" After escaping, being recaptured, and reescaping (and thus displaying the tenacity that thenceforth distinguished the screen's toughest inmate heroes), Allen is corrupted by circumstance and injustice. Hissing "I steal!" he becomes the criminal he was alleged to be. While few subsequent prison films blame the state so explicitly for inducing criminality, most at least hint at this theme.

I Am a Fugitive from a Chain Gang was a product of Warner Bros., the outstanding crime film studio in the 1930s. Unlike Paramount and MGM, it did not circumvent the Great Depression, instead churning out cynical, daring, and streetwise films such as *I Am a Fugitive, Scarface,* and *Marked Woman* (1937). Into the 1940s this same studio continued to make important crime films, competing with the other studios by hiring a fleet of talented young directors (Michael Curtiz, Howard Hawks, John Huston, and William Wyler), many of whom specialized in "A" noirs and crime pictures (including *Mildred Pierce* [1945], *Casablanca* [1942], *The Big Sleep* [1946], and *The Maltese Falcon* [1941]).

In spite of Warner Bros.' influence, however, Hollywood movies of the 1930's typically relied on conventional ideas of criminality. Although murder mysteries abounded during this period, few subscribed to the psychoanalytical themes and bizarre characterizations of European films. Some American-made movies featured antiheroes, and others, such as John Ford's *The Informer* (1935) and Fritz Lang's

Fury, were unusually cynical, psychological, and stylistically sophis-ticated, anticipating film noir. On the whole, however, there were few signs that crime films were on the cusp of radical change.

About 1940 the gangster film entered a period of relative dor-mancy, one brought on by America's involvement in World War II and the decreasing relevance of the Great Depression. For the next two decades, mobsters appeared mainly in secondary roles or as des-perate, aging representatives of a dying breed, as in Raoul Walsh's *High Sierra* (1941) and *Key Largo* (1958). In *High Sierra,* Humphrey Bogart stars as a middle-aged gangster trying to do one last job be-fore retiring to an honest life. The honorable mobsters of his genera-tion, who killed only when double-crossed, are being replaced by a younger, brasher type. His last stand in the mountains, outnumbered and outgunned, is thus emblematic of the decline not only of tradi-tional gangsters but also of the gangster film itself. The genre remained largely moribund until revived about 1970 by *Bonnie and Clyde* (1967) and *The Godfather* (1972).

Film Noir, ca. 1940–1955

As the gangster film declined, the movie industry reached a dramatic turning point: the advent of a new film style that transformed Holly-wood and later became known as film noir. Noir was not a genre but rather what Spencer Selby calls "a historical, stylistic and thematic trend . . . within . . . the American crime film of the forties and fifties."[10] Thus, its emergence went unremarked, and years passed before critics (first French, then American) began to agree on a set of defining attributes. (They are working on it still.) James Naremore, in his important study of film noir, *More Than Night: Film Noir in its Contexts,* chooses not to look for the essential features that define this group of films but instead tries to explain the paradox that "film noir is both an important cinematic legacy and an idea we have projected onto the past."[11] Cynical, daring, and risqué, noir was worldly in its themes and sophisticated in style. The term (literally, "black" or "dark" film) refers to the mood of these productions, their shadowy, nighttime settings, and the black-and-white film stocks with which they were made. As Naremore points out in his history of the idea of film noir, the term has become a metaphor for these movies' preoc-cupation with nocturnal settings, the underworld, eroticized violence, existential misery, exotic nonwhite characters, death, and nightmarish irrationality.[12] Noir inverted Hollywood traditions, ushering in a heightened emphasis on form and a new kind of viewing experience. While noir changed the way many types of films looked and sounded, it affected crime films most profoundly.

Of the sources that fed the development of film noir, one of the most influential was American filmmakers' growing interest in European techniques and styles. The importation of European approaches such as German expressionism accelerated with the arrival in Hollywood of foreign-born directors (Billy Wilder, Fritz Lang, and Alfred Hitchcock, among others). Moreover, a new generation of American directors, including Orson Welles and William Wyler, began using innovative techniques such as deep focus and long camera takes. Open to stylistic experimentation, these filmmakers welcomed the artistic approaches of European directors, and their attention to style revolutionized the industry.

A second factor contributing to noir's development was that Hollywood had become home to some of the country's better writers, including Raymond Chandler, William Faulkner, Dorothy Parker, and Dashiell Hammett, many of whom produced fluent and original screenplays about crime. Noir's dark characters and complicated subplots replaced the simple narrative structures that had hitherto been synonymous with American filmmaking. Criminals now blended with the innocents, confusing the moral order. Previously linear, chronological plots became labyrinthine, at times chaotic. Criminal motives, limited in the 1930s gangster movies to money and power, became increasingly cryptic and pathological, reflecting a cynical, almost hopeless disillusionment with society.

New gender relationships also contributed to the development of noir and came to characterize it. Although strong women had achieved star status in the 1930s, they had been all but excluded from crime films. In the 1940s the barriers began to erode, a reflection of women's changing roles in the larger society. As World War II siphoned men out of the labor market and into the armed forces, women moved into jobs traditionally held by men. But as soon as the war ended, women were sent back into the home, a sign of Americans' uneasiness about women's (temporary) emancipation. Film noir echoed this uneasiness. While it created a niche for women—sometimes very powerful women—for the most part it portrayed them disparagingly, as vamps and psychotics.

John Huston's *The Maltese Falcon* and Howard Hawks's *The Big Sleep* exemplify the early noir detective thrillers. Adapted from seminal mystery novels—the former by Hammett and the latter by Chandler—these films introduced the "private dick" (deftly played in both cases by Humphrey Bogart, the male icon of noir): sardonic, nocturnal, and corruptible, a glass of bourbon in one hand and a married woman in the other. He lives in an ethical limbo, working both sides of the law, navigating between the justice system and the underworld. Not all noirs revolve around a private investigator, but film noir quickly became famous for its hard-boiled, tough-guy leads, particularly the detectives Sam Spade and Philip Marlowe. "The ideal noir hero," Naremore observes, "is the opposite of John Wayne."[13]

The female counterparts in these two films also set early examples, creating classic models of the femme fatale: conniving, double-crossing, and smooth-talking, traps waiting to ensnare men who fall for their beauty and skin-deep charm. In *The Maltese Falcon,* where she is played by Mary Astor, the femme fatale almost lures detective Sam Spade to his doom. The main female character in *The Big Sleep,* played by Lauren Bacall, is more lovable and indeed had to be, as Bogart and Bacall were already one of America's most famous couples. However, she, too, is a powerful character who plays hardball in a traditionally male game. Most femmes fatales originate from the mystery pulp fiction made popular in the late 1920s and the 1930s by the likes of James M. Cain, Hammett, and Chandler. In *Farewell, My Lovely,* for instance, private dick Marlowe describes his ideal woman in typical noir terms: "I like smooth shiny girls, hardboiled and loaded with sin."[14] Hammett's *Red Harvest* provides another early model of the sly, money-hungry seductress who inhabits most film noir: "She's money-made, all right, but somehow you don't mind it. She's so thoroughly mercenary, so frankly greedy, that there's nothing disagreeable about it."[15] "The noir heroine," Naremore points out, "is no Doris Day."[16]

When the cagey detective and seductress share the screen, fireworks ensue. In some cases the couple battle to the death with elaborate strategies and merciless determination. In Billy Wilder's *Double Indemnity* (1944), starring Barbara Stanwyck and Fred MacMurray, the heartless femme fatale arranges to eliminate her newest lover (with whom she killed her second husband for his insurance policy); discovering her scheme, he responds with a chess move of his own, arriving at her house armed. Bullets fly, she dies, and he stumbles out the front door mortally wounded. When not at each other's throats, however, noir's male and female leads are usually in each other's beds. Sexual relations, while not explicitly shown, are implied more strongly than ever in these noir thrillers, defying the censors' injunctions against big-screen sex.

Injecting a bleakness into American cinema, film noir countered Hollywood's tendency to provide comforting resolutions. Noir's desolate, cynical qualities distinguish it from the more optimistic productions synonymous with classical Hollywood's well-lit sets, tidy narratives, and more-or-less happy conclusions. Appropriately, most noirs take place at night, usually in the shadowy city but sometimes in the loneliness of middle America. In Nicholas Ray's *They Live By Night* (1949), a young married couple on the run from the law travel only at night—as the film's title suggests—passing through a series of small towns. The likable young man (Farley Granger) aspires to right his wrongs and live out the Hollywood dream, but his criminal past won't let him. Gunned down in a blaze of bullets, he leaves behind his young, pregnant wife.

Integral to noir's pessimism is its famously terse and hard-boiled dialogue, whether uttered in conversation or voice-over narration. Take, for instance, Jacques Tourneur's important contribution to the cycle, *Out of the Past* (1947), starring Robert Mitchum and Jane Greer. In a casino, while on the run from a mob boss, Kathie (Greer) asks Jeff (Mitchum), "Is there a way to win?" to which Jeff responds, in a perfect display of noir's detached fatalism, "There's a way to lose more slowly." Many other films exemplify the cycle's cynical fatalism through narrative structure. Edgar Ulmer's *Detour* (1945), Robert Siodmak's *The Killers* (1946), and Billy Wilder's *Double Indemnity* and *Sunset Boulevard* (1950), for instance, all begin where most crime films "end," after the lead (whether criminal or victim) is either dead or about to die; then, through flashbacks, these films travel back in time to a happier day, only to wind forward, in conclusion, to their doomed finales. Although Jules Dassin's *Night and the City* (1950) does not employ the same narrative structure, it imposes a similar sense of impending doom upon the film's trajectory: Richard Widmark plays an ambitious but hapless character who commits one costly blunder after another until his luck, if you can call it that, runs out for good in the fateful conclusion.

In *Hollywood Genres,* Thomas Schatz attributes the bleakness that is central to so many films noirs to social conditions in World War II America:

> This changing visual portrayal of the world . . . reflected the progressively darkening cultural attitudes during and after the war. Hollywood's *noir* films documented the growing disillusionment with certain traditional American values in the face of complex and often contradictory social, political, scientific, and economic developments.[17]

Previously clear divisions between good and evil now grew murky. Everyone appears criminal in the shadowy land of film noir, hopelessly tainted by sin, lust, and greed. Even the innocents and the detectives succumb to corruption. In *The Maltese Falcon,* for example, detective Sam Spade is the prime suspect in his partner's murder, and he seems more concerned with finding a scapegoat than identifying the actual killer. The once-honest insurance detective of *Double Indemnity* devolves into a ruthless, duplicitous killer.

Another characteristic distinguishing noirs from earlier crime films and typical Hollywood fare is their highly expressionistic style. They exploit the infinite possibilities of low-key lighting, high-contrast shadow, frame depth, and the versatile camera, creating complex compositions that extend the film's themes and central dilemmas. Day-for-night shooting[18] and deep focus, popularized by Gregg Toland, William Wyler, and Orson Welles, contributed to noir's distinct aesthetic. This emphasis on style appears in literally hundreds of films of this era, not all of them crime movies or conventional noirs.

By midcentury, mainstream Hollywood embraced the aesthetics of noir. Directors such as Michael Curtiz (*Casablanca*), John Ford (*The Grapes of Wrath* [1940]), Howard Hawks (*Red River* [1948]), John Huston (*The Treasure of the Sierra Madre* [1948]), George Stevens (*A Place in the Sun* [1951]), Orson Welles (*Citizen Kane* [1941]), and Billy Wilder (*The Lost Weekend* [1945]) made expressionistic, well-crafted films of all genres. Likewise, noir crime films, earlier limited mainly to detective thrillers, broadened in theme and story line. Remaining noir in tone and style, they shifted attention from the detective to the criminal. And, anticipating later crime films, they became increasingly pathological, erotic, and violent (*Detour, The Postman Always Rings Twice* [1946], *Sunset Boulevard, Kiss Me Deadly* [1955], *Touch of Evil* [1958]).

Crime films thrived for about a decade after World War II, out-numbering even retrospective war pictures and expanding their commentary on social issues. These films evoked the spirit of the era and reflected the period's transitions. In the war's aftermath, after reveling in victory and apparent stability, America entered the Cold War years, a period of difficult adjustment and division. Beset by self-doubt, suspicion (McCarthyism and the Red Scare), anxiety (threats of war with the Soviet Union and of nuclear catastrophe), and rapid change (suburbanization), Americans embraced social and cultural conformity. Builders created look-alike housing developments such as Levittown, and advertisers targeted the faceless American suburbanite.

In reaction to these developments, an insurgent avant-garde arts movement burgeoned on all fronts. Abstract expressionist painting, bop and post-bop jazz, and Beat Generation poetry and prose introduced new styles of dissonance and rebellion. Without becoming avant-garde itself, Hollywood was deeply affected by the new social and cultural currents. Senator Joe McCarthy's demagogic campaign against communists led to witch hunts for Hollywood leftists and to the blacklisting of moviemakers. With the stakes raised, some directors felt impelled to do more than merely entertain viewers.

Audiences, in turn, were ready for more challenging and daring films. In society at large, resistance to depictions of sex and obscenity was weakening, with the U.S. Supreme Court, for example, narrowing the definition of obscenity in the mid-1950s. *Playboy* hit the market in 1952. Americans began accepting the central tenets of Freudian theory, which led to new interpretations of criminality, and a more liberal view of sex. In response to these social shifts, and in an attempt to lure television viewers out of the home and back into the theater, the Production Code in 1956 loosened its stance on taboo topics such as drug abuse and prostitution. For Hollywood in general, this meant more productions geared to adult audiences, a change that helps explain the rise of the melodrama (*East of Eden* [1954], *All That Heaven Allows* [1955], *Giant* [1956], *Peyton Place* [1957]) and the sex comedy (*Gentlemen Prefer Blondes* [1953], *The Seven Year Itch* [1955], *Some Like it Hot* [1959]). For the crime film, these developments meant shocking, highly psychological productions, replete with new kinds of killers, offenses, and motivations, and a brasher display of screen violence.

Joseph Lewis's *Gun Crazy,* released in 1949, shows how crime noirs changed in the postwar period. Written by a blacklisted screenwriter,

Figure 1.1. *Gun Crazy* (1949) became a model for subsequent lovers-on-the-lam films. Peggy Cummins's character, halfway between the femme fatale of 1940s noirs and the independent woman of 1990s films, reflects changing roles of women in the broader society. Photo used by permission of Photofest.

Dalton Trumbo, *Gun Crazy* delves into perversion and ends in tragedy. Alarming and extremist, it tells the story of a man and woman united by their obsession with guns. They meet while she—a modern-day Annie Oakley with an attitude—is performing in a carnival shooting show. They marry, and he dreams of a job with a gun manufacturer; but she wants more than middle-class suburbia. Threatening to end the relationship, she persuades him that crime alone will provide the kind of life she needs. As the young criminals roam the countryside, robbing banks and warehouses, they come to revel in a life of lust and depravity. When the law catches up with them, they flee to his childhood stomping ground, only to be gunned down by a lakeside in the early morning mists.

At first glance, *Gun Crazy* seems to provide merely another portrait of noir's femme fatale, driven by greed and luring a good-hearted man to his destruction. As her character develops, though, it transcends the conventional femme fatale, becoming overtly sadistic. Against her husband's wishes, she kills an innocent clerk, her eyes widening with excitement. Although more a pathological she-devil than a liberated woman, she stands on equal ground with her male counterpart, wielding weapons as well as any and masterminding their crimes.

Gun Crazy was received as little more than a cheap "B" picture, but in retrospect we can see that it marked an important stage in crime films' evolution. Presaging *Bonnie and Clyde,* which in turn influenced a generation of crime films, *Gun Crazy* was one of the first movies to feature the now familiar male-female crime team. Even though it perpetuates misogynist notions of the criminal woman, it expands her character. Its memorable camera work and deftly staged robbery of a meat warehouse, with hundreds of dangling carcasses, push viewers to a new closeness in identification with the bad guy. Moreover, *Gun Crazy's* bold inclusion of aberrant psychology and sexuality, as well as its focus on the criminals' degeneration, make it a precursor of more recent crime films such as *Taxi Driver* (1976) and *Boogie Nights* (1997).

Other postwar crime noirs (Otto Preminger's *The Man with the Golden Arm* [1955], for instance) brought the new social concern of drug addiction to the big screen. *White Heat* (1949), *The Asphalt Jungle* (1950), and *The Desperate Hours* (1955) reveal the period's newfound fascination with the psychology of crime.[19] Even more relevant to the times was *Kiss Me Deadly,* an archetypal noir detective film with a distinctly Cold War twist. Mike Hammer, a trash-talking detective, finds himself in the middle of a security crisis, searching for a mysterious box containing radioactive uranium. In the final sequence, the Pandora-like femme fatale succumbs to curiosity and opens the box, releasing the sinful by-products of modernity and ushering in the nuclear age. Burdened by small budgets, no-name actors, and pulpy dialogues, few postwar noirs equaled *Double Indemnity* or *The Big Sleep* in production values. Yet their bravura aesthetic and thematic relevance captivated audiences and critics alike, changing the direction of the film industry. The detective noir has inspired countless remakes and homages (among them *Devil in a Blue Dress* [1995] and *L.A. Confidential* [1997]). That subsequent directors as disparate as Carl Franklin, Jean-Luc Godard, Tom Kalin, Akira Kurosawa, Quentin Tarantino, and Francois Truffaut have been influenced by these films suggests their impact not only on crime movies but also all cinema.

Transition and Development, 1955–1967

In the mid-1950s, crime films underwent considerable change. Film noir, which for nearly two decades had defined crime films, was entering a period of quiescence, its scenarios and leitmotifs having grown not only worn but also untimely. The classical Hollywood studio system, with its oligopolistic control over all phases of the movie industry, was coming to an end. The increasing popularity of television in American households cut into Hollywood's profits. The movie industry responded with new attractions: drive-ins, Cinemascope and wide-screen movies, and Technicolor. The civil rights movement, the advent of rock and roll and youth marketing, entrenchment of the Cold War, and space travel redirected Hollywood toward espionage thrillers (the James Bond series, *The Manchurian Candidate* [1962], *The Spy Who Came in from the Cold* [1965]), stylized epics (*Ben-Hur* [1959], *The Guns of Navarone* [1961], *The Sound of Music* [1965]), romance and folly pictures (*Love Me Tender* [1956], *Pillow Talk* [1959], *Beach Blanket Bingo* [1965]), sci-fis (*The Blob* [1958], *The Castle of Fu Manchu* [1968]), and race-oriented melodramas (*Imitation of Life* [1959], *A Raisin in the Sun* [1961], *Guess Who's Coming to Dinner* [1967]).

In spite of these midcentury transitions, crime films did not disappear. Several types, in fact, thrived during this period, with two cycles in particular, courtroom dramas and heist movies, enjoying great popularity during the Cold War. Also notable was the rise of Hollywood's most prolific and renowned director of crime movies, Alfred Hitchcock.

In the early 1950s, the British-born Hitchcock emerged as a leading director of American crime movies. More than most of his contemporaries, he incorporated psychological aberration and Freudian theories, a tendency most overt in *Spellbound* (1946), the tale of a man whose troubled past surfaces with the help of an analyst. Known in particular for his polished, sophisticated crime thrillers (*Rear Window* [1954], *North by Northwest* [1959], *Vertigo* [1958]), Hitchcock also made a number of noirish films centered on the psychology of crime.

Hitchcock's *Shadow of a Doubt* (1943) tells the story of Uncle Charley, played memorably by Joseph Cotten, who makes a surprise visit—from the big city—to his sister and her family in the clean and quiet town of Santa Rosa, North Carolina. Most surprising of all, however, is that the charming and lovable Charley is a notorious killer, the "Merry Widow Murderer," on the run. In *Rope* (1948), starring James Stewart and based loosely on the infamous Leopold and Loeb case, Hitchcock follows two wealthy bachelors as they plan and execute what they conceive as the "perfect" murder. They have no motive other than to boast of having gotten away with the crime. Their twisted psyches (and Hitchcock's delight in the perverse) come to the fore when they serve dinner on top of the trunk containing the body. Hitchcock's 1951 masterpiece, *Strangers on a Train,* opens as a tennis player named Guy meets the deranged Bruno on a commuter train. When Guy halfheartedly wishes that his two-timing wife were dead, Bruno suggests that they swap murders, as he happens to be tiring of his father. Guy agrees, mainly to placate the persistent Bruno. Bruno follows up on his half of the bargain, however, strangling the woman in an extended and grisly scene. The son of a doting mother and despotic father, Bruno is a version of the maniacal killer whose violent rages stem from a dysfunctional family. Thereafter, Hitchcock went on to make other well-crafted hits such as *Dial M for Murder* (1954), *Rear Window,* and *The Wrong Man* (1956) before crowning his career with *Psycho* (1960).

Psycho introduced a new kind of screen violence: gory, graphic, and sexually charged. To heighten the effect, Hitchcock allows the viewer no escape or relief. Early in the film, for example, he kills off Marion Crane (Janet Leigh), the person we are most likely to relate to, in a shower scene that quickly became one of the most celebrated moments in cinematic history. During the scene, moreover, Hitchcock flagellates viewers with shrieking violin sounds that we can no more evade than Marion can the slashing knife. The killer—the seemingly meek, clean-cut Norman Bates—is in fact contorted by psychosis and dual personality syndrome, acting out his homicidal urges in the guise of his dead mother. *Psycho* opened a door in the Hollywood crime film for the grisly, lurid, and violently deranged. It also emphasized the elements of wit and playfulness that came to characterize crime films of the late 1990s.

An important midcentury development for the crime film was the rise of trial dramas. This type, as Carol Clover reminds us,[20] first emerged during the silent era (*Falsely Accused* [1907], *By Whose Hand* [1913], *A Woman's Resurrection* [1915], Cecil B. DeMille's *The Whispering Chorus* [1918]). Yet the biggest flurry of courtroom pictures on record did not come until the silent era gave way to talkies (*The Trial of Mary Dugan* [1929], starring Norma Shearer; two Greta Garbo vehicles, *The Kiss* [1929] and *Mata Hari* [1931]; Fritz Lang's *M; An American Tragedy* [1931]; and *Account Rendered* [1932]). This cycle continued through the 1930s, with titles such as *Manhattan Melodrama* (1934), starring Clark Gable and Myrna Loy; *Fury;* the prototypical film noir, *Marked Woman;* and John Ford's *Young Mr. Lincoln* (1939). A more cynical breed of courtroom movies emerged in the wartime 1940s, exemplified by what Norman Rosenberg aptly terms "law noirs" (William Wyler's *The Letter* [1940]; *Scarlet Street;* Orson Welles's *The Lady from Shanghai* [1947]; *A Place in the Sun;* and Hitchcock's *The Wrong Man*). As the Cold War heated up during the 1950s—a decade that saw McCarthyism take hold of America in a series of nationally televised witch-hunt trials by the House Un-American Activities Committee—so too did trial movies about the limitations of the judicial process.

Like prison films, courtroom dramas often hinge on the accused person's innocence while exploiting the dramatic potential of the courtroom setting. The protagonist, whether defendant, defense attorney, or jury member, restores justice, sometimes by exposing the true culprit in the course of the trial and sometimes by defining justice broadly, in terms of "natural" law (*Anatomy of a Murder* [1959], *Inherit the Wind* [1960], *Witness for the Prosecution* [1957], *Judgment at Nuremberg* [1961]). Integral to the classic trial dramas of the mid-twentieth century, however, was not so much their indictment of the justice system as their indictment of society at large.

Above all, these films criticized narrow-mindedness and other social ills, portraying the trial as an effective means of discovering the truth. *Twelve Angry Men* (1957) concentrates on a closed jury session in which a young Hispanic man's guilt is all but assumed. Gradually, though, a lone juror (Henry Fonda) convinces his doltish and quick-to-judge peers otherwise, in the process revealing flaws in the prosecution's arguments and a subtle racism among the jury. *Twelve Angry Men* portrays this holdout's victory as a triumph for the American judicial process while condemning the irresponsibility, racism, and selfishness of the other eleven jurors. *They Won't Believe Me* (1947), a weaker film, makes the same basic point: The justice system, though perhaps imperfect, is not to blame for the world's injustices. The jury members recognize the defendant's innocence, but he, expecting them to convict, jumps from a window to his death just before they announce their verdict.

To Kill a Mockingbird (1962), filmed in the midst of the civil rights movement, directly attacks a racist America struggling to reconcile its diversity and differences. (The previous year, John Ford released *Sergeant Rutledge,* a Western trial picture about a black cavalry sergeant falsely accused of raping and murdering a white woman.) The jury is blind to all details of the case except that the accused is a black man and the plaintiff a white woman. Her mendacious charge of rape is confirmed by the town, jury, and judicial system, but the fact that Atticus Finch (Gregory Peck), the heroic defense attorney, has defended the man is a sign that the system can be redeemed.

In *A Place in the Sun,* the accused on trial is a working-class man entangled in the paradoxes and hypocrisies of America. Aspiring to higher status, as his society demands, George Eastman (Montgomery Clift) is unable to cross class lines, having impregnated a lower-class woman (who in turn is denied access to an abortion). The ambiguities of Eastman's alleged crime—the drowning of his pregnant girlfriend (Shelley Winters) and the thwarting of his relationship with his debutante lover/fiancée (Elizabeth Taylor)—reflect the insurmountable class barriers that ultimately condemn Eastman to execution. American values as well as the young man were put on trial by *A Place in the Sun.* As more recent courtroom dramas demonstrate, this element of social critique is often the constant, while the specific charge (class inequities, greed, racism, sexism) varies according to the era of production.

Also popular during this period were heist or caper films. This movie cycle, like trial and prison movies, overlapped with film noir at first and then blossomed on its own in the late 1950s and throughout the 1960s and 1970s, to be resurrected again by later generations. Several important noirs serve as prototypes for the caper film, but none was as influential as *The Asphalt Jungle,* which more than any previous noir focused on the intricate planning and execution of a robbery. Thereafter, many noir-inflected heist movies followed this formula, including *White Heat,* Stanley Kubrick's *The Killing* (1956), Robert Wise's *Odds Against Tomorrow* (1959), and two French masterpieces of 1955, Jean-Pierre Melville's *Bob le flambeur* and Jules Dassin's *Rififi.*[21] These were imitated by countless subsequent caper films, beginning with Britain's droll hit *The Ladykillers* (1955), starring Alec

Guinness and Peter Sellers and remade by the Coen brothers in 2004. True to noir sensibility, all of these filmed robberies end in failure and death.

In keeping with the turn toward youth pop culture and Hollywood's new love affair with the epic, heist movies of the 1960s tended to be glitzy, glamorous, and (for crime films) relatively cheery. Several, exploiting the popularity of World War II escape epics (*The Bridge over the River Kwai* [1957], *The Great Escape* [1963]), transported the heist formula from city streets to European battlefields (*Dirty Dozen* [1967], *Kelly's Heroes* [1970]). Even lighter was a string of comedic capers. *Ocean's Eleven* (1960) starred the Rat Pack (Frank Sinatra, Sammy Davis Jr., and Dean Martin) as World War II vets who plot to rob the five biggest casinos in one Las Vegas night. *The Italian Job* (1969) comically depicts a plot to steal gold from Turin by causing a large traffic jam, while *The Doberman Gang* (1972) shows an ex-con and his friends training a pack of large dogs to rob a bank. That same year Robert Redford starred in Peter Yates's comedy *The Hot Rock* (1972), about an unlucky crew of thieves on the trail of a large diamond, while the following year George Roy Hill's upbeat favorite, *The Sting* (1973), starring Paul Newman and Robert Redford, won the Oscar for Best Picture. Yet other heist films, such as Norman Jewison's *The Thomas Crown Affair* (1968), tapped into the era's fondness for dapper men and international intrigue.

In a sign of its formulaic success, the heist movie revived at the turn of the century in a series of popular remakes (*The Thomas Crown Affair* [1999]; *Ocean's Eleven* [2001], which then spawned *Ocean's Twelve* [2004]; and *The Italian Job* [2003], which is due to be followed in 2006 by *The Italian Job II*). Regardless of whether heist movies end tragically or happily, audiences are always positioned to favor the criminals—a position that seems to come easily to moviegoers around the world and across generations. This sympathy stems in part from the heist film's tendency to give viewers the criminals' perspective and in part from its almost exclusive concentration on inventive planning of the crimes.[22] Merely through following the plotline, viewers build allegiances to these characters and their circumstances. Another explanation for the heist film's popularity lies in the populist appeal of Robin Hood underdogs, who are shown stealing money from a faceless source that may have too much to begin with. In addition, heist films play out a quintessential capitalist fantasy.

Renewal: 1967–ca. 1980

As the 1960s came to an end, several important crime film genres re-vived. The 1967 release of *Bonnie and Clyde* almost single-handedly revitalized the gangster genre. At the same time, detective and prison movies reemerged, complemented by an entirely new genre, the cop film, which materialized from the remains of noir's private investiga-tors. The antihero was reborn, this time in the guise of the psychotic loner and vigilante police officer. Crime films again flooded the silver screen, with American youth readier than ever before to idolize heroic rebels. In retrospect, however, we can see that even in the suppos-edly radical 1970s, few moviemakers were willing to actually chal-lenge the status quo. At best, they kept up with the transformations wracking American society.

In 1967 the United States was in the midst of one of its most tumultuous periods, with no reprieve in sight. Radicalism came to a head with riots in the big cities and street warfare between resent-ful minorities and the predominantly white police. The assassina-tions of John F. Kennedy, Martin Luther King Jr., Robert Kennedy, and Malcolm X exacerbated already deep divisions, raising fears for the stability of the social order. Other eruptions occurred over the increasingly unpopular Vietnam War and hypocrisies of the Nixon administration. As baby boomers came of age, many turned to drugs, street celebrations, and political demonstrations, forming a counter-culture and warning one another to mistrust anyone older than thirty. A new generation of directors, including Francis Ford Cop-pola, George Lucas, Martin Scorsese, and Steven Spielberg (the so-called movie brats), began making films attuned to modern times. In addition, crime was again looming as a major public concern, with presidential commissions calling for overhauls of the criminal jus-tice system.

Hollywood eased up on its suppression of sex and vice, freeing di-rectors of the late 1960s from constraints. Since the early days of silent film, moralists had worried that movies could corrupt youth by ex-posing them to sin and crime. Hollywood had reacted creatively, agreeing to self-regulation in order to avoid government censorship. In 1922 the industry established the Motion Picture Producers and Distributors of America to serve as its censor and public relations arm. The association imposed strict standards, but filmmakers and producers were not held accountable for the content of their films until the adoption, in 1934, of the Motion Picture Production Code, which ruled out depictions of sex, vulgarity, and some types of crime. "Totally forbidden," writes Jack C. Ellis,

> were presentations of drug traffic or the use of drugs, sexual perversion, white slavery, sex relations between the white and black races, and nudity. . . . Proscribed were [such terms as] "alley cat," or "bat" or "broad (applied to a woman)." Also prohibited were: "Bronx cheer (the sound); . . . cripes; fanny; fairy (in the vulgar sense); finger (the)."[23]

Hollywood began to loosen these self-imposed rules in the 1950s and 1960s in a bid to attract youthful audiences away from television. Otto Preminger's *The Man with the Golden Arm* ignored the censors to become the first Hollywood film to deal openly with drug addiction, for example. In the late 1960s Hollywood abandoned the Production Code in favor of a rating system that classified films by letters such as G (suitable for general audiences), R (restricted; people under sixteen years old had to be accompanied by a parent or guardian), and X (restricted entirely to people over sixteen). Hereafter theaters would have to do the policing, leaving filmmakers free to depict almost anything they chose.

Arthur Penn's *Bonnie and Clyde* made its bold debut in 1967, a politically tumultuous year when anger against the state and authority neared its peak. In this context (and with help from influential reviewers and an unusual distribution history), the film about youthful rebels netted $20 million. Based loosely on the lives of bank robbers Bonnie Parker and Clyde Barrow (played by Faye Dunaway and Warren Beatty), the film follows their crime spree across the Southwest, venerating the criminals as populist folk heroes. (In one bank robbery scene, for instance, Clyde gives back money to a poor farmer.) Thoroughly modern and brazen, the movie appealed to youth defying authority and tradition. It also reflected recent shifts in gender relations, with Faye Dunaway playing an equal to Warren Beatty. Instead of luring an innocent man into trouble, like the standard femme fatale, or standing passively by, she works as his partner-in-crime.

The bloody conclusion of *Bonnie and Clyde* seemed paradigmatic to 1960s youth. Betrayed by a friend's father, the amiable couple is gunned down in a horrific scene of police overkill. Beautiful, young, and in love, they become martyrs for an era. But this tragic ending failed to provide a coherent or specific critique of institutions of power, instead offering dramatic violence and aimless rebellion.

Figure 1.2. *Bonnie and Clyde* (1967) created heroes for 1960s youth: a young, egalitarian couple in revolt against authority, mowed down by representatives of a corrupt older generation. Photo used by permission of Photofest.

In addition to setting the stage for explicitly modern, violent crime films, *Bonnie and Clyde* triggered a revisionist movement in American cinema. Hollywood began to produce genre films that, like *Bonnie and Clyde,* relied on but updated older conventions. Directors of the late 1960s and early 1970s, many of them products of newly instituted film schools, emulated the classics in style, story line, and characterizations but modernized them for a new generation of viewers. Musicals now kept time to rock and roll, westerns presented a Native American perspective, and a new wave of crime pictures, from gangster sagas to private detective and police films, made overt reference to the golden age of noir while also reflecting the tumult and disillusionment of the Vietnam War era. Crime movies had long been cynical, but these latest additions embraced a futility matched only by a few films noirs.

In previous decades the central conflict had usually been resolved with the criminal's capture or demise. Crime pictures of the Vietnam War era and beyond, in contrast, redefined the problem of crime as systemic in origin and, often, as insurmountable (*A Clockwork Orange* [1971], *Straw Dogs* [1972], *The Conversation* [1974], *Chinatown* [1974], *Straight Time* [1978]). (Here begins the alternative tradition of the critical crime films discussed in the introduction.) Contributing to the darker mood of these new crime films was, once again, Hollywood's elimination of the Production Code's "decency" standards, a change that enabled movies to become more violent, risqué, and gory.

If *Bonnie and Clyde* revived the gangster genre, Francis Ford Coppola's *The Godfather* restored it to a position of primacy in American cinema. Critically acclaimed, *The Godfather* reinstated the gangster saga not only in Hollywood but also in America's mythic imagination. The film follows the changing of the guard in a prominent gangster family—from a more orderly and traditional rule, which abided by a strict set of codes (no drugs, for example), to one less chivalrous, more violent, and embittered. This transition is easily likened to the one America was undergoing at the time of the film's making: from a relatively unified nation characterized by popular leadership, peace, and orderly succession, to one rendered cynical and divided by war, civil protest, assassinations, and political corruption. Starring Marlon Brando and Al Pacino, *The Godfather* presented the family as a surrogate state, the source of the Corleones' morality, security, stability, and sense of purpose.

In Coppola's sequel, *The Godfather, Part II* (1974), the family no longer provides a refuge from governmental ineptitude. Like Nixon's inner circle, the family fails morally, degenerating until it serves only one purpose: ensuring its own survival. Despite this moral bleakness, however (or perhaps partly because of it), *The Godfather, Part II* reinforced the stature of the gangster genre, which continued its revival into the 1990s with such films as Brian De Palma's 1983 version of *Scarface, Once Upon a Time in America* (1984), *The Untouchables* (1987), *Miller's Crossing* (1990), *Goodfellas* (1990), and *Donnie Brasco* (1997).

Noir-inspired detective films and prison movies also experienced revival in the late 1960s and 1970s. Robert Altman's *The Long Goodbye* (1973), based on a Chandler novel, stars Elliot Gould as a modern-day Philip Marlowe, while Roman Polanski's *Chinatown* initiated what some critics have termed "neo-noir"[24] and evoked Howard Hawks's *The Big Sleep* (another Philip Marlowe movie).[25] Like the original *Big Sleep, Chinatown* takes place in Los Angeles, and its cocky private detective, Jake Gittes (Jack Nicholson), is a direct descendant of *The Big*

Sleep's detective. Both movies are sinuous, psychological, and stylish. However, *Chinatown* includes far more sexual violence than its predecessor (its plot hinges on intergenerational incest), and its conclusion—in which the heroine is killed, her sexually abusive father lays claim to his daughter/granddaughter, and the detective stands by despairing—is far more cynical.

The new prison films, too, closely followed the formulas of earlier classics while piling on profanity, violence, and sex. Nearly all of them backed the inmates, portraying government authorities as despotic crooks, even while failing to raise objections that might lead to specific prison reforms. *Cool Hand Luke* (1967) inaugurated this revival, followed by *Midnight Express* (1978), *Papillon* (1973), *Escape from Alcatraz* (1979), and—one of the few prison films that does provide a constructive critique—*Brubaker* (1980). This renaissance carried prison films into the 1980s and 1990s, where they continued to attract audiences, comment on the times, and denigrate authority. *Kiss of the Spider Woman* (1985), for example, uses the prison setting to critique homophobia and to attack U.S.-backed Latin American dictatorships. More recently, *The Shawshank Redemption* (1994) won critical acclaim and financial success by resurrecting nearly every convention and theme of the prison genre.

Clint Eastwood's *Dirty Harry* films gave birth to the cop movie, an entirely new genre within the crime film category. Eastwood brought his inimitable tough-guy persona to these films, reinventing the police detective as (in the words of the hostile critic Pauline Kael) an "emotionless hero, who lives and kills as affectlessly as a psychopathic personality."[26] A vigilante, at least initially, Harry Callahan is fed up with a corrupt and inept system. In the first film of the series, Donald Siegel's *Dirty Harry* (1971), the hero battles a serial killer who repeatedly slips through the system due to legal niceties or departmental ineptitude. Refusing to let this killer escape, Harry defies orders, pursuing and shooting the crazed murderer himself, in cold blood. Harry's anger, and that of the film, differs from the anger of 1940s and 1950s rebel films, which protest against the boring, homogenized life of middle-class America. In the *Dirty Harry* films, anger is directed against the state for leaving citizens defenseless, and it is mixed with fear and fantasies of vigilante justice.

In the first sequel, *Magnum Force* (1973), Harry faces an even more dangerous threat, an inside ring of neofascist cops who assassinate not only offenders who evade the law but also ordinary citizens whose lifestyles offend them. Significantly more violent than *Dirty Harry*, *Magnum Force* evokes the period's strong mistrust of authority while at the same time making a conservative statement about the need for more law and order. Other cop films of the era, such as *The French Connection* (1971) and the factual *Serpico* (1973), also expose corruption among municipal officials and keepers of the peace. Although few later ones are as good as these early examples, cop films have continued to flourish ever since. In the 1980s, for instance, buddy-cop movies (*Beverly Hills Cop* [1984], *Lethal Weapon* [1987], *Stakeout* [1987]) did very well at the box office, in many cases spawning sequels. More recent cop films include Abel Ferrara's *Bad Lieutenant* (1992), starring Harvey Keitel as a morally corrupted, spiritually adrift police officer, and *The Pledge* (2001) and *Insomnia* (2002), both of which are also in part serial killer films.

Beyond developing genres, the 1970s produced an intriguing and unusual kind of crime film in which the antihero is deranged. Apocalyptic in vision, movies such as *The Wild Bunch* (1969), *Straw Dogs*, and *The French Connection* turned the everyday world on its head by presenting a violent vigilante as savior. In Martin Scorsese's *Taxi Driver*, Robert De Niro plays Travis Bickle, one of the screen's most riveting characters. A Vietnam vet turned cabdriver, Travis cannot stand the "filth" of New York City, describing it as "sick, venal." Here the state has failed completely: By sending Travis to Vietnam, it turned this innocent into a pathological monster. New York has become a sewer, a vision of hell, and Travis drives through the night disgusted by the garbage, the whores, the drug pushers, hoping that someday "a real rain will come and wash all the scum away." With no one to trust or believe in (certainly not the politician, with his empty promises, or the invisible police), Travis turns vigilante, deciding that he must do his own part to "clean up the mess."

Having purchased an arsenal of handguns and given himself a menacing-looking mohawk, Travis plots to rescue Iris (Jodie Foster), a child prostitute. In a graphic (and publicly vilified) scene, Travis raids her pimp's turf, slaughtering downtown lowlife. Fingers are blown off, and blood coats the floor and walls. Later with Iris safely (though unwillingly) returned to her small-town family, Travis is hailed as a hero, even though he is clearly unstable and on the verge of psychosis through much of the film. Ironically, though, he is the only character who seems concerned that teenage girls are turning tricks on the streets. By the mid-1970s, the traditional screen hero,

Figure 1.3. The release of Martin Scorsese's *Taxi Driver* (1976) signaled the death of the traditional hero and start of the critical or alternative tradition in crime films. Its deranged protagonist, Travis Bickle (Robert De Niro) is at once a vigilante, would-be assassin, and messiah. Photo used by permission of Photofest.

who once had gotten by with good looks, brawn, and bravery, was obsolete. He had been replaced by a pathological outcast, embittered and impulsively violent, left to his own devices in a town without a sheriff.

Developments since 1980

When Ronald Reagan was elected president in 1980, he ushered in a conservative era with promises of increased defense spending, lower taxes, and boosts for big business. Hollywood reacted, in part, with films that implicitly criticized Reagan's social and political policies, both domestic and international. For crime movies this meant a spate of political films that portray historical and fictional incidents of corruption and demagoguery. A decade earlier, Watergate, environmentalist concerns, and the women's and civil rights movements had created a social context conducive to politically charged films (*All the President's Men* [1976], *Norma Rae* [1979], *The China Syndrome* [1979]), so that by the 1980s the political crime film was coming of age. Moreover, spy vehicles such as the popular James Bond series and John Frankenheimer's *The Manchurian Candidate* had earlier hinted at political crimes without targeting specific policies or political parties. But in the 1980s, films overtly critiqued official policies and citizens' political apathy—and in this way were the only sort of crime film to question systemic oppression. Post-Reagan examples include *Missing* (1982), *Silkwood* (1983), *No Way Out* (1987), and *In the Name of the Father* (1993).

Silkwood, based on actual events and starring Meryl Streep, documents Karen Silkwood's battle to expose the misdeeds of her employer, an Oklahoma nuclear power plant. Hoping to conceal hazardous defects, the management tries to silence Silkwood, but despite her meager resources and the resistance of both her friends and her labor union, she smuggles information incriminating the power plant to the newspapers. Her mysterious death in a single-car crash implicates not only the power plant but also America's nuclear policy for disregarding and covering up public safety concerns. In *No Way Out*, a CIA liaison discloses a murder covered up by an elite group in the federal government. Whether these films expose political or corporate corruption, white-collar crimes or murder, they tend to indict the same crowd: wealthy, white, conservative men who hold the reins of power in America's business and political establishments.

During the 1980s there also emerged a new crop of politically charged prison and courtroom dramas that indirectly attacked the U.S. international agenda or domestic policies. Two prison films, *Kiss of the Spider Woman* and *Cry Freedom* (1987), implicitly question American foreign policy by depicting oppressive regimes promoted by the United States. *The Accused* (1988), a trial film, comments on the legal and social abuse endured by women who attempt to bring rape charges. Based on the notorious Big Dan rape case of New Bedford, Massachusetts, *The Accused* focuses on the presumed ambiguities of what is typically called a date-rape situation, asking whether a victim sometimes precipitates sexual assaults. In this instance, before the rape, Sarah Tobias (Jodie Foster) had been drinking and dancing provocatively with her assailants in a bar. The film highlights issues of victim "character" that had recently been brought to public attention by rape-law-reform activists: Sarah lives in a trailer with her boyfriend, uses vulgar language, and smokes marijuana. Clearly, she is not the pristine virgin required by traditional rape prosecutions, which forced accusers to prove unblemished innocence. Yet the film insists on Sarah's truthfulness, her experience of violation, her need to tell her story in the courtroom, and her right to be legitimated through official procedures. It ends with her successful testimony in court and the conviction of three men who stood by cheering while others raped her.

Addressing urban and racial dilemmas, Hollywood now produced numerous gang and ghetto pictures. Many fared well at the box office, demonstrating an appeal due at least in part to their apparently authentic portrayals of inner-city streets. Often reinforcing the antidrug and antiviolence themes of the period, these include *Bad Boys* (1983), *Colors* (1988), *New Jack City* (1991), *Boyz N the Hood* (1991), *South Central* (1992), *Menace II Society* (1993), *Fresh* (1994), and *Kids* (1995).

The serial killer film, too, began to solidify as a specific type in this period. Serial killers had been depicted in earlier movies, of course (*M, Psycho, Peeping Tom* [1960], *The Boston Strangler* [1968], *10 Rillington Place* [1971], *Frenzy* [1972], *Badlands* [1974]), but rarely in a way that emphasized the serial nature of their crimes. Starting in the 1980s, in contrast, a large number of films began to dwell on the repetitive nature of some murders. While many of these films were teen terror flicks, they also included adult fare: Brian De Palma's *Dressed to Kill* (1980); *Henry: Portrait of a Serial Killer* (1986); *Silence of the Lambs* (1991); the documentary *Aileen Wuornos: The Selling of a Serial Killer* (1992)[27]; and two Morgan Freeman films, *Seven* (1995) and *Kiss the Girls* (1997). Atom Egoyan's provocative *Felicia's Journey* (1999), the grisly *American Psycho* (2000) (an adaptation of Bret Easton Ellis's 1991 novel of the same name about a snooty business executive with murderous impulses) and *Monster* (2003) (another film based on the life of Aileen Wuornos, the Florida prostitute who became a serial killer) are more recent examples. The increased production of serial killer movies reflects the expanding coverage of serial crimes in the media. Their popularity suggests that such films have become a medium for working through widespread fears of and fascination with unpredictable voilence.

In a prescient 1979 article on "*Chinatown* and Generic Transformation in Recent American Films" (reprinted as part of an edited volume on film theory in 1992), John G. Cawelti analyzed changes signaled by movies such as *Chinatown* and *The Wild Bunch*. Older genres were being transformed, Cawelti argued, by some newer films' tendency to parody established genre patterns, their cultivation of nostalgia, and their critique of the myths (such as the myth of hero) on which traditional genres were based. Cawelti's observations proved to be prophetic of a new type of crime film that, because it goes so far in the burlesque of traditions, might best be labeled *postmodern,* a term used to describe cultural responses under late capitalism to demands for aesthetic originality, demands that force artists to borrow, quote, remake, and otherwise engage the market of popular culture.

Pop art may be the best illustration of the postmodern aesthetic, one in which Andy Warhol and others created forms that simultaneously deconstruct, celebrate, and imitate practices of mass production and commodification. Postmodernist aesthetics generally interrogate assumptions, such as the modernist sense of originality—long considered inherent to artistic creation—or "boundaries," as in those among genres or between high and low culture. In a postmodern context, genres blur, pastiche prevails, and once-fixed ideals, such as time and meaning, are subverted, destabilized. In the case of crime movies, postmodernism signals a rejection of linear storytelling, of expectations about genre conventions, and of easy distinctions between right and wrong. In these respects, postmodernism is closely aligned with what this book refers to as the alternative or critical tradition of crime films.

In the aftermath of World War II, there were a few early signs of the postmodernist turn ahead in the production of crime movies. Film noir, for instance, though first and foremost an American expression of European modernism, introduced elements of postmodernism, thus serving as an early prototype of the alternative tradition in crime films. Like many noirs, *Detour* moves through narrative time and space disjunctively. Its highly subjective (and potentially mendacious) flashbacks, rather than merely filling in story gaps, encourage viewers to distrust the narrator's version of events and therefore the entire enterprise of the film. Although the desperate protagonist may have us believe that he is the victim of circumstance and a heartless, conniving femme fatale, the film's construction casts doubts upon itself. In this upside-down world, who is telling the truth and how can justice ever be restored, since the parameters of good and evil are so skewed?

Perhaps the most important postmodernist prototype of the alternative-tradition crime film is Akira Kurosawa's *Rashomon* (1950). Almost cubist in its fragmentation of perspective and meaning, it provides several conflicting accounts of a woman's rape in a forest. In the process, *Rashomon* never gives its viewers the satisfaction of declaring any version more truthful than the others, thus interrogating assumptions about objectivity and truth. Rather than restoring justice, the film's ending leaves viewers wondering how justice can ever be attained. *Rashomon* was a groundbreaking film for many reasons, not least of which is the influence it has had on crime films made since.

Beginning in the 1970s, in particular, the alternative-tradition crime film played an important role in a burgeoning independent cinema, which in Europe fed off New Wave practices and in the United States provided an alternative to Hollywood. In 1970 Bernardo Bertolucci released *The Conformist,* a film about a spiritless man, an ally of Italy's Fascist government, who participates in the assassination of a former teacher turned political dissident. Blending aspects of film noir with absurdism, the movie reflects Bertolucci's recurrent interest in breaking down reality (and thus one's sense of justice) to a series of illusions and confusions. Michelangelo Antonioni's *Blow Up* (1966) (a highly ambiguous and existential reworking of Hitchcock's *Rear Window*), *Zabriskie Point* (1970), and *The Passenger* (1975) similarly deconstruct the world of crime, evidence, and absolutes upon which the justice system depends for dealing with criminals and the crimes they commit. At the same time, films by American directors such as *Taxi Driver* blurred the lines between hero and villain, justice and chaos, laying the foundation for a string of critically acclaimed crime films that have tested the limitations of genre and the traditional Hollywood narrative.

By the 1980s the postmodernist pattern was becoming established in the United States, with filmmakers such as David Lynch, Joel Coen and Ethan Coen, and Brian De Palma leading the way. De Palma made a series of movies in the early 1980s—*Dressed to Kill; Blow Out* (1981), a reworking of Antonioni's *Blow Up; Scarface* (1983), a bold and bloody remake of Hawks's 1932 classic; and *Body Double* (1984)—that pays homage, somewhat obsessively, to the styles of classical Hollywood and to earlier directors (Hitchcock, in particular). Yet these films do much more than imitate: They realign and blend genres and, more noticeably, they approach the absurd.

David Lynch and the Coen brothers produced stylized yet gritty and dryly humorous pictures evoking dream states. Lynch's *Blue Velvet*

(1986)—and, later, *Wild at Heart* (1990), the *Twin Peaks* television series (1990), *Lost Highway* (1997), and *Mulholland Drive* (2001)—provide surrealistic glimpses into the dark, strange netherworlds of suburban and small-town America. The Coen brothers' first feature, *Blood Simple* (1984), provides another striking example of the alternative-tradition crime movie. At one and the same time honoring and spoofing classical film noir, this memorable debut film includes a crafty femme fatale (Frances McDormand's Abby), brilliant hard-boiled voice-over narration, and a hopelessly dim male protagonist (John Getz's Ray), who is unable to grasp the dangers that surround him.[28] In each of these movies a paper-thin semblance of normality belies a comical yet perverted underworld, dysfunctional and deadly to the core. Nothing is as it appears: Seemingly innocuous suburbs are overrun with psychopaths, and because normality never presided in these unpredictable realms to begin with, justice and escape are always just beyond reach.

More recent absurdist and postmodern crime films such as *Fargo* (1996), *Natural Born Killers* (1994), *Pulp Fiction* (1994), *Reservoir Dogs* (1992), *True Romance* (1993), and *American Psycho* share this taste for fantastical, semicomical violence but are considerably more brash and slick. They reach out to a younger audience more tolerant of screen violence and its comedic potential and more likely to have been bred on the rapid-fire editing of MTV and on commercials' disjunctive style. While they, like the earlier *Blue Velvet,* continue to display a surrealistic tendency, their exaggerated violence and aberrant crime sequences mirror an all-too-familiar aspect of American society. In an age when teachers wanting to kill their spouses enlist students' help, schoolchildren pack guns, and twenty-four-hour news stations report an endless barrage of kidnappings, arsons, and murders, nothing, it seems, is too foul for contemporary films and their audiences.

Incorporating the trends Cawelti detected, these crime films are nostalgic yet undeniably modern, conventional yet radical. They simultaneously venerate and poke fun at genre tradition. Garnering large followings and critical acclaim, postmodernist movies have now extended the crime film category, spawning a renaissance that continues to inspire movie production decades after Cawelti's essay was first published. These films have taken many forms recently, but they are typically characterized by playfulness (sometimes deadpan, as in *Fargo*), multiple points of view (*Reservoir Dogs*), concern with identity and identity politics (*Natural Born Killers*), irreverence (including a refusal to take themselves too seriously), eclecticism, and self-reflexivity.

In Oliver Stone's *Natural Born Killers,* the most controversial of the postmodern crime films, two romantic misfits hitch up and wreak havoc, killing everyone in their path. They are out for not money but notoriety, not revenge but media attention. Products of abusive families and media violence, Mickey and Mallory Knox vent their anger by slaying innocent citizens. They intermix love and violence, flaunting a deviant psychosexuality, much like the couple in *Gun Crazy.* Whereas Bonnie and Clyde toured the country as populist folk heroes, robbing from the rich and mocking authority, Mickey and Mallory have no allies other than their fans. Stone, mounting an extended attack on the vapid sensationalism of modern media and society, ridicules the frothing reporters who chase after the couple for their newsworthiness. But his critique, its manic energy and inventiveness notwithstanding, is not entirely persuasive, given the film's tendency to reproduce the sins it condemns.

Quentin Tarantino, the boy wonder of absurdist crime films, scored three direct hits in three consecutive years with *Reservoir Dogs* (which he wrote and directed), *True Romance* (which he scripted), and *Pulp Fiction* (which he coauthored and directed). (Tarantino also had a hand in the script for *Natural Born Killers.*) His slice-of-life films treat violence and crime lightly, often prompting laughter at displays of carnage and mutilation. In *Reservoir Dogs,* for example, one criminal slices off a cop's ear while dancing to the upbeat song "Stuck in the Middle with You." Similarly, in *Pulp Fiction,* when John Travolta's character accidentally blows someone's brains out, his main regret is for the mess in the back of the car; and the heroine of *True Romance* sets an assailant on fire with a hair dryer.

Wisecracking violence, however, constitutes only a fraction of the appeal of Tarantino's densely layered, allusive movies. *Reservoir Dogs* observes the unities of place and time in a gesture toward Greek drama made ridiculous not only by the disparities in heroism but also by cinema's freedom from time and space constraints. *Pulp Fiction,* on the other hand, slides around in time as inventively as any film since *The Terminator* (1984). (Two other crime films that exhibit this playful experimentation with time and sequence are *Magnolia* [1999] and *Memento* [2001].) In an homage to the noir *Kiss Me Deadly,* the two mercenary killers of *Pulp Fiction* carry a case that seems to contain drugs but when opened emanates a shining glow, like the earlier film's box of uranium. At the end of *True Romance,* the lead characters become lead characters in a movie.

Joel and Ethan Coen's *Fargo* illustrates many of the new developments in crime films. Like Tarantino's movies, *Fargo* elicits laughter at odd moments, as when one of the hired killers stuffs his partner's body into a wood chipper. Weird and yet plaintive, it leaves viewers confused and disoriented, unsure of how they're supposed to react. The characters lack emotion, strength, and moral standards: a husband responds to business debts by bumping off his wife; the criminals kill a cop on an open highway, dragging the body away as cars whiz by; and the wealthy father, though determined to rescue his abducted daughter, thinks mainly in terms of profit margins and dies in a parody of the classic crime film shoot-out. Even Marge Gunderson (Frances McDormand), the savvy and pregnant cop, at times seems no more than a lifeless apparition. Married to a clod, sinking with him in a stupor before their TV set, Marge is fiercely moral but personally vapid. Whether "good" or "bad," all of *Fargo*'s characters seem lost in a snowy world without direction or stimulus.

An important but subdued moment emphasizes this point: As Marge drives the captured killer to the station, she asks whether his criminal deeds are worth the money he was promised. The film then gives us a point-of-view shot from the kidnapper's perspective as he looks out the car window at the giant plastic statue of Paul Bunyan and his blue ox—a monument to the artificiality and banality of modern society. He doesn't answer her pointed question. In fact, there is no answer. The criminal has as much reason to kidnap for money as he has to spend the rest of his days toiling at a dead-end job or aging in a prison cell. In this vacuous realm, both avenues lead to the same place: futility. Whereas in many films this type of sequence is the defining moment, the point when the movie delivers its moral, in *Fargo* and its absurdist, postmodern contemporaries, the moral is that there is no moral.

While some directors were striking out in directions forecast by Cawelti's essay, others adhered more closely to crime film traditions. Martin Scorsese, whose *Mean Streets* (1973) and *Taxi Driver* were among the most perfectly realized crime films of the 1970s, produced three crime films in the 1990s, two of them rather lifeless (*Cape Fear* [1991] and *Casino* [1995]) but the third a landmark: *Goodfellas,* based on the biography of gangster Henry Hill. As high-spirited as *Pulp*

Fiction, manic as *Natural Born Killers,* and violent as either, *Goodfellas* nonetheless stays within the realm of the possible, indeed miring us in the quotidian as Henry cooks spaghetti sauce with one hand and tries to move a cocaine shipment with the other.

Even more traditional are the recent offerings of Sidney Lumet, a director who has produced provocative crime films since his 1957 debut with *Twelve Angry Men.* Lumet, the director of such classics as *Serpico, Dog Day Afternoon* (1975), and *Prince of the City* (1981), more recently made *Q & A* (1990), a very dark film about a crooked cop, and *Night Falls on Manhattan* (1996), the first film since *Knock on Any Door* (1949) to successfully feature a prosecutor as hero. Eschewing the razzle-dazzle camera work, frenetic pace, and whacked-out characters favored by other directors, Lumet, who won an Academy Award for lifetime achievement in 2005, continues his straightforward, earnest explorations of the weaknesses and strengths of the criminal justice system. At the same time, directors such as Taylor Hackford (*Dolores Claiborne* [1995]), Tom Kalin (*Swoon* [1991]), Troy Duffy (*Boondock Saints* [1999]), Ridley Scott (*Thelma and Louise* [1991]), Carl Franklin (*Devil in a Blue Dress*), Andy Wachowsky and Larry Wachowsky (*Bound* [1996]), Tom Tykwer (*Run Lola Run* [1998]), Alejandro González Iñárritu (*21 Grams* [2003]), and Joshua Marston (*María Full of Grace* [2004]) are expanding the boundaries of crime films with heroes who are female, people of color, and gay or lesbian. Yet others, following the example of Errol Morris's *The Thin Blue Line* (1988), are devising radical new approaches to crime film documentaries (*Brother's Keeper* [1992], *Capturing the Friedmans* [2003]).

A final development was a popular cycle of pictures made just before and after the turn of the twenty-first century but set in the 1970s. A surprising number of Hollywood hits took advantage of renewed interest in the "me" decade. Popular television shows (*That Seventies Show*) and the resurrection of 1970s music (disco and the popular Swedish band, Abba, for instance) help generate the trend. Hollywood, always tuned into popular culture, was quick to follow suit. In most cases, these movies focused on "celebrity" crimes and drew on stereotypes of the 1970s as a period of fast living where anything went. Paul Schrader's *Auto Focus* (2002), for instance, looked at the life of Bob Crane, the star of the popular television show *Hogan's Heroes,* who became a sex addict and paid with his life. Another sex-oriented hit was Paul Thomas Anderson's epic *Boogie Nights,* starring Mark Wahlberg as Dirk Diggler, a relatively innocent porn star sucked into a dangerous world of cocaine addiction, greed, and vapid commercialism. *Studio 54* (1998) followed the rise of Manhattan's notorious disco club and starred Mike Myer as club owner Steve Rubell, whose exploits included being stoned most of the time and vomiting on piles of fifty-dollar bills. Other drug-oriented movies in this cycle included *Traffic* (2000), which strongly evoked the 1970s, and *Blow* (2001), about the man who established America's cocaine market. Other popular films, though not as crime-oriented, followed a similar pattern: *The Virgin Suicides* (1999), *Almost Famous* (2000), and *Confessions of a Dangerous Mind* (2002). Regardless of subject or theme, these movies were linked by their fetishization of the 1970s, projecting popular stereotypes and memories of this historical era. They provided turn-of-the-century filmmakers and audiences the chance to make sense of a past that was, paradoxically, simultaneously demonized and glamorized.

This cycle of crime films entertained audiences by devoting the first three-quarters of the narrative to decadent, hedonistic lifestyles filled with drugs, sex, booze, money, fame, and rock and roll. But, betraying their moralistic intentions, these same movies became traditional by the end, when the consequences of living too fast and too hard led to the same tragic place: the morgue (or, if one was lucky, prison). As with the classical gangster film, which followed the ethnic gangster's rise to riches and power but ended in moralizing tragedy, the question lingers: Do these movies intend to preach at us, or are they simply interested in showing us hedonistic people at work and play? Regardless of the answer, the retro-seventies crime movie struggled to reconcile, on one hand, audiences' thirst for spectacle and, on the other, anxieties about social order.

Taking advantage of popular appeal, Hollywood studios and independent directors have turned crime and its consequences into one of the most frequently depicted topics in American film. Criminality, rivaling romance for general interest, has long dominated film plots and fascinated audiences, eliciting sympathy as well as loathing, and nourishing latent voyeuristic desires. One key to this fascination lies in the subject's seemingly limitless horizon—from crimes themselves, in their near-endless variation, to the causes of crime; from the work of cops, detectives, judges, attorneys, and jurors to dark prison cells and the glaring walls of the gas chamber. But if crime and its consequences are inherently interesting, crime films also owe their ongoing success to the ways they represent crime. In each decade, crime films have shocked and bewildered, angered and appeased their audiences by offering a window onto contemporary society, the workings of law and justice, and the latest permutations in chicanery and cruelty. Ultimately, these films give us a way of examining our world and ourselves. Because crime films are so clearly linked to social norms, values, rules, and everyday practices, they mirror and reflect back on a society in constant motion, evoking more saliently than any other film type our culture's deep and shifting attitudes toward morality and the state.

Notes

Drew Todd received his Ph.D. in film studies from the Department of Communication and Culture at Indiana University, Bloomington. He has published on film technology, director Satyajit Ray, and dandyism and masculinity in classical Hollywood. He teaches film studies at San José State University.

1. Roffman and Purdy 1981: 10.
2. McCarty 1993a: 1.
3. Maltby 1995: 117, citing research by Charles Musser. For a scene-by-scene analysis of *The Great Train Robbery,* see Ellis 1979: 42–43.
4. For fuller discussions of *The Musketeers of Pig Alley,* see McCarty 1993a: 1–4 and Clarens 1980: 15–21. The latter source includes stills.
5. McCarty writes: "Raoul Walsh's *The Regeneration* (1915) is the oldest surviving *feature-length* gangster film; in his autobiography, *Each Man in His Time,* Walsh contends that it was the first full-length gangster film ever made, which may well have been the case" (1993a: 5; emphasis in original). Other crime film historians (e.g., Clarens 1980: 31) recognize Josef von Sternberg's *Underworld* (1927), which runs eighty minutes, as the first gangster film. The difference may lie in the definition of *feature-length; Regeneration* lasts fifty minutes.
6. McCarty 1993a: 5.
7. Warshow 1974a: 131.
8. Gomery 1991: 164–165.
9. J. Edgar Hoover, as quoted in Barnes and Teeters 1944: 633.
10. Selby 1984: 1.
11. Naremore 1998: 11.
12. Naremore 1995–96: 19.
13. Ibid.: 19.
14. Chandler 1992 (1940): 196.
15. Hammett 1972 (1929): 26.
16. Naremore 1995–96: 19.
17. Schatz 1981: 113.
18. This was a cost-effective method of depicting nighttime situations. Requiring special filters that gave the impression of twilight, day-for-night shoot-

ing was typically done on studio lots during the day. One way to tell these sequences from actual on-location night shots is to look for more glare than may be provided by the fullest moon.

19. In *White Heat*, James Cagney plays Cody Jarrett, a psychopathic criminal who has chronic headaches and a mother complex. In the famous climax, he stands atop a burning chemical plant, facing imminent death, and yells, "Top of the world, Ma!" *The Asphalt Jungle* ultimately attributes the Sterling Hayden character's life of crime to his family's decision to sell his boyhood farm. In the film's bizarre denouement, after having driven for days, he staggers onto his old farm's pasture, where he dies of a gunshot wound, in sight of his childhood horse.

20. Clover 2000.

21. After making several remarkable films noirs in the United States, Dassin left the country in the early 1950s to escape the Red Scare and the McCarthy witch hunts. For *Rififi* he won that year's Cannes award for best director.

22. This same process of humanizing criminals occurs in prison movies that focus on the inmates plotting their elaborate escapes.

23. Ellis 1979: 198.

24. Other important examples of the neo-noir include Scorsese's *Raging Bull* (1980) and the Coen brothers' *Blood Simple* (1984).

25. An updated *Big Sleep* starring Robert Mitchum was released in 1978, but its tired treatment of older themes mainly provoked jokes based on the title.

26. Kael 1991: 452. For a more favorable view of Harry Callahan's character, see Schickel 1996.

27. Director Nick Broomfield recently followed this up with another documentary on Wuornos, *Aileen: Life and Death of a Serial Killer* (2003).

28. One scene has Ray burying the near-dead body of his boss (and Abby's husband) in the middle of a crop field at night—his tire tracks, in an otherwise unblemished plot of land, leading right to the mound of dirt that now covers the body.

2 Why They Went Bad
CRIMINOLOGY IN CRIME FILMS

A psychopath ain't a professional. . . . You don't know what
those sick assholes are going to do next.
— Mr. White, speaking of Mr. Blond in *Reservoir Dogs*

In this country, you gotta make the money first. Then when
you get the money, you get the power. Then when you get
the power, then you get the woman.
— Tony Montana in *Scarface*

Crime films serve as a cultural resource, creating a reservoir of images
and stories on which viewers draw when they think about the causes
of crime. Many crime films also endorse a particular explanation of
crime. Whether they merely hint at a criminological theory or beat
us over the head with one, crime films expose viewers to national
(even international) debates about the causes of crime. Films draw on
popular criminological explanations and in turn embody these explanations, feeding them back to mass audiences.

Films constitute an ideal tool for probing the nature and causes of
deviance. Depicting bad deeds done in secret, movies can dig down
to the bedrock motives for an offender's behavior. Through flashbacks they can reveal the childhood traumas that warped a character's outlook; through settings, they can argue that the filth, chaos,
and violence of bad neighborhoods induce criminality. Films can
show us the calm rationality of offenders who calculate their misdeeds and the bitter slide into criminal ways of an unjustly convicted
prisoner. They can also explore the psyches of famous criminals of
earlier decades, interpreting and reinterpreting the motives of historic figures such as Nathan Leopold, Bonnie Parker, and Charlie Starkweather, thus giving us stories with which to remember and understand our own past.

Ultimately, crime films' remarkable capacity for explaining criminal behavior works on an ideological level, feeding our assumptions
about the nature, extent, and significance of crime. Crime films help

shape beliefs so fundamental that we are scarcely aware that we have them: the belief that crime *can* be explained, for instance, and opinions about who is qualified to explain it; our view of the world as basically benign or threatening; and unstated and unexamined stereotypes about who is likely to be dangerous. They tell us not only what to think but also how to feel about crime, criminals, and criminal justice.

True, many crime films show little interest in the causes of law-breaking. Movies that focus intently on crime detection, court processes, or prison life are usually indifferent to the causes of crime,[1] as are postmodernist films such as *Blood Simple* (1984) and *Pulp Fiction* (1994). In noirs, too, crime is often just part of the scenery, a fact of life or an excuse for showing a private detective in action. But other movies explore the causes of crime in depth, and a few (*I Am a Fugitive from a Chain Gang* [1932], *Trainspotting* [1996], *A Simple Plan* [1998], *María Full of Grace* [2004]) seem to have been written primarily to make a criminological point.

Crime films tend to reflect the criminological theory or theories in vogue at the moment they are produced. During the 1930s, when criminologists pointed to inner-city conditions and immigration as causes of crime, films depicted ethnic mobsters struggling for control against a backdrop of brutal urbanization. In the late 1940s and 1950s, when Freudian explanations of crime became fashionable, films presented a host of morally twisted characters, in effect using the camera to psychoanalyze them. In the 1960s and 1970s, when nonconformity became heroic and criminologists taught that there are few fundamental differences between deviants and the rest of us, films glorified characters who turned to crime to escape the monotony of poverty or bourgeois life. And in the 1980s and 1990s, when criminologists and the public alike indicted drugs and family violence as causes of crime, films such as *Scarface* (1983) and *River's Edge* (1987) endorsed these theories. In an intriguing development, some 1990s films, echoing the message of parent groups and pundits, began blaming the media—including movies themselves—for crime. But while movie explanations of crime tend to parallel current criminological theories or concerns, they have greater staying power. Criminologists drop discredited theories; movies recycle them. Once used, a movie explanation of crime turns up time and again, irrespective of scientific credibility. Filmmakers' choices of theory tend to be opportunistic, dictated less by enthusiasm for a particular criminological position than by a hunch about what will play well.

The most successful crime movies are often those that are one step ahead of popular opinion—films that burst the current criminological framework to introduce new ways of thinking about crime. The big-three gangster films of the 1930s—*Little Caesar* (1931), *Public Enemy* (1931), and *Scarface* (1932)—appeared just as the Chicago School of criminology, which emphasized the criminogenic nature of inner-city neighborhoods, got under way.[2] *Bonnie and Clyde* was released in 1967, just as criminologists were normalizing criminal behavior, while *Dirty Harry,* one of the earliest signs of reaction against this normalization and a harbinger of conservative theories to come, appeared in 1971.[3] *Natural Born Killers* (1994) was the first mass media production to vehemently condemn the mass media themselves for inducing criminal behavior.[4] Instead of following criminological trends, these films helped set them, at least among the general public.

As a rule, the more ambiguous or complex the criminological message, the better the film. People enjoy debating movies' meanings. Did Michael Corleone's motives change between *The Godfather* (1972) and *The Godfather, Part II* (1974)? Did Claus von Bulow, as portrayed in *Reversal of Fortune* (1990), try to kill his wife? In *They Made Me a Criminal* (1939), did the cop act ethically when he freed the young criminal who had so clearly reformed, allowing him to escape justice? If the message is too explicit or ham-handed in its delivery, there is less to analyze. Similarly, if there is but a single explanation for a character's behavior, or if the main interpretation is morally simplistic, viewers will leave dissatisfied. (Critics complained, for instance, that in *Boyz N the Hood* [1991], the character of the father, Furious Styles [Laurence Fishburne], is little more than a didactic device, a mouthpiece for writer-director John Singleton's own views on the causes of inner-city crime. Similarly, the environmentalist explanations of *American History X* [1998] may strike viewers as too pat to be persuasive.) The best films brim over with complexity, challenging viewers intellectually and imaginatively to participate in the act of interpretation.

Movies on the Causes of Crime

Although movies attribute criminality to an enormous range of factors, they favor three basic explanations. One set of films emphasizes environmental causes, illustrating how criminalistic subcultures or other situational factors can drive people to crime. A second set stresses

psychopathy or mental illness, demonstrating that psychological abnormality is a source of criminal behavior. Aspirations for a better
life (more money, more excitement, more opportunity to rise through
the class structure) dominate the motives of a third set of film criminals, those who freely choose crime over dull conformity. A fourth
explanation of crime, bad biology, is favored by neither moviemakers
nor criminologists but is nonetheless treated occasionally by both,
forming a significant explanatory substratum and giving us yet another window on the relationship of crime films to society.

Born Bad: Biological Theories of Crime

Films that attribute criminality to bad biology rely frequently (though
not necessarily consciously) on the work of Cesare Lombroso, the
nineteenth-century Italian physician who claimed to have identified
the "born" criminal. [Born criminals, according to Lombroso, are
throwbacks to an earlier evolutionary stage, biological freaks whose
hereditary defects are mirrored in their apelike bodies and primitive
morality] Unlike more ordinary offenders, born criminals are doomed
to commit crimes repeatedly, for they are criminal by nature.[5]

Vestiges of Lombroso's theory turn up in *Frankenstein* (1931), where
a demented scientist experimenting with the brain of an executed murderer creates a criminalistic monster (Boris Karloff), his face scarred,
arms dangling, gait clumping, and instincts primitive. The next year,
in *Scarface,* Paul Muni played the lead character as a violent and lust-
ful primitive, incapable of lawful behavior. (Muni was even made up
to look a bit like a gorilla, with heavy eyebrows and sloping brow.)
Similarly, *Murder, My Sweet* (1944) features a brutish gangster named
Moose Malloy whom detective Philip Marlowe describes as "a dopey
ape." (The director had Mike Mazurki, the six-foot-tall actor who
played Moose, stand on boxes and walk around on risers to make him
loom even larger.) Echoes of Lombroso sound again in *Born to Kill*
(1947), in which a thug (Lawrence Tierney) who is huge in body but
small in brain shoots people who annoy him. "Why did you do it,
Sam?" his best friend (Elisha Cook Jr.) asks after one of the killings.
"I've been scared something like this would happen, the way you go
off your head, and it's been worse . . . since that nervous crack-up
last summer. Honest, Sam, you go nuts about nothing, nothing at all,
you got to watch that, you can't just go around killing people when-

ever the notion strikes you. It's not feasible." To which the unre-deemably brutish Sam replies, "Why isn't it?"

Cannibals, sodomists, and murderers in particular are endowed with Lombrosian traits. In the *Texas Chainsaw Massacre* series (1974 and following), the barbaric faces of the Sawyer family indicate that they are genetically predisposed to their crime of choice: dismember-ing teens. The backwoods sodomists of *Deliverance* (1972), based on James Dickey's novel about a river exploration gone awry, resemble Lombroso's born criminals mentally, morally, and physically. Biologi-cal explanations of crime reach their movie apogee in *The Bad Seed* (1956), in which a sinister tot named Rhoda commits serial murder. Dr. Reginald Tasker, a friend of Rhoda's mother (and, conveniently, a psychiatric criminologist), explains that there is "a type of criminal born with no capacity for remorse or guilt." Offenders of this type have "no feeling for right or wrong," he continues, because they are "born with the kind of brain that may have been normal in humans fifty thousand years ago." Such people, Dr. Tasker concludes, are "bad seeds," creatures "absolutely doomed to commit murder after mur-der." This explanation, already close to Lombroso's criminal anthro-pology, moves even closer as we learn that Rhoda's ferocity is heredi-tary: Her maternal grandmother, too, was a homicidal maniac.

Lombroso's theory of criminal anthropology codified a set of im-ages and ideas about inherent criminality, arguing that the worst criminals bear on their bodies specific signs ("stigmata," Lombroso called them) of their degenerate nature. Lombrosian images and ideas have worked their way into movies and, in turn, are perpetuated by film. That Lombroso's theory, and not another biological explanation of crime, has over time been favored by filmmakers is a function of its visual appeal. (The idea that the causes of crime lie hidden in the genes lends itself less readily to the big screen.) The visual codes of crimi-nal anthropology have become part of the vocabulary of crime films.

Made Bad: Environmental Theories of Crime

Other films depict offenders whom circumstances have forced into crime, and in these films (in sharp contrast to those with biological explanations), criminals are essentially normal. Offenders may end up as hardened misfits, but initially they are like everyone else: blank slates on which the social environment engraves behavioral patterns.

Films of this type are highly deterministic; arguing that escape from one's situational fate is unlikely or impossible, they offer their characters few alternative courses of action, a point they drive home with images of entrapment (a big fish in a little bowl, a dead-end alley filled with garbage). While criminologists subdivide environmentalist explanations into subcultural theory, social control theory, social learning theory, and the like, filmmakers blur such distinctions to speak generally about the negative impact of unsavory environments or ill-fated circumstances on character and behavior.

Badlands (1974), Terrence Malick's celebrated film of a teenage couple's murder spree, provides a pure example of this type. Based on the 1950s case of Charlie Starkweather and his girlfriend, it opens with Holly (Sissy Spacek) recounting how circumstances turned her into the emotionally deadened, love-starved fifteen-year-old that she is:

> My mother died of pneumonia when I was just a kid. My father'd kept their wedding cake in the freezer for ten whole years; after the funeral he gave it to the yard man. He tried to act cheerful, but he could never be consoled by the little stranger he found in his house. Then, one day, hoping to begin a new life, . . . he moved us from Texas to Ft. Dupree, South Dakota.

Holly's father punishes her for a minor infraction by shooting her beloved dog, thus intensifying her emotional brutalization and giving her a motive for escape. The boy Holly falls in love with, Kit (Martin Sheen), is similarly a product of his environment, a trash collector so poor that he bums cigarettes and peddles junk from garbage cans. (Later, working in a stockyard, he learns to kill steers.) Almost inevitably, the two run away and begin killing people. Holly finishes the story in the same flat, dispassionate tone with which she's narrated it from the beginning: "I got off with probation and a lot of nasty looks. I married the son of the lawyer who defended me. Kit was sentenced to die in the electric chair, . . . and he did." She seems to be describing events over which they had no control.

Environmental explanations dominate in the best of Martin Scorsese's crime films. The credits for *Mean Streets* (1973) roll over a movie-within-the-movie, a crudely made home video that shows the main character, Charlie (Harvey Keitel), in his usual haunts and that more generally reveals the forces that turned Charlie into a street hustler.[6] Charlie's friends, too, are involved in crime, most of them for the same environmental reasons, as demonstrated by early scenes of sleazy

Figure 2.1. *Badlands* (1974), based on the life of an actual serial killer, shows poverty and brutalization turning Kit (Martin Sheen) into a cold-hearted psychopath. Movies often endorse bad-environment explanations of criminality, which encourage sympathy with even violent protagonists. Photo used by permission of Photofest.

bars, drug addicts, and fencing stolen property. Similarly, *Taxi Driver*'s (1976) Travis Bickle is the product of limited opportunity and a tour of duty in Vietnam, where he learned to save the world by shooting people. One of the other cabdrivers, known as the Wizard (Peter Boyle), observes, "You are your job," and ironically, Travis does become his job at the end, despite interludes as a would-be political assassin and vigilante. *Goodfellas* (1990), the Scorsese film about mobster Henry Hill, starts with Henry explaining that as a kid, he lived across the street from gangsters. Looking back fondly on his misspent youth, Henry recalls:

> To me, being a gangster was better than being the president of the United States. . . . I knew I wanted to be a part of them [the local mob]. To me it meant being somebody in a neighborhood that was full of nobodies. They did what they wanted; they parked in front of a fire hydrant and nobody ever gave them a ticket. . . . People like my father could never understand, but I belonged, I was treated like a grown-up. Every day I was learning to score.

For such Scorsese characters, criminality is preordained by their life situations.

Bad-environment explanations also turn up frequently in movies about ghetto crime such as *Menace II Society* (1993) and *Boyz N the Hood*. The latter starts by showing us what typical ghetto children encounter on their way home from school: uncollected trash, dead bodies, unemployed young men, crack-addicted mothers. The only boy to escape, Tre Styles (Cuba Gooding Jr.), has been raised by parents who actively oppose ghetto values and the racism that breeds them.[7] Likewise, most juvenile delinquency films emphasize subcultural factors that turn good kids into bad ones, although some, such as *Rebel Without a Cause* (1955), supplement this environmental explanation with one of intergenerational conflict. Many movies about organized crime—*Angels with Dirty Faces* (1938), *Donnie Brasco* (1997), *Once Upon a Time in America* (1984), *Prizzi's Honor* (1985)—also emphasize environmental explanations, and for the same reason: They want us to sympathize with their characters. Occasionally a story will stress unfortunate personal circumstances as well. In *The Bicycle Thief* (1948), the desperately poor father is driven to steal a bicycle when his own is stolen, making it otherwise impossible for him to keep his job; and in *American History X*, Derek Vinyard becomes a neo-Nazi skinhead under the influence of, first his father and, later, a neighborhood white supremacist. But these are little more than variations on the bad-environment theme.

Bad-environment movies tell us that violence originates in a violent society. Even the most murderous characters start as innocents, no worse than the rest of us but with fewer chances to escape the destiny that circumstance decrees. Or if, like *Straw Dogs* (1972), the film begins with adults, we are shown other conditions that make it all but impossible for the lead characters not to become violent. Of all criminological theories, the bad-environment explanation is the one that movies draw on most frequently, no doubt because it takes the blame off criminals, enabling scriptwriters to glorify them, or at least to portray them as normal men and women, sinned against as well as sinning.

Twisted Psyches: Abnormal Psychology as a Cause of Crime

Almost as numerous are films that explain crime in terms of psychological abnormality, a type that includes *White Heat* (1949), about an epileptic gangster who is in love with his mother[8]; *The Jagged Edge* (1985), about a man who loves to kill women; *Seven* (1995), about a man who loves to kill sinners; *American Psycho* (2000), about a young stockbroker who is unable to love anything except his own body; and *The Woodsman* (2004), about a sex pervert who loves little girls. The offenders in twisted-psyche films suffer from a range of psychological impairments, from obsessive-compulsive disorder through sadomasochism and narcissism to homicidal mania. A favorite diagnostic category is psychopathy, a particularly photogenic condition in which the protagonist lacks a conscience. (The next chapter examines psychopath movies in detail; here my interest lies in what they say about the causes of crime.)

It is useful to distinguish between movies with a cameo psycho— a loony included merely for local color—and those with an explanatory psycho, a crazy included to account for crime. Cameo psychos appear in dozens of crime films (Clu Gulager as the hit man who loves his work in *The Killers* [1964]; Robert De Niro as Johnny Boy in *Mean Streets;* Michael Madsen as the dancing slasher in *Reservoir Dogs* [1992]). The Evil Woman who drives the plot of so many noirs is often no more than a cameo psycho; her criminality, though profound, is a given. She supplies the lead male with his motives (most frequently, sex and greed), but noirs are seldom interested in the origins of the Evil Woman's psychopathy.

Movies with explanatory psychos reach back to German expressionism (*The Cabinet of Dr. Caligari* [1919], *Nosferatu* [1922]). Fritz

Lang's *M* (1931) perpetuated the expressionist tradition by using labyrinthine streets and deep shadows to mirror the tortured mind of the child-murderer. Noirs revived the expressionist tradition and incorporated Freudianism, developments that encouraged their representations of mental pathology. While noirs tend to depict male criminals as repugnant but normal characters, their female criminals are often icons of abnormality, infantile and morally depraved. In *Kiss Me Deadly* (1955), for instance, the male criminals are ordinary mobsters and scientists, but one of the three female characters is a fugitive from a mental institution, the second a childish psychotic, and the third a nymphomaniac.

Gun Crazy (1949) draws delicately nuanced portraits of two criminal psychopaths who, as one of them observes, go together "like ammunition and guns."[9] Annie Laurie Starr (Peggy Cummins) and Bart Tare (John Dall) meet at Annie's carnival sideshow, where she bets onlookers that they can't outshoot her. Bart accepts the challenge and wins, thanks to a fixation on guns that he has had since childhood (and that had earlier landed him in reform school for stealing a revolver). At the point when he meets Laurie, however, Bart is essentially a decent guy, obsessed by guns but far from criminal. Laurie, however, has already killed a man (although neither we nor Bart learn that until later). It is she who pushes Bart into robbery (she wants more money than he can earn), and it is she who kills, starting with a supervisor who forbade her to wear slacks to work. At the end, when Laurie and Bart are run to the ground in a marsh, we can hear two of Bart's old friends coming in a boat to capture them. Laurie prepares an ambush, but Bart, although he loves her dearly, shoots her to prevent this and is then mowed down by his friends. Psychopathy is not the only cause of crime in *Gun Crazy,* which adds love, ambition, greed, and elements of the Evil Woman explanation to the causational picture. However, from the start we are shown that mental abnormality, in the form of Bart and Laurie's fascination with firearms, is the key cause of their downfall.

The most celebrated cinematic investigation of the criminal psyche—the classic that set the standard for subsequent films in this vein—is Alfred Hitchcock's *Psycho* (1960), starring Anthony Perkins as the young man who has murdered and mummified his mother and continues to murder guests in his motel, dumping their bodies in the swamp out back. Toward the end of *Psycho,* a psychiatrist tries to explain Norman Bates's mental pathology:

His mother was a clinging, demanding woman. . . . Then she met a man. . . . [Norman] killed them both. . . . He had to erase the crime, at least in his own mind. . . . He hid the body in the fruit cellar. . . . She was *there,* but she was a corpse, so he began to think and speak for her. . . . At times, he could be both personalities . . . but other times, the mother-half took over completely. . . . If he felt a strong attraction to any other woman, the mother-side of him would go wild. . . . *Mother* killed the girl.

Some viewers accept the psychiatrist's explanation; for others, however, his glib prattle about split personalities fails to account for Norman's mental peculiarities.

Deeply influenced by the symbolic geographies of German expressionism, *Psycho* objectifies Norman's psychoses: in the motel, with its overtones of illicit sexuality; in the cesspool-like swamp out back, with its hints of toilet training gone awry; and in the dark, decaying mansion, which, harboring a nasty secret in its innermost recesses, becomes an image of both Norman's convoluted mind and his mother's body. The haunting terror of *Psycho,* and a factor that lifts it far above other psychological thrillers, lies in the way it implicates viewers in Norman's beastly acts. Through the very act of watching the film, we emulate Norman's creepy voyeurism, a parallel he forces us to acknowledge in his closing scene as he (and his mother), smiling complicitly, return our gaze.

A key transitional scene occurs in the parlor of the Bates Motel, where Norman gives Marion her last supper. One of the most remarkable settings in film history, the parlor is filled with stuffed birds that anticipate both Marion's death and Mrs. Bates's taxidermic condition. Predators with cruel eyes and frightening beaks, the birds also stand for Norman, who will soon be peering at Marion in the shower and tearing at her flesh. Moreover, the camera looks up at the birds (as it does at Norman), intensifying their menace. All elements of the setting reinforce Hitchcock's message about psychological abnormality as a cause of crime.

Movies that correlate criminality with deviant sexuality form a noteworthy subtype of the film of psychological abnormality. The child-murderer in *M* is a sex psychopath, and Norman Bates, with his babyish face, wispy body, and fussy manner, is coded for effeminacy. The vigilante cops with whom Clint Eastwood contends in *Magnum Force* (1973) are described as sexually "queer" while Buffalo Bill, one of the serial killers in *Silence of the Lambs,* is a transsexual, and the homicidal preacher of *Night of the Hunter* (1955) is a sexual sadist. In the case of female characters, films sometimes present sexuality itself as deviant, then use it to explain why the woman deserves to be harmed. In *Psycho*, for instance, the moment we see Marion Crane—in her bra! in a hotel room with a lover! in the afternoon!—we know she is going to be punished.[10]

Aspiration and Longing: Rational Choice Explanations of Crime

Many films attribute crime to aspiration and longing—ambition, lust, or simply a desire to escape boredom. *The Asphalt Jungle* (1950) falls into this category, as do *House of Games* (1987), *A Place in the Sun* (1951), and the majority of heist and caper films. Criminals in aspiration-and-longing movies, like those in bad-environment films, are normal human beings, driven by the mundane motives of need and greed, but they have more choice. Whereas bad-environment films give characters few if any alternatives, arguing that their behavior has been determined by outside forces, aspiration-and-longing films endow their criminals with free will. Their characters survey their circumstances and decide to commit crimes. These decisions are rational—logical (if ill-advised) solutions to the problems at hand. Characters in these films tend to be complicated, people torn by ethical dilemmas. Because they make choices, and because those choices are wrong, some become tragic figures, damning themselves.

The Postman Always Rings Twice (1946), for example, harshly punishes its main characters for making bad decisions: The woman dies in an auto accident, the man in the gas chamber. The film starts when Frank (James Garfield), a charming if unfocused young hitchhiker, is dropped off near a roadhouse in rural California. The owner, Nick, needs a helper, and Frank takes the job; but he immediately falls for Nick's glamorous wife Cora (Lana Turner, resplendent in platinum hair and spotless white outfits). Cora, who longs for a more interesting husband than the oafish Nick and for a better life than that of hash-slinger, reciprocates Frank's interest, and off they go for a moonlight swim.

Cora and Frank eventually kill Nick, motivated by desire for his money and one another. The movie portrays them sympathetically, revealing their admirable qualities along with the bad, showing that they deserve a better hand than the one they've drawn, and giving them every excuse for the murder. At the same time, though, it condemns them for it. Forcing viewers into the young couple's moral position, the movie makes us share their ethical predicament.

The inevitability of punishment is reflected in *The Postman*'s enigmatic title, the meaning of which emerges when, in the last scene, the district attorney drops by Frank's death cell. Court officials, the DA reports, have discovered that Frank was in fact not responsible for the death of Cora (the crime for which, ironically, he was sentenced), but they have also discovered new evidence proving that he and Cora conspired to kill Nick. Better go to the gas chamber now, the DA advises, and save California the cost of a trial that is certain to lead to conviction for Nick's murder. Accepting his fate, Frank agrees, remarking,

> There's something about this that's like—well, it's like you're expecting a letter that you're just crazy to get, and you hang around the front door for fear you might not hear [the postman] ring. You never realize that he always rings twice. . . . The truth is, you always hear him ring the second time, even if you're way out in the backyard. . . . I guess God knows more about these things than we do.

In this metaphor, the postman becomes the god of retribution, calling again for Frank.

The Killing (1956), an early film of director Stanley Kubrick, also shows likable characters making bad choices and bringing down consequences on themselves. This story concerns a racetrack heist, a very elaborate scheme that fails during the getaway when a suitcase falls off an airport luggage cart, flies open, and spills stolen money over the airport tarmac. Starring Sterling Hayden as Johnnie Clay, the ex-con who plans the heist as one last job before he and his girl get married and go straight, *The Killing* develops Johnnie as an appealing character: smart, handsome, and cool. But Johnnie is captured in the end, and we realize that he has thrown his life away, tossed it, like the floating bills, into the wind.[11]

More recent films, too, stress the element of rationality in the choice of a criminal lifestyle. *As Tears Go By* (1988), Wong Kar Wai's film of gangster brothers, shows the older man deliberately returning to Hong Kong to help the younger one, fully aware that the result is bound to be death. In *To Die For* (1995), a young television broadcaster (Nicole Kidman) hires teenagers to kill her husband in order to further her career. The money-hungry conspirators of *The Usual Suspects* (1995) are so purposeful that one can hardly follow their plotline, while the bored young businessman of *Fight Club* (1999) intentionally constructs a life full of sadomasochistic thrills. Two recent drug movies emphasize participants' free choice in marketing illegal substances: *Traffic* (2000) and *María Full of Grace* (2004). In fact, rational choice has now become one of Hollywood's favorite criminological theories, pulling ahead of the bad-environment explanations favored a generation ago.

The Alternative Tradition and the Fallen World

So far this chapter has discussed the causes of crime in traditional crime films, the usual moral pattern of which is violation, discovery, punishment, and resolution. Someone breaks the law—due to bad biology, bad environment, abnormal psychology, rational choice, or some less frequently cited cause. The violation is discovered and attributed to the criminal who, no matter how likable, innocent, bright, and brave, is then punished, restoring the world to its former equilibrium. But what of films in the alternative tradition, those critical crime movies that refuse the pat endings and feel-good morals of traditional films? Films in this tradition, as observed in the introduction, lack conventional heroes and tend to be alienated and bleak. What do they have to say about the causes of crime?

Criminologically, alternative-tradition films hark back to noirs, movies that are relatively uninterested in specific causes of crime but take a dim view of human nature in general. Corruption is intrinsic to noirs such as *Double Indemnity* (1944), *The Lady from Shanghai* (1947), and *The Maltese Falcon* (1941); it forms the metaphysical foundation for their being. Noirs, critic Leonard Quart writes:

> projected a world that was almost universally corrupt and morally chaotic. . . .
> Many characters in film noir were impotent and helpless in the face of
> evil, bending to its force, which seemed to reside in an inalterable human
> nature. Others struggled against it but in the process were tainted by evil
> even when they achieved a victory. And there were still other characters
> who acted as if they were the personification of that corruption.[12]

In this Fallen World, crime is not the exception but the rule, and fate, as the doomed lead character of *Detour* (1945) observes, is likely to stick out its foot to trip us up no matter which way we turn.

In alternative-tradition films, the atmosphere is saturated with menace and depravity. To be sure, movies such as *Chinatown* (1974), *The Grifters* (1990), *Normal Life* (1996), and *Q & A* (1990) present char-

Figure 2.2. Noirs such as *The Lady from Shanghai* (1947), by starting from the premise that people are innately wicked, bypass the need to explain criminality—all they need do is depict it. Photo used by permission of Photofest.

acters with specific motives such as lechery and covetousness, but in them, as in noirs, the entire context is one of corruption. Alternative-tradition crime films incorporate the Fallen World of noirs, modernize it with drug factories and female mobsters, and make it their own. In them, righteousness and salvation are impossible.

Romeo Is Bleeding (1993), starring Gary Oldman as Jack, a degenerate cop, illustrates the way alternative-tradition movies ultimately explain crime in terms of a Fallen World and inevitable sinning. The film opens with Jack already taking bribes, doing favors for mobsters, and cheating on his wife; there are no introductory Edenic scenes to contrast with Jack's post-Fall condition. He deteriorates, partly out of greed but mainly because self-destructiveness is part of human nature. Toward the end, as he sends his wife (Annabella Sciorra) out of town to protect her, he arranges to wait for her every May 1 and December 1 at a certain Arizona roadhouse. Realizing how much he loves her and how completely he has wrecked his life, Jack extricates himself from various subplots and moves to Arizona, where he waits for his wife in the desolate restaurant that symbolizes his (and the human) condition. Naturally, she never appears.

Movies, Crime, and Ideology

Beyond their criminological messages, movies communicate other meanings that are best defined as ideological because they contribute to our taken-for-granted beliefs about the causes of crime. One of crime films' most potent ideological messages is, simply, that crime can be explained. This assumption is such a familiar part of our thinking that we rarely stop to examine it. We accept it partly because, sub rosa, nearly all crime films imply that lawbreaking, even in its most bizarre and heinous forms, is comprehensible. Films get into the minds and lives of criminals, including violent offenders, offering narratives that account for their misdeeds. In addition, to the extent that they endorse specific explanations of crime, movies lend credence to those theories. Only alternative-tradition films raise the grim possibility that crime cannot be explained, that it may simply be a form of evil or a mysterious fact of social life. They alone suggest that crime may be unfixable.

A second ideological message of crime films is that there are certain individuals who are able and, indeed, specially equipped to figure out the causes of and solutions to crime. Who these individuals are differs from film to film. In *Psycho, The Bad Seed,* and *Silence of the Lambs* they are psychiatrists. In *Boyz N the Hood* it is Furious Styles, the wise father, and in *American History X* it is the wise father-substitute, the high school principal; in noirs it is often a private investigator; and in cop, court, and prison films, it tends to be a criminal justice official or private attorney. The point is that crime films usually assume that there is some cultural authority who can explain crime and knows what to do about it—an assumption they pass on to audiences.

This is a comforting message. Crime films raise anxieties and instill fear, but they usually conclude by sending experts to our rescue. In movies, few criminals are so monstrous that they cannot be understood or so clever that they elude the authorities forever. For decades, crime films assumed that the authority figure would be a white, middle-class male—another aspect of their ideology. More recently, in keeping with the movement to recognize cultural pluralism, the specialist's identity has broadened to include black men, white women, and other nontraditional authorities. The possibility that *no one* can cope with crime is raised only by a few bold, alternative-tradition movies such as *187* (1997), *State of Grace* (1990), and *To Live and Die in L.A.* (1985).

Third, crime films feed ideology by defining "the crime problem." In reality, the most common types of crime are nonviolent property offenses, but one could watch movies for a week before finding a petty theft. Instead, murder seems to be the most common offense, followed closely by attempted murder and serial murder. In a study of how crime is portrayed by news media, Michael Welch and his colleagues point out that "crime news is . . . shaped according to the dominant ideology," according to which

> street offenses are the most costly, most dangerous, and most threatening form of crime. . . . Financial losses assessed for different types of offenses, however, contradict this image of crime. It is estimated that the cost of street crime hovers around $4 billion per year, whereas the cost of white-collar and corporate crime reaches $200 billion. . . . Further, approximately 24,000 homicides were committed in the United States in 1995 [but in] the same period, more than 56,000 workers died as a result of injuries or diseases caused by unsafe working conditions.[13]

The news media, Welch and his colleagues conclude, stress street crime but neglect such social harms as white-collar and corporate offenses "because of ideological constraints." Precisely the same point could be made about crime films.

In "Predator Criminals as Media Icons," Ray Surette writes that "one result of the media's central role is the construction of mass media-supported crime myths" that have almost nothing to do with crime actualities but nonetheless "provide knowledge that becomes permanently incorporated into our socially constructed world models."[14] Surette focuses on the myth of the violent predator who does little but prey on innocent citizens, but there are other criminological myths as well, such as the one that we live in constant danger from serial killers (an offender type that, statistically, is in fact exceedingly rare). In addition, movies reinforce the myth of a close association between mental illness and crime (in fact, mentally ill people are more likely to be victimized than victimizers) and the age-old myth of the Evil Woman who leads men astray, a figure perpetuated by noirs and more recently by *Body Heat* (1981), *The Grifters,* and *Basic Instinct* (1992). Movies generate these skewed perceptions of crime not to deliberately mislead the public but to attract audiences with lures of proven efficacy: action, emotional thrills, blood and gore.

Even though movies' emphasis on violence and death may distort public perceptions of "the crime problem," films also have the potential to correct such misunderstandings and increase public awareness of the effects of crime. The representations of prison rape in *An Innocent Man* (1989), *Short Eyes* (1979), *The Shawshank Redemption* (1994), and *American History X,* for instance, probably increased public sensitivity to the problem of prison violence, while the depictions of family violence in films such as *River's Edge, Dolores Claiborne* (1995), and *Eye of God* (1997) probably heightened public awareness of the consequences of this type of crime. But only alternative-tradition films (and just a few of them) actually challenge dominant ideological understandings of "the crime problem." *Bad Lieutenant* (1992), *Q & A,* and *Romeo Is Bleeding* suggest that cops may be part of the crime problem, while *Falling Down* (1993) and *L.I.E.* (2001) show us a white, middle-class, patriotic man as dangerous as any street criminal.

Finally, films tell us how to feel about crime and the contexts in which it occurs. Killing and armed robbery may be crimes, *Bonnie and Clyde* explains, but sometimes they are committed by innocents—an explanation repeated twenty-five years later by *Thelma and Louise* (1991). While films do not determine our emotions, they do provide narratives that we use to frame our emotional responses to actual criminal events. *A Simple Plan* suggests that we all are capable of grand larceny; *Judgment at Nuremberg* (1961) maintains that there are no circumstances under which crimes against humanity can be excused. Movie narratives may fade in memory, cancel one another out, modify previous narrative lines, or pile up to create a cumulative impression. Some glorify lawbreakers; others encourage us to look for a psychopath in every cabdriver and motel clerk. Collectively, however, film narratives shape our attitudes toward crime and its contexts.

Few crime films simultaneously perform all these ideological functions: assuring us that crime *can* be explained; identifying criminological authorities; defining "the crime problem"; and shaping our beliefs about crime. But all crime films contribute to the tool kits or sets of mental images viewers use to think about crime and crime control.

Beyond the ideological messages already discussed, many crime films have more specific ideological content, a point that can be illustrated by comparing three movie versions of one of the twentieth century's most notorious crimes, the 1924 killing of Bobby Franks. When they were still young men, Nathan Leopold and Richard Loeb killed this boy from their Chicago neighborhood on the theory that as unusually intelligent people, they were above the law. The context of the murder story included a number of intriguing elements—homosexuality, debates over mental illness and criminal responsibility, Nietzsche's idea of the superman, issues of wealth and religion (Leopold and Loeb both came from well-to-do Jewish families), and the spectacle of the most famous defense attorney of the day, Clarence Darrow, staving off death sentences; as a result, the Bobby Franks killing has inspired a play, a novel, and other books, as well as the three film versions.

The first movie version, Alfred Hitchcock's *Rope* (1948), skirts the murderers' Jewishness and relegates their homosexuality to a subtext in order to focus on the crime itself and the superman theories that inspired it. Derived from a play, this version locates the events in a Manhattan penthouse where the Leopold and Loeb figures (John Dall and Farley Granger) serve dinner to their victim's family, using as a table the wooden chest in which they've hidden the body. Also present is their old prep school headmaster (James Stewart), who figures out what has happened and brings in the police. This version is concerned with the crime itself and with the relationship of fathers and sons, especially that of the headmaster father figure who catches the bad boys and will see that they are punished. On a deeper level it is concerned with self-destruction, not only by the young men but also by the headmaster, who, because he taught the superman theory to killers, is partly responsible for their deed.[15]

Ideologically, *Rope* conveys messages about the desirability of being powerful and in control. The setting, atop Manhattan, is one of power and privilege. The young men attempt to exercise power but fail to control themselves in the aftermath, thus revealing what they have done. Through his intelligence and sleuthing ability, the headmaster gains power over the other two, but even his control is suspect in the end due to his triangulation with the killers. The figure who is most powerful and most in control, *Rope* implies, is the filmmaker. As often happens in Hitchcock films, the movie ends up being about the relationship between viewer and director, with Hitchcock playfully underscoring his control over us, his audience.

The second movie, based on a novelized version of the story, was director Richard Fleischer's *Compulsion* (1959). This movie hints broadly at homosexual attraction between Leopold and Loeb, although (perhaps to confuse the censors) it also gives them girlfriends. Its ide-ological emphasis falls not on sexuality but on the law. *Compulsion* sings a sustained hymn of praise to the law, personified by three male characters: the district attorney (E. G. Marshall) who solves the crime; the defense attorney (Orson Welles, playing Darrow) who argues successfully against the death penalty; and the judge who, heeding the defense, tempers justice with mercy by sentencing the young men to prison for life plus ninety-nine years. These lawyers' tireless pur-suit of justice is contrasted with the despicable superman theories of the killers. Inexorably, the majestic, heroic law bears down, showing them an impartiality and compassion they cannot even comprehend.

The third and most recent version, *Swoon* (1991), is writer-director Tom Kalin's postmodernist retelling of the Leopold and Loeb story. *Swoon* starts the story at an earlier point in time than the other two movies, follows it through Leopold's death in 1971, and reanalyzes the young men's identities as Jewish and gay, all the while commenting visually on the two previous films. Kalin asks questions about the re-lationship of film to history and about the nature of illusion and film documentary. He explores the role of film in the social construction of past events and in our ideas about sexuality, gender, and race. Unlike *Rope,* which stays out of the courtroom, *Swoon* includes court scenes, but there are no heroic lawyers here, only the psychiatrists who patholo-gized the young men's homosexual relationship. Witty, self-conscious, and stagy, *Swoon* rescues Leopold and Loeb's love from the coy slanders of the two earlier versions, normalizes it, and brings it to the fore. The film ends up making a statement about movies themselves—what they can be, stylistically, and what they can reveal both about characters' inner lives and about events in the nation's past.

Movies, as these three examples show, never simply tell a story but, through the choices they make about character, setting, and theme, also convey ideological assumptions about what is and what is not important. These assumptions derive partly from the social context in which movies are made and partly from the filmmakers' own sen-sibilities. In the aftermath of World War II, neither *Rope* nor *Compul-sion* dared address the fact that Leopold and Loeb were Jews who had embraced the superman theory that inspired the Holocaust. Nor, at a time of widespread ignorance and fear of homosexuality, could they portray the young men's love relationship. *Rope,* drawing on then-modish psychoanalytic concepts, emphasizes guilt, self-destruction, and intergenerational complexities. *Compulsion,* positioning itself among the classic law films of the 1950s, concentrates on courtroom drama and heroic lawyering, while *Swoon*'s roots in the identity-politics of postmodernist theory enables it to be more frank about the men's ethnicity and sexuality. Although the three films build on a single incident in American history, they encapsulate very different ideologies.

Do Movies Cause Crime?

A recurrent controversy concerns whether movies encourage people to behave violently and engage in other sorts of criminal activities. Sociologists and psychologists design studies to determine whether the media influence actual behavior, and newspapers and television carry frequent allegations of copycat criminality. Thus, it seems fitting to conclude this chapter on criminology in movies with a discussion of the question "Do movies cause crime?"

There are good intuitive reasons for suspecting a relationship between movie-viewing and criminal behavior. Advertisers and politicians spend billions annually on the assumption that media influence behavior. Violent crimes seem to be ubiquitous; so do violent films. Furthermore, we know that movies can set trends—in dress, speech ("make my day"), alcohol consumption (sales of pinot noir shot up after the release of the wine-tasting film *Sideways* [2004]), and even career choices (as when, after the release of *Silence of the Lambs,* young women flocked to join the FBI). The assumption that films can induce antisocial behavior, moreover, lies behind the history of film regulation and censorship.

Anecdotal evidence seems to support the notion that movies cause crime. The night *Boyz N the Hood* opened, audience violence after the screening left two viewers dead and more than thirty injured. Films sometimes inspire copycat crimes, as when John Hinckley Jr., imitating *Taxi Driver*'s Travis Bickle, attempted to assassinate President Reagan in the hope of impressing Jodie Foster, one of the film's actors.[16] Similarly, in 1998 in Olympia, Washington, five young women who had repeatedly watched *Set It Off* (1996), a movie about female bank robbers, held up the local bank. "Bank heist mimics film," proclaimed one headline, while another touted the event as a "movie rip-off heist."[17] Such anecdotes suggest that at least under some circumstances, movies lead directly to crime.

Social science research, however, indicates that the relationship between media and criminal behavior is not that simple. For decades, social scientists have been trying to determine whether the media influence behavior and, if so, how. Their studies have produced evidence that some media influence the behavior of some people some of the time.[18] However, this evidence is difficult to interpret, and it does not necessarily apply to movies. In fact, most of the studies have focused on the effects of television violence on children and of advertising campaigns on consumers and voters. Many have been conducted under conditions (for example, in psychology laboratories) very different from those in which people view movies, and some have concentrated on measuring aggression (for example, the number of punches delivered to an inflatable doll), not actual criminality. While experiments indicate that media violence does tend to increase aggressive behavioral outcomes, these effects are often short in duration, and they do not show up in all viewers. Summarizing these studies, Surette writes:

> The evidence concerning the media as a criminogenic factor clearly supports the conclusion that the media have a significant short-term effect on some individuals. . . . The more heavily the consumer relies on the media for information about the world and the greater his or her predisposition to criminal behavior, the greater the effect. . . . [V]iolence-prone children and the mentally unbalanced are especially at risk of emulating media violence.[19]

But it is premature and even simplistic to suggest that movies cause people in general to commit crime. Human behavior is influenced by multiple factors, in combinations so complex that no one has yet devised a way to isolate them from one another.

As for incidents in which movie-watching apparently has led specific individuals to criminal behavior, details of these cases suggest other, more plausible explanations. John Hinckley Jr. was one of those "mentally unbalanced" people whom Surette identifies as "especially at risk of emulating media violence." The female bank robbers seem to have been unusually naive and even stupid. (They left a copy of the film in their house and boasted about their heist both before and after the event.) In the case of *Boyz N the Hood,* it seems odd to blame this antiviolence movie for the violent incidents that accompanied its opening. Because *Boyz* deals with racism, it may well have inflamed some viewers' frustration with racism, leading them to post-screening violence; but the underlying cause of the violence is likely to have been racism itself rather than the movie. In any case, only an infinitesimally small fraction of the people who saw *Boyz* committed assults immediately thereafter.

The best way to think about movie-crime relationships, as I suggested in the introduction, is by drawing on theory offered by cultural sociology. Movies give us cultural fragments that serve as "tool kits" from which we construct strategies for action.[20] Because viewers perceive and recall movies differently, they store up somewhat different cultural information, even from the same film. However— since nearly all movies deliver an anticrime message—most such fragments will aggregate into schemata that constrain criminal activity. Only in rare cases (those bizarre exceptions reported in news stories) will movie information interact with other factors (some peculiar to the individual, as in John Hinkley's case, and some unique to his or her external world) to enable criminal behavior; and even then, the movie contribution will be but one factor among many.[21]

We probably store most of the bits of cultural information that we derive from movies as narrative fragments or (in the case of the larger structures termed *schemata*) as master narratives—shared, generalized story lines, such as that of the hero with a weapon who rescues the maiden in distress. Narratives seem to be crucial to our efforts to make sense of our lives. Donald E. Polkinghorne, a specialist in this area, holds that narrative is "the primary form by which human experience is made meaningful."[22] We are constantly bombarded with stimuli, none of which has obvious meaning; we make sense through self-talk, mulling over the meaning of these stimuli in internal conversations and then organizing the fragments of experience into stories. Films are one source of our narrative lines. As Australian film scholar Graeme Turner writes, "The world 'comes to us' in the shape of stories. . . . This is not to say that all our stories *explain* the world. Rather, story provides us with an easy, unconscious, and involving way of constructing our world . . . and sharing that 'sense' with others."[23] Movies, then, do not cause crime, but they do create narratives, giving us images and scenarios that we store in our mental reservoirs of narrative lines.

In sum, crime films give us narratives for thinking about the nature, causes, and consequences of crime. Many incorporate a theory of crime, but most do so opportunistically rather than in order to promote a specific interpretation. Crime films influence ideologies of crime and justice through their assumptions about the comprehensibility of criminal behavior, who is best qualified to cope with it, and its distribution by offense type. Instead of asking "Do movies cause crime?" we should be asking how they work to contain or prevent it, for most films preach from an anticrime pulpit, and their power to facilitate criminal behavior is apparently limited to nudging crime-prone individuals in directions they are already headed. What movies do produce is narratives, stories that help us interpret both crime and our lives. They form a bridge, with heavy traffic in both directions, between "the real world" and our imaginations, between social experience and its interpretation.

Notes

1. But for contradictory examples see *Knock on Any Door* (1949), a courtroom film that endorses the bad-environment theory of crime, and *The Onion Field* (1979), a cops-courts-and-prison film that attributes crime to the killer's psychopathic personality.

2. On the Chicago School, see Shaw 1929 and Shaw and McKay 1931. In another example of movies anticipating criminology, these three films also provide examples of anomie theory, years before it received its classic formation by Robert Merton in 1938.

3. *Straw Dogs,* the tale of a math professor goaded into extreme violence, both normalizes violent behavior and condemns it; significantly, it appeared in 1972, a tipping-point year when movies could still have it both ways.

4. On the mass media and crime, also see *RoboCop* (1987) and *To Die For* (1995).

5. Lombroso 2006 (forthcoming); Lombroso and Ferrero 2004. For a related argument, see Mitchell 1995.

6. "The research on *Mean Streets* was my life," Scorsese has said. "There was no research. I literally took one step out of the neighborhood and made that movie" (Gussow 1997).

7. A film about white delinquents, *They Made Me a Criminal,* proceeds similarly. The main character, a prizefighter played by John Garfield, is framed for a murder, but he has been so brutalized by his environment as to make the false accusation look likely. However, fleeing the law, he ends up on an Arizona ranch, a kind of Eden where two dedicated women are working with delinquent boys, and at that point Garfield's character reforms. He goes on to reform the kids and even to redeem an embittered cop who tracks him down in Arizona.

8. The epilepsy is a biological touch inspired by Lombroso, according to whom many born criminals have fits.

9. More recent movie psychos are seldom drawn with such a fine brush. Contrast the leads in *Gun Crazy* with the vivid but blatant psychos in *Silence of the Lambs* (1991): Buffalo Bill, who is making a dress out of his victims' skins, and the cannibalistic Dr. Hannibal ("I'm having a friend for dinner") Lecter.

10. For more on movie sex criminals, see chapter 8.

11. The floating bills echo the close of *Treasure of the Sierra Madre* (1948). *The Killing,* which replays an early scene over and over, showing us ever more clearly what was really going on, may have inspired Quentin Tarantino's *Jackie Brown* (1997), another movie in which a key scene is repeated from different points of view.

12. Quart and Auster 1991: 29–30.

13. Welch, Fenwick, and Roberts 1998: 223.

14. Surette 1995: 133.

15. On *Rope's* homosexual subtext and its ideological meanings, see Lawrence 1999 and Wood 1989.

16. For a fuller discussion of copycat crimes, see Douglas 1999 and Surette 1998: 137–51.

17. *Boston Globe,* 13 August 1998: A10. *Burlington Free Press,* 13 August 1998: A2.

18. This evidence, along with various models of the nature of media's effects on behavior, is presented at length in Straubhaar and LaRose 1996: 411–33; also see the essays in Goldstein 1998, many of which carefully evaluate the effects of media on behavior, and Surette 1998.

19. Surette 1998: 152–53.

20. Swidler 1986.

21. On the nature of this interaction, see DiMaggio 1997, a work discussed in more detail in the introduction.

22. Polkinghorne 1988: 1.

23. Turner 1993: 68 (emphasis in original).

3 Slasher, Serial Killer, and Psycho Movies

Psychopaths sell like hotcakes.
—Hack screenplay writer Joe Gillis in *Sunset Boulevard*

First principles, Clarice. Read Marcus Aurelius. Of each particular thing ask: What is it in itself? What is its nature? What does he do, this man you seek?
—Hannibal Lecter in *Silence of the Lambs*

Cody Jarrett, the gangster protagonist of *White Heat* (1949), kills seven people in the course of his movie (not counting himself, in the final explosion); Bonnie Parker and Clyde Barrow, the bank robber protagonists of *Bonnie and Clyde* (1967), kill almost a dozen. Yet we do not think of these characters as serial killers or of their films as serial killer films, for their directors (Raoul Walsh and Arthur Penn, respectively) did not frame the films that way. They created multifaceted characters, not unidimensional killing-machines, giving Cody, Clyde, and Bonnie admirable as well as negative traits and thus enabling viewers to identify with them. Moreover, the stories are not "about" killing, *White Heat* being a study in criminal psychopathology, *Bonnie and Clyde* a saga of rebellion against authority, mediocrity, and anonymity. The films depict even violent criminals as sympathetic figures, attractive and heroic—a message that is fundamentally ideological in that it keeps these killers within the human fold.

This chapter pries open the ideological frameworks of violent films to explore what they say about criminal nature.[1] Examining three types of violent cinema—slasher, serial killer, and psycho movies—it tries to see how these differ in their constructions of the archcriminal and to catch them in the act (so to speak) of generating popular beliefs and mythologies about serious crime. Conversely, it identifies some of the scandals, debates, and preoccupations in the broader culture that helped bring these movies into being.

Slashers

The slasher film made its debut in 1974, with Tobe Hooper's *The Texas Chainsaw Massacre,* in which a cannibalistic family preys upon a group of teenagers until one, Sally, ingeniously evading their efforts to dismember her, escapes. The genre found its footing with the 1978 release of *Halloween,* the story of another heroic teenage girl, Laurie (Jamie Lee Curtis), eluding the homicidal Michael, who has escaped from his mental institution. These formula-setters were followed by a string of *Friday the 13th* films (1980, 1981, 1982, and so on), *Nightmare on Elm Street*s (1984, 1985, 1987), *Slumber Party Massacre*s (1982, 1987, and 1990), and other variations, and elaborated again by Wes Craven's *Scream* offerings (1996, 1997, and 2000). These low-budget teen horror films feature villains with names such as Freddy and Jason who kill over and over again but cannot themselves be killed; Amazonian heroines who survive through a combination of wit and self-discipline; settings that isolate their teenager protagonists in dangerous situations; and plots that on the one hand punish sexually active teens with death and on the other reward the virginal Final Girl with victory.[2]

On the surface, slashers resemble serial killer and other crime movies: they have villains who kill repeatedly (here, mainly with knives) and almost-victims who scramble up from the depths of disaster to vanquish the villain and save the day (although that day may pass rapidly before the villain returns for the sequel). It is further tempting to include slashers in the crime films category because not only do they have roots in the horror tradition (*The Omen* [1976]; *Carrie* [1976]) but also in crime film history, especially *Psycho* (1960), in which Norman Bates, the weird repeat killer, is tracked down in a hideous isolated place (the root cellar of the decaying mansion) by a heroic victim-surrogate (Marion Crane's sister, Lila)—tracked down but, like Michael, Jason, and Freddy, not conclusively immobilized. Slashers are in fact close enough to crime films to have influenced subsequent movies in the latter category, such as *The Accused* (1988), in which a rape victim gets her revenge, and *Silence of the Lambs* (1991), in which an FBI agent overcomes the serial killer who has trapped her in yet another cellar. Slashers showed Hollywood how to adopt victims' points of view and freshen up its depictions of slaughter.

Notwithstanding these parallels and overlaps, however, slashers are not true crime films. They are not interested in crime and justice but chills and thrills—the ineffable pleasures of threat and revenge. Their action consists primarily of ambushes and mutilations, and their formulaic characters are interchangeable. Moreover, while these characters may look like ordinary teenagers, they are modeled after figures of folklore and myth: vampires, werewolves, creatures who dwell at the bottoms of lakes, maidens in distress, and pure knights with magic swords who invariably win their struggles. Like folktales, slashers revel in repetition and other narrative rituals; if they tell the same story over and over, they do so because individually they are no more than variants on a fundamental tale of threat and salvation, of meeting the monster and overcoming it. Moreover, unlike most crime films, slashers leaven their plots with elements of camp. Scary but ludicrous, satirical and sometimes wry, they ask to be taken seriously and lightly at the same time. Although they punish teenagers for violating the parental No Sex rule, slashers do so gleefully, inducing their own type of orgiastic excitement.

In sum, slashers are fairy tales or fables for adolescents. Folklorist Maria Tatar traces the origins of fairy tales to "an irreverent folk culture that set itself in conscious opposition to the official ecclesiastical and feudal order"; similarly, slasher audiences and even their characters participate in a teen culture different from and consciously opposed to that of authorities. Tatar locates the pleasures of fairy tales in the "charms" of "transgressive curiosity"—in children's fascination "with catastrophic events, with perilous encounters" and their delight in "burlesque violence, which depends for its effect on distortion and exaggeration." Slashers, too, simultaneously punish and reward transgressions; and they, too, are pleasurable because they are silly, encouraging audiences to laugh at themselves even while they cringe in terror. Again like fairy tales, slashers are highly stylized in their violence: No one behaves like Freddy in real life; his killings entertain because they signal, through their excesses, that they are unreal. In both mediums, the meaning of violence is determined by the way it is framed.[3]

The slasher film, then, is a subgenre of horror that is closely related to fairy tales and folklore and has a comic edge. Although it outwardly resembles the serial killer film, the slasher has a different audience and different social functions.

Serial Killer Films

The serial killer figure began to emerge in the late 1970s, in the context of a seismic political shift in American attitudes toward crime and criminals. After a century of liberal efforts to explain criminality in terms of social or medical causes, a more conservative approach began to argue that criminals are not so much disadvantaged or sick as evil—people who are fundamentally immoral, perhaps due to some sort of innate biological defect.[4] At the same time, conservatives redirected crime control policies toward severe punishments and the immobilization of repeat and violent offenders. One sign of the rejection of the rehabilitative philosophy appeared in a 1981 speech in which President Ronald Reagan declared that "the solution to the crime problem will not be found in the social worker's files, the psychiatrist's notes, or the bureaucrat's budget; it's a problem of the human heart, and it's there we must look for the answer."[5]

Another sign of the change showed up in the ideological gap between two movies, both depicting a series of killings, released just three years apart: *The Boston Strangler* (1968) and *Dirty Harry* (1971). *The Boston Strangler,* based on the real-life story of Albert deSalvo, a laborer thought to have raped and murdered up to thirteen women, stars Tony Curtis as not only "a sick animal" with a split personality but also as a rather sweet, befuddled family man. For the last third of the movie he walks around in pajamas and a bathrobe, a patient in a mental hospital who has the full sympathy of his psychiatrist and the district attorney. A text box at the conclusion announces, "This film has ended, but the responsibility of society for the early recognition and treatment of the violent among us has yet to begin." In *Dirty Harry,* in contrast, the sex murderer, Scorpio, is a drugged-out hippie monster who cackles manically and elicits nothing but contempt ("punk," "madman," "creep") from the detective who pursues him. *Dirty Harry* is concerned with not a series of murders but a serial murderer—a person defined by his behavior. Scorpio became a progenitor of a long line of essentially evil serial killers created by late twentieth-century cinema.

Among the factors encouraging this shift in attitudes were improvements in forensics and computerized communications that made it easier to identify the repeat murderers who, in an earlier period, could disappear into a new locale. Another factor was the Federal Bureau of Investigation's willingness in the1990s to fund the psychological profiling of offenders deemed particularly dangerous.[6] (Troubled by recent public relations fiascos, in the 1990s the FBI seems to have deliberately adopted the image of Jack Crawford, the supersleuth of films based on Thomas Harris's popular novels *Red Dragon* and *Silence of the Lambs*.[7]) Notorious cases such as those of Jeffrey Dahlmer, John Wayne Gacy, and Ted Bundy further heightened the serial killer's profile, especially when they became the basis for movies. In addition there seems to have been an increase in the actual incidence of serial killer cases, although according to Philip Jenkins, the increase merely took the rates back to their early twentieth-century level after a period of decline.[8] Yet another factor was the commodification of the serial killer by criminologists, Hollywood, novelists, and producers of soft porn who recognized a marketing opportunity. Thanks to all these influences, by the 1990s a new criminal stereotype had taken hold in the public imagination, that of the superpredator, more monster than human, psychopathic, sexually deviant, and ubiquitous.

Serial killer films are essentially slashers for adults. Centrally concerned with seriality or regular repetition, they portray killing as a compulsive, recurrent behavior—with the result that they themselves tend to be episodic, little more than a string of similar scenes that build toward neither a climax nor a denouement. These episodes of violence, much more so than the out-of-the-blue attacks of slasher films, are designed as sadomasochistic fantasies, orgies of calculated pain and calibrated bloodletting that invite viewers to identify with the killer, the victim, or both. Gone are the supernatural bad guys of slashers, but the demonic serial killers who replace them are not much more believable.[9] (Some movies do explore the psychology of repeat murderers, but these fall into the psycho films category discussed in the next section.) The thrust of serial killer movies is to construct a stereotype of the violent predator: abnormal, incomprehensible, beyond the pale of humanity, bloodthirsty, sexually twisted, and lurking in our midst, a threat to us all.[10]

In its purest form, the serial killer film focuses solely on the murderer and his (rarely her) exploits. *American Psycho* (2000), for instance, follows the robotic Patrick Bateman (Christian Bale), a young New York City stockbroker, through a spate of recreational killing. Self-indulgent, rich, and bored, Patrick wakes up emotionally only long enough to exterminate someone. *American Psycho* hints, halfheartedly, at various explanations—success has come too easily to Patrick; the slick superficiality of the modern world has deadened him; maybe he

Figure 3.1. Serial killer films such as *American Psycho* (2000), featuring flat, unredeemable characters, echo and reinforce the lock-em-up rhetoric of contemporary crime control agencies. Unlike earlier psycho films, these movies portray criminals as incomprehensible monsters. Photo used by permission of Photofest.

is mentally ill—but none is persuasive, and as Patrick himself observes, "There is no real me. I simply am not there." At the end, he tries to confess, but his companions, lost in their own vapidity, ignore him. The main character of *Henry: Portrait of a Serial Killer* (1986) is similarly soulless and amoral. Even when serial killer films are based on actual cases—*In the Light of the Moon* (2000) (a biography of Ed Gein), *Ted Bundy* (2002), *Dahmer* (2002), *Gacy* (2003)—they fail to create plausible characters.[11]

While the "pure" serial killer film concentrates on a single character, a common hybrid grafts the serial killer onto the cop movie. The plot in which a police detective pursues a serial killer has a long cinematic history, deriving ultimately from the archetypal plot of the maiden in distress who is saved by a hero from the monster's clutches. This narrative line appears in one of Alfred Hitchcock's first works, a silent film called *The Lodger* (1927) in which a detective roams through the fogs of London in search of a serial killer, the Avenger, who is doing in blondes. Other examples include *Dirty Harry, Jennifer Eight* (1992), *Copycat* (1995), *Kiss the Girls* (1997), *Resurrection* (1999), *The Bone Collector* (1999), and *In the Cut* (2003). One might go so far as to include a civilian example, *Collateral* (2004), in which a taxi driver who is impressed into chauffeur duty by a serial killer overcomes him in the end and saves the woman.

In some cases, the cop discovers a kinship with the murderer, just as Henry Jekyll long ago discovered a kinship with the revolting Mr. Hyde. This plot twist shows up in *The Offence* (1973), a film made in England by American director Sidney Lumet and starring Sean Connery as a detective brutalized by decades of dealing with violent crime. While questioning a man in the sex murders of young girls, the detective punches the suspect to death. Arrested and questioned, the detective comes to recognize his own potential for violence, including the rape-murder of little girls. A dark film, literally and metaphorically, *The Offence* uses settings (the brutalist concrete architecture of 1960s England, the old heaths being eaten up by expressways and airports) with great effect and constitutes Connery's most interesting film. Because it never clarifies the original suspect's status, we are left wondering if the detective himself might have been the villain. Other movies in which a cop discovers his inner serial killer include *Tightrope* (1984), which follows a detective (Clint Eastwood) stalking a sex-murderer with whom he has close affinities, and *Manhunter* (1986), a Michael Mann film in which the detective tries to catch the serial killer by adopting his thought processes.

However it is constructed, the typical serial killer film markets a stereotype: that of the superpredator who murders on the installment plan and scatters bones in his wake (or body parts in his fridge). All of the "pure" serial killer films and most of the hybrids have been made since the 1970s swing toward conservative criminal justice policies. With their portraits of the criminal as Other and of crime as personal depravity, these films mesh well with the lock-em-up policies of the last thirty years. They not only reflect such policies; they reinforce them with their spectacles of the unrepentant, incurable killer.

Psycho Films

Many authors have written about psychopath films, but because no one has specified what should and should not be included in the category, the result has been a confusion of psycho movies with slashers and serial killer films. Christian Fuchs's *Bad Blood: An Illustrated Guide to Psycho Cinema* illustrates one aspect of this problem: Organized around forty-seven real-life "serial killers and murderers" who turn up in movies, the book groups the cases into incoherent subdivisions such as "amok killers," "weirdos," and "Sadean monsters." Such sensationalist, overlapping categories tell us little about either psychopaths or movies. John McCarty's *Movie Psychos and Madmen* focuses more clearly on films, but its very broad reach (from *Fatal Attraction* [1987] through *Friday the 13th*) obscures whatever it is that is distinctive about the psycho film. Philip L. Simpson's more rigorous *Pyscho Paths: Tracking the Serial Killer through Contemporary American Film and Fiction* locates serial killer films in the Gothic tradition and relates them to detective fiction, but it concentrates almost exclusively on three films (*Natural Born Killers* [1994], *Kalifornia* [1993], and *Seven* [1995]), and it is no clearer than the other books about what to include in the psycho movie category.[12]

The clinical literature on the condition of psychopathy offers a way out of this definitional morass. The leading researcher in this area, psychologist Robert Hare, and the leading professional body, the American Psychiatric Association (APA), define psychopathy as a state characterized primarily by a lack of conscience: Psychopaths are incapable of remorse, an incapacity that frees them to offend repeatedly—not necessarily to kill but to prey on others without experiencing guilt.[13] Hare and the APA speak of psychopathy as a constellation of symptoms, including deceitfulness and manipulation, egocentricity, grandiosity, emotional shallowness, impulsivity, shortness of temper, craving for excitement, and irresponsibility. Neither authority expects every psychopath to display every symptom; rather, they apply the *psychopath* label to those who score high on a diagnostic scale by exhibiting a certain number of psychopathic traits.

Drawing on this clinical literature and using its terminology as a heuristic device, we can quite precisely define psychopath movies as films in which the main character lacks a conscience and exhibits other symptoms of psychopathy. If we restrict the analysis to movies that either explore the psychopathic personality in depth or follow a psychopath over a period of time, it becomes clear that these films have their own set of stock characters and their own, distinctive message about the nature of and need for law.[14]

The Stock Protagonists of Psycho Films

Psycho films, unlike slasher and serial killer movies, are not a recent development but have appeared since the first talkies. Thus, they now exist in considerable numbers, giving us a large group of films to analyze. The most revealing way to classify them is by types of protagonists and the impulses that lie behind their evil deeds.

Most rational of the psychos are predators, characters who have an excuse such as money or revenge for their psychopathic behavior, even though that behavior is by definition an overreaction. For instance, the gangster protagonist of the first *Scarface* movie (1932), as his simian face suggests, is animalian in his cruelty, someone who lives ruthlessly by the law of tooth and claw. (Al Pacino closely followed this role model for predacity in the 1983 remake of *Scarface*.) Similarly, Tom Udo, the psychopathic gangster of the first version of *Kiss of Death* (1947), is after money, dames, and underworld power. As played by Richard Widmark in the role that made him famous, Tom Udo combines fatuous stupidity with menace. "You know what I do to squealers?" he asks. "I let 'em have it in the belly, so they can roll around for a long time, thinking it over." In the 1995 remake of *Kiss of Death,* Nicolas Cage is equally chilling as the psychopathically brutal Little Junior Brown.

Predatory psychopaths aren't necessarily gangsters, however. In *The Hand that Rocks the Cradle* (1992), the psychopath is a nanny, out for revenge. John Christie, the sex psycho whose necrophilia is the focus of *10 Rillington Place* (1971), is apparently a perfectly ordinary homeowner who occasionally offers his services as a physician, while the main character of *The Talented Mr. Ripley* (1999) is an amateur musician. The protagonist of *Night of the Hunter* (1955; played by Robert Mitchum) is an ersatz preacher who has killed twelve widows so far and, as he explains to God in the opening sequence, is now after another "widow with a little wad of bills hidden away in the sugar bowl." Sexually perverted as well, he loathes "perfumed things with curly hair" who weaken his self-control and make him feel unclean. Another memorable Mitchum predator is the ex-convict Max Cady of *Cape Fear* (1962), in which Cady torments Sam Bowden, a lawyer (played by Gregory Peck) who helped send him to prison eight years earlier. Although Sam did nothing more than testify as witness to a rape, Cady's thirst for revenge, overwhelming and unstoppable, can be slaked only by raping Sam's teenage daughter.

Pacific Heights (1990) brings new meaning to the concept of predation with its story of a young couple who rent part of their Victorian fixer-upper to a lodger (Michael Keaton) who, as it turns out, plans
to drive them mad and assume ownership of the mansion himself. To
this end he destroys his quarters in the house, frightens the owners
out of their wits, and tricks them into making blunders, for example
by goading the landlord into assaulting him so he can play the victim when the police arrive and have the landlord evicted. *Body Heat*
(1981), too, rings changes on the theme of predation by forcing the
viewer to share the viewpoint of Ned Racine (William Hurt), the poor
chump whom the glamorous Mattie (Kathleen Turner) persuades to
kill her rich husband. Not until the end do we realize that Mattie
prearranged everything, including her initial encounter with Ned.
Even while Ned is off bludgeoning her husband, she is destroying
his alibi so she can dump him in prison.

Predatory psychos are Machiavellis—cold, cunning, and calculating. Monomaniacal in pursuit of their goals, abnormal by dint of what
they will do to achieve those goals, they are antisocial types who
scheme and plot to satisfy their desires. In their single-minded selfishness they resemble the protagonists of serial killer films, but predatory psychos are better developed as characters, and they have ex-
cuses for what they do. Moreover, as *Pacific Heights* and *Body Heat*
indicate, killing is not necessarily their central purpose in life.

Another type of psycho, gripped by insane desires and incapable
of self-control, is far less rational. While these characters, too, are often
predatory, their movies emphasize psychological deviation, unpre-
dictability, and lack of self-control. One example can be found in *The
Bad Seed* (1956), the tale of blond-haired, goody-goody little Rhoda
who has inherited a homicidal gene from her maternal grandmother.
Rhoda kills again and again, until she is finally struck dead by lightening. Boris Karloff created another classic example in the role of
Frankenstein's monster. Even though *Frankenstein* (1931) is usually
classified as a horror film, it is a seminal psycho movie as well, for its
monster became a model for subsequent irrational psychopaths. Infantile, only half human, and cursed with a criminaloid's brain, the
monster yearns for goodness and light but clumsily destroys the things
he loves. Like Norman Bates of *Psycho* (his most famous descendant),
the monster is drawn to blonds but impulsively murders them. And
like Norman Bates, he is not fully responsible for his criminal acts. In
keeping with the psychiatry of the early 1930s, his irrationality is

explained partly in terms of mental retardation, while Norman is more of a 1950s sex psycho. But both films are visually structured around alternating bright and dark scenes that symbolize the main characters' losing struggle between rationality and madness.

The unpredictable, impulsive type of psychopath has generated a host of remarkable film characters. One is Mark Lewis, the obsessive-compulsive scopophiliac of *Peeping Tom* (1960), who photographs women as he impales them. Another is the failed novelist Jack Daniel Torrance (Jack Nicholson) of *The Shining* (1980) who, like little Rhoda and Frankenstein's monster, is governed by homicidal impulses over which he has no control. In *Silence of the Lambs,* Buffalo Bill, too, is helpless in the face of his obsessions. (Hannibal Lecter, in contrast, is a predatory psychopath, and thus able to stay on top of his madness.) Alex (Malcolm McDowell), the exuberantly delinquent protagonist of *A Clockwork Orange* (1971), engages in crime because hurting people is the most amusing activity he can think of.

The differences between predatory and irrational psychos come into focus through a comparison of *Black Widow* (1987) with *Single White Female* (1992). Theresa Russell's predatory widow is motivated solely by greed; the film is organized around her searches for rich husbands and by the hunt for her by a federal agent (Debra Winger). On the other hand, Hedy Carlton (Jennifer Jason Leigh), the psychopath of *Single White Female,* is psychologically twisted. Desperate for a friend, she tries to make her apartment-mate, Ally, more dependent on her by tossing Ally's dog out the window and braining Ally's lover with a stiletto shoe heel. Whereas the Black Widow is unflappable and unchanging, Hedy ricochets among personalities and trips over her own lies. *Black Widow* stresses the cold rationality and extraordinary patience of its predator while *Single White Female* concentrates on Hedy's frantic nuttiness.

A third version of the psychopathic protagonist assumes the right to toy with others and inflict pain. Characters of this type aspire to be supermen, gods who decide the fate of others. They, too, are predatory and mentally unbalanced, but their films emphasize their Nietzschean ambition to rise above the human condition. In *White Heat,* Cody Jarrett (James Cagney) assumes powers of life and death over others by virtue of his leadership of a criminal gang. But, egged on by his ambitious, doting mother (herself a predatory psychopath), Cody aspires even higher, to the "top of the world." Taking this goal perhaps too literally, Cody achieves it in the theatrical final scene where, cornered by cops, he climbs an oil tank and blows it up, yelling, "Made it, Ma! Top of the world!"—dying in a triumph of deluded egotism.

Bruno, the psychopath of Hitchcock's *Strangers on a Train* (1951), explicitly articulates his sense of entitlement to decide life and death matters for others. Like Cody, Bruno (Robert Walker) is a mama's boy; like Cody, he suffers from strange spells or fits. But Bruno is much more arrogant, a spoiled rich guy, vain, insensitive, presumptuous, and greedy. During the first scene, in the lounge car of the train, Bruno presses his new acquaintance, Guy Haines (Farley Granger), to "Ask me anything, I know the answer." Later, Bruno responds to a remark by Guy with "Oh, I've got a wonderful theory about that." He explains that his absurd father wants him to get a job and

> work my way up. . . . I want to kill him. . . . I want to do something—everything. Now, I've got a theory that you should do everything before you die. Have you ever driven a car blindfolded, at 150 miles per hour? . . . I did. . . . And I'm going to make a reservation on the first rocket to the moon.

It turns out that Bruno is serious in suggesting that he and Guy switch victims, with Guy murdering Bruno's father and Bruno getting rid of Guy's floozy of a wife. "What is a life or two, Guy? Some people are better off dead."

The psychopath of *Seven*, John Doe (Kevin Spacey), plays God by turning New York City into a stage for the production of a medieval morality play. Inflamed by the city's indifference to the seven deadly sins, John Doe creates a Dantesque hell on earth as he punishes one sin at a time, working his way through gluttony, greed, sloth, lust, and vanity. Playing God to himself as well, John Doe arranges to be struck down for his envy of the younger detective's normalcy. On another level, John Doe controls the movie's plot as well, generating this morality play for the edification of Detective Lt. William Somerset (Morgan Freeman) and the movie's viewers, much as God generated the world for the edification of Everyman.

Most Nietzschean of all psycho protagonists is Raymond Lemorne (Bernard-Pierre Donnadieu), the central figure in the Dutch/French version of *The Vanishing* (1988). This tightly wrought film single-mindedly explores the motivations of Lemorne, who appears to be an innocuous man, a chemistry instructor with a wife and two daughters. Despite his bland exterior, however, Lemorne is obsessed with

control, as we gather from his constant counting, measuring, and timing of things. To Rex Hofman, his second victim, Lemorne explains
that at age sixteen he realized that he could go beyond "what is predestined" by forcing himself to jump from a high balcony. Although
he broke an arm and lost two fingers, he has always been glad that he
jumped, because it proved he can defy fate. Then Lemorne tells Rex
about a family holiday during which he saved a child from drowning.
When one of his daughters congratulated him, Lemorne recalls, he
responded, "Watch out for heroes. A hero is someone who is capable
of excess." His daughter's admiration, Lemorne continues, encouraged him to think of the worst thing he could imagine doing ("since
there is no white without black"). Killing, he casually observes, is
not the worst thing he can conceive of.

What makes *The Vanishing* devastating is not just the nature of
Lemorne's "worst thing" but the fact that Rex becomes like his killer
in his own Nietzschean defiance of fate. After his girlfriend vanishes
during a holiday in southern France, Rex spends three years trying to figure out what happened, in the process becoming obsessed
and unhinged. Lemorne finally comes to him and starts driving Rex
through the night to the spot where Saskia disappeared. At any point
during the car trip, Rex could kill Lemorne, or at least break out and
escape. But he remains of his own free will. Similarly, in order "to go
against what's predestined," Rex agrees to drink the drugged coffee
that Lemorne offers him. Lemorne knows all along that Rex will try
thus to defy fate. Like the stick insects in the opening and closing
shots, Lemorne has learned to catch his prey while remaining mo-
tionless and blending in with the landscape.[15]

The Secondary Characters of Psycho Films

Most psycho movies include a predictable secondary character or set
of characters. Often these are what we might call good bad-guys, secondary characters whose lesser moral flaws throw the psychopath's
monstrosity into higher relief. In *M* (1931) we find an entire underworld of ordinary criminals, all of them shocked to the bone by Hans
Beckert's sex murders and anxious to help the authorities hunt him
down. Similarly, both versions of *Kiss of Death* contrast their psycho
with a criminal who is trying to go straight for the good of his family. In both versions the good bad-guy struggles with the bad bad-
guy in a battle that signifies the psychological struggle within the

reforming offender as well as the universal struggle of good against evil. *Night of the Hunter* compares the evil preacher with Willa's first husband, Ben Harper, an essentially decent man who, made desperate by financial woes, began robbing to feed his family. The two criminals share a prison cell together, which is where the preacher learns that Willa and her children are sitting on a pile of stolen money. But whereas Ben, the good criminal, gave money to the family, the other intends to take it away. *Body Heat* makes the good bad-guy, Ned Racine, the unwitting accomplice of Mattie, the psycho-predator. In stark contrast to Mattie, Ned is lovable and straightforward. He's not very smart, as Mattie immediately remarks, and he is unsophisticated, an ordinary fellow with simple lusts. Mattie chooses him for these qualities, which differ dramatically from her own.

Another common secondary character in psycho movies is the pure innocent, a figure who illustrates the weakness of virtue when faced with malice, and hence the need for law. *M* opens with a mother making lunch for a little girl who (it turns out) will never return from school; this maternal figure, along with all the child victims, underscores Hans Beckert's destructiveness. Children again fill the role of lambs-in-danger in *Kiss of Death,* in both versions of which the psycho attempts to prevent the milder criminal from reforming by threatening the latter's offspring. *Night of the Hunter,* casting the psychopathic preacher as a stepfather and the innocent children as his prey, takes on a mythic dimension in which a Bad Father is intent on destroying childhood itself.

The figure of the innocent child matures slightly in *Cape Fear,* becoming sixteen-year-old Nancy, Max Cady's intended rape victim. The innocent is again a very helpless young woman in *Seven,* in which Gwyneth Paltrow's ingenue is overwhelmed by the noise, confusion, and crime of New York City and, eventually, by the psychopath who represents them. Her film husband, Detective David Mills (Brad Pitt), while less innocent, is also young and extremely naive, traits that inspire psychopath John Doe to teach him a lesson. *Frankenstein* includes two innocents, first Little Maria, the playmate whom the monster accidently drowns, and then the bride in full regalia, her gown and long, white train contrasting vividly with the ill-fitting black worsted suit of the figure clambering through her window.

Thanks to the women's movement, the Pure Innocent increased in complexity during the 1990s. First came *Silence of the Lambs,* with

Figure 3.2. Fritz Lang used *M* (1931), based on an actual case, to explore the psychology of a child rapist and murderer. Here we look out of a toy store at the psychopath (Peter Lorre) and his next victim, past dangling marionettes that hint at what is about to happen. Photo used by permission of Photofest.

Clarice Starling, the clear, birdlike naïf who is nonetheless eager to learn and ends up coping heroically with two psychopaths at once. On its heels came *Pacific Heights,* which portrays Patty (Melanie Griffith), the female half of the victimized couple, as a lot smarter and tougher than her partner, Drake. Whereas Drake fights back physically, thus earning a restraining order that forbids him from coming within 500 feet of his own house, Patty combats the psychopath with cunning. She realizes that, if she is to save her house and her life, she must take the law into her own hands. Equally impressive are the transformations of the Pure Innocent in *Single White Female.* Ally Jones (Bridget Fonda), the apartment owner who advertises for a "single white female" roommate, is a bit of a Barbie Doll but no ethereal maiden. Her competence, independence, and generosity contrast with Hedy's mean-spirited dependency. Whereas Ally is poised and self-confident, Hedy is mousy, dreary, and (who can blame her?) filled with self-loathing. Hedy is consumed with guilt about having killed

her twin in childhood, but Ally has the fortitude to kill when neces-
sary and get on with life. The Pure Innocent, perhaps with slasher
film's Final Girl in mind, has become a psycho-slayer.[16]

Legal Themes in Psycho Films

Psycho movies are animated by a fundamental dialectic of disorder
and control, a struggle that plays out partly through the deployment
of stock characters and partly in the films' discourses about law: the
need for law; the inadequacy of law in extreme circumstances such
as those posed by psychos; and means through which the lawful
order can be restored. These legal discourses often revolve around
the theme of intrusion. A psycho penetrates a previously lawful space,
creates havoc, and immobilizes the law. Rendered helpless, other
characters have no idea how to react. They turn to traditional legal
means only to find these ineffective. Gradually they conclude that
they must take the law into their own hands.

In *M* the psycho intrudes on the nurturing, quotidian world in
which mothers fix lunch for children who return from school; Hans
Beckert shatters this world with his sex slayings. The first *Scarface*
opens with the shadow of an armed man gliding along a wall; Tony
Camonte is about to intrude violently on a late-night party. In *Pacific
Heights* lodger Carter Hayes not only intrudes into the normal world
of the young property owners; he also lures their fluffy white cat, an
emblem of Patty and Drake's innocent domesticity, into his own
apartment. This happens innocuously, but we know it means doom.
Similarly, in *Single White Female* Hedy makes her first entrance into
Ally's apartment unannounced and unnoticed. Here, as in most psycho films, the victim is someone with simple aspirations, trying to
repair an old house, fixing lunch, arguing with a lover, sobering up
after a party. What the psychopath intrudes on, ultimately, is the
normality of our ordinary lives. Often the psycho is discovered at the
center of a placid family or community, hidden there after the initial
intrusion, working (like the nanny of *The Hand that Rocks the Cradle*)
malignantly from within.

In *Frankenstein* the key scene of intrusion comes relatively late in
the film, when the monster penetrates the bride's bedroom. Usually,
however, the most powerful images of intrusion occur near the start
of a movie, where they start the plot rolling. The preacher in *Night
of the Hunter* drives into the movie in an open-topped convertible,

his broad-brimmed hat tilted back, on his way to Willa Harper's place; the cataclysm is about to begin. *Cape Fear* opens with a tracking shot of Mitchum, wearing that hat again, ambling across a town square to the courthouse. More than an intrusion of lawlessness into the territory of law, this is a sexual invasion as well, as the huge cigar protruding from Max Cady's mouth signifies. Cady removes the cigar for a puff, cooly checks out some women passersby, and takes his first step into the court building. Climbing the stairs (and rudely ignoring a librarian struggling with a stack of law books), Cady strolls into Sam Bowden's courtroom. Its intense, multilayered rendering of the theme of intrusion makes this one of the most effective opening scenes in movie history.

The point of these intrusions is not just that the psychopath kills people and sows disorder. The psychopath *is* disorder, the destroyer of predictability in the ordinary world. We need law because the ominous-looking men under the streetlight may be Alex and his droogies from *A Clockwork Orange,* preparing to beat us up and wreck our expectations of normalcy. (Underscoring the anonymous, ubiquitous nature of the psychopath, *Seven* names him John Doe and even denies him fingerprints.) The psychopath is always there, waiting to intrude, to knock innocent people off their feet and take over. What can protect us, if not law?

But even law, we find, is powerless to contain the psychopath, and in fact, it can turn a situation from bad to worse. Two films make this point with special acerbity by featuring a lawyer as the psychopath's main victim and showing that he simply cannot cope.

Ned Racine of *Body Heat* is a lawyer with little ambition, few skills, and almost no integrity. Before he met Mattie, we learn, he botched a case involving a will. He fails to guess that Mattie will use a loophole in Florida inheritance law to walk away with her murdered husband's entire fortune.[17] *Body Heat* concludes with a faint gesture toward the restoration of law and order when Ned, in prison, manages to get hold of a copy of Mattie's high school yearbook and figure out her true identity. But as hunts for the psychopath go, this one lacks promise.

Cape Fear's chief victim is not just a lawyer but Gregory Peck, an actor whose very appearance conveys moral and legal rectitude.[18] Sam turns for help to his old friend the police chief, who uses police harassment to encourage Max Cady to leave town. But Cady has been studying law in prison for eight years and outsmarts them, bringing in a sleazy lawyer to halt the chief's campaign. Sam, who of course knows his rights, then warns Cady to "stay off my property." Moments later in the garden of his house, Nancy's dog starts yelping and expires, poisoned, with Bernard Herrmann's violins screeching in the background. Evidently Cady is unimpressed by property rights and lawerly injunctions. Sam and the police chief begin wondering whether law should be able to "prevent" crime through denial of civil liberties. "Either we have too many laws," one of them observes, "or not enough." Later, after Max Cady has beaten a girlfriend to a pulp, the police beg her to press charges; but she refuses—another round for Cady in his match against the law.

Cady has figured out how to use the law against Sam: If his daughter is raped, Sam will not ask Nancy to testify. "It's the clinical reports and the questions and the detailed answers that she'd have to give," Sam explains to his wife. "Cady *knows* we'd never put her through an ordeal like that." Running out of lawful solutions, Sam has Cady beaten by thugs, but the moment they leave, Cady goes to a pay phone, calls Sam's house, and announces, "You just put the law in my hands, and I'm going to break your heart with it. I've got something planned for your wife and kid that they'll never forget, and neither will you, counselor." At this point Sam realizes that to save his family, he may have to kill Cady himself. As a lawyer, he is helpless.[19]

Nonlawyer victims, too, discover that the law cannot help. In the first version of *Kiss of Death,* ex-con Nick Bianco (Victor Mature) decides to go straight and turn state's evidence. Encouraged by a good-hearted district attorney, he even testifies at Tom Udo's trial. Justice miscarries, however. Udo walks, and Nick's life is in danger, along with that of his new wife and kids. Realizing that the law has only gotten him into hotter water, Nick takes the law into his own hands and ends up doing what the DA was unable to do by bringing Udo to justice. The second version of *Kiss of Death,* evidently hesitant to portray a good-hearted district attorney, splits this figure into two other characters, one an overly slick DA, the other a compassionate plainclothes cop. Jimmy, the punk who wants to go straight, wears a wire and collects evidence against not only the psychopath but also the DA who cares more about his own career than justice. Order is restored, but with little help from the law. In fact, in this version of *Kiss of Death,* law is incompetent, chaotic, and deadly, incapable of protecting even its own representatives from violence.

In *Pacific Heights* as in some other psycho movies, the law actually protects the wicked. Beset by Carter, their psychopathic lodger, Patty and Drake turn to a lawyer for help; she has to inform them that, unfortunately, the law ties their hands. At another point the law in the form of a restraining order prevents Drake from going back to his own house, leaving Patty stranded there with the psychopath. Carter, they learn from his executor, has "been out of control for a long time"; law has never been able to contain him, though he has a long history of scamming landlords and bilking heiresses. At one point, Patty and Drake do manage to get an eviction order against Carter; but when the bailiff unlocks the lodger's apartment, they find a scene of total destruction—even the toilet is gone. Law fails again. Only when Patty fully realizes the powerlessness of law does she conclude that she herself must act. Rex, in *The Vanishing,* after a similar realization of law's impotence, decides to go after the psychopath himself. In *Seven* the psychopath's lawyer sets up the final scene of the morality play, and the impetuous younger detective allows himself to be manipulated into breaking the law, thus enabling the psycho to win.

The legal order is restored at the end of most psycho movies. In some cases the agent of restoration is a legal authority, such as a law enforcement officer. Examples include *Frankenstein,* in which townsfolk led by local bigwigs pursue the monster to the Old Mill; *White Heat; Black Widow; Silence of the Lambs; Seven,* in which the world-weary older detective decides to remain on the police force; and *Badlands.* In *The Bad Seed,* Nature itself restores law and order. A bolt of lightening wipes out little Rhoda, and this is no doubt fitting since Nature, in the form of a bad gene, created this monstrous brat in the first place. Nature plays a role in *The Shining,* too, where a fortuitous snowstorm freezes the psycho to death, enabling his family to flee the cursed hotel. But most of the time the psycho-slayer is either one of the psycho's victims or a victim surrogate: in *Night of the Hunter,* the elderly woman who saves the children; in *Strangers on a Train,* Guy Haines, who kills Bruno; in *Psycho,* Lila Crane, Marion's sister; in *Cape Fear,* Sam Bowden; in *Pacific Heights,* Patty Palmer, the brainier half of the home-owning couple; in *Single White Female,* Ally Jones, who fittingly wipes out Hedy in the apartment building from which she initially advertised for a roommate.

Psycho movies, then, begin by demonstrating that danger lurks everywhere, even in apparent normalcy. Like death itself, a psycho may intrude upon us at the next roadside rest stop, or by ringing the doorbell one evening, or by creeping up while we're out bowling with the family. The very randomness of the threat intensifies the need for law. But, the movies go on to observe, law is often powerless, at least initially, against such intruders; thus psychos turn ordinarily pacific people into vigilantes, forcing even lawyers to take up arms. Eventually, the world returns to normalcy with the defeat and punishment of the psycho. In a few interesting exceptions, however, the psycho is not really defeated. Holly survives in *Badlands* to tell the tale. The end of *Body Heat* finds Mattie sunning herself on an exotic beach with a new hunk, almost beyond the reach of Ned in his prison cell. In *Seven,* psycho John Doe engineers his own arrest and death, even while punishing the law in the form of the younger detective. *Psycho* closes with a complicitous smile that may mean that Norman Bates has triumphed after all. More grimly, *The Vanishing* concludes with not the law but the psychopath savoring victory.

By distinguishing among slashers, serial killer films, and psycho movies, then, we gain understanding of the meanings and reception of cinematic violence, and a sense of how violent films vary in their subtexts about criminal nature. The subtextual meanings derive in part from the context in which a film is made, with, for instance, the 1990s sensationalization of serial killing and rhetoric of incapacitation shaping the messages of *American Psycho*. The meanings of violent cinema are shaped as well by the anticipated audience (most obviously in the case of slashers) and even unanticipated audiences (the filmmakers could not have guessed, for example, that a generation of youthful rebels would adopt Bonnie and Clyde as role models). By making the distinctions, we are better equipped to understand what violent movies say about the nature of crime, law, and criminals; we are also better able to understand them as films. We can see why it does not occur to viewers to register *White Heat* or *Bonnie and Clyde* as serial killer films, despite those works' brutal and sequential killings.

Notes

1. For a study that aims at these same ends while using a different kind of film, see Tzanelli, Yar, and O'Brien 2005.
2. The term "Final Girl" comes from Clover 1992.
3. Tatar 1998: 71, 86, 69, 72, 83.

4. On authorities' increased willingness to explain criminal behavior in terms of evil—a willingness that would have been unthinkable only a decade ago—see Carey 2005.

5. Ronald Reagan, as quoted in Jenkins 1994: 10. Jenkins provides an excellent, in-depth analysis of the social circumstances that gave rise to the serial killer boom.

6. Jenkins 1994: chap. 3.

7. Jenkins (1994: 73) writes,

> Thomas Harris provided the FBI's violent-crime experts with invaluable publicity and unprecedented visibility, both crucial in the aftermath of the *Iowa* disaster. As Ressler [Robert Ressler, the FBI profiler who claimed to have originated the term "serial murder"] has written in his remarkably candid autobiography, "The media have come around to lionizing behavioral science people as supersleuths who put all other police to shame and solve cases where others have failed."

On Harris and his influence on the FBI, also see Simpson 2000, esp. pp. 70–73. Harris's novel *Red Dragon* was originally made into a film in 1986 under the title *Manhunter;* the film version of Harris's *Silence of the Lambs* appeared in 1991.

8. Jenkins 1994: 40.

9. See Jenkins 1994: chap. 5 ("Serial Murder as Modern Mythology").

10. Picart and Greek 2003 argue that the serial killer and vampire cinematic traditions converge in "gothic" criminology. While this argument illuminates some serial killer films, it does not apply to them all, and it tends to wash out what is distinctive about the two traditions.

11. Spike Lee's *Summer of Sam* (1999) has more animation than most true-story serial killer movies because, instead of unilaterally focusing on the serial killer (here, David "Son of Sam" Berkowitz), it explores his historical and social context. Another exception, as mentioned previously, is *The Boston Strangler,* based on the deSalvo case; but due to its probing of the killer's psychology, it is better classified as a psychopath movie than as a serial killer film.

12. Fuchs 2002, McCarty 1993b, Simpson 2000; also see Douglass 1981. Another work, Wayne Wilson's *The Psychopath in Film* (1999), defines the psychopath category so loosely as to include Nurse Rached of *One Flew Over the Cuckoo's Nest* (1975), Goldfinger in the *James Bond* movies, and the carouser in *Hud* (1963).

13. Hare 1993; Hare 1994; Hare, Hart, and Harpur 1991; American Psychiatric Association 2000. The American Psychiatric Association's current term for psychopathy is *antisocial personality disorder.*

14. A longer version of this analysis appears in Rafter 2005.

15. The second version of *The Vanishing* (1993), by the same director but with a different cast, is a serial killer film with a slasher ending.

16. A lot of ink has been spilled in discussing why Martin Scorsese's remake of *Cape Fear* is less successful than the original. The basic problem, I think, is

that the characters of both the Pure Innocent and the psycho are diluted. Lawyer Sam Bowden (Nick Nolte in the remake) is more flawed than the original character, just as the other innocent, his young daughter, is less lamblike. Meanwhile, Max Cady (Robert De Niro in the second version) is given a stronger motive for coming after Sam. The net result is loss of the psycho movie's stock characters and with it, loss of the stark struggle between good and evil that one expects to find in this type of film.

17. This same legal loophole is invoked in *Black Widow,* another psycho film in which law protects the lawless.

18. *Cape Fear* was released in April 1962, eight months before *To Kill a Mockingbird,* in which Peck stars as the heroic lawyer Atticus Finch. Anyone who saw *Cape Fear* after 25 December 1962, then, might also have associated its lawyer, Sam Bowden, with Atticus, the very model of legal integrity. On Atticus's image, see Thain 2001.

19. Law is even less effective in the second version of *Cape Fear,* where Cady beats Sam in the race to hire "the best criminal lawyer in the state" and a judge issues a restraining order against Sam.

4 Cop and Detective Films

> We need a twenty-four-hour-a-day police officer. A cop who
> doesn't need to eat or sleep. A cop with superior fire power
> *and* the reflexes to use it.
>
> —*RoboCop*

Trying to bring conceptual order to cop and detective movies is like
trying to classify a proliferating form of life—one with hundreds of
individual examples—using an obsolete taxonomy. Detective movies
alone encompass half a dozen subtypes: amateur sleuth films; films
about private eyes, private security agents, and plainclothes police
detectives; victim-turned-hunter films; and movies more generally
classified as noirs, neo-noirs, and whodunits or mysteries. Cop movies
include even more subtypes: action films; aging cop films; the blaxploitation or black cop films of the early 1970s; films about buddy
cops, corrupt cops, female cops, and rogue cops; cyborg or science-
fiction cop films; serial killer cop films; cop comedies; postmodernist
cop films; and what I call alternative cop films. All are concerned with
detection—seeing, penetrating, interpreting, apprehending—but they
differ considerably in characters, theme, and relationships to the
broader society. The challenge is to bring order to this antic prolif-
eration and discover how these mutating film types evolved, which
species are dying out, and how others are adapting for survival.

Their evolution, which for decades closely paralleled developments
in mystery fiction, began with whodunits and progressed through
noirs until, around 1970, it reached the cop-film era. Early twentieth-
century whodunits, echoing the stories of Sir Arthur Conan Doyle
and the "cozy" mysteries of Agatha Christie, picture crime as a dis-
ruption of a safe world of settled routines. An eccentric amateur detective who is part of that world deciphers the clues and identifies
the criminal, whose expulsion restores the world to snug familiarity.
(This pattern of internal discovery, expulsion, and restoration contrasts with that of later detection films, in which criminality is woven
into the fabric of daily life and therefore can be neither fully excised
nor exorcised.) Most famous of the amateur sleuths was Sherlock
Holmes, Sir Arthur Conan Doyle's Victorian gentleman who, with his

buddy Dr. Watson, solves the mystery in dozens of silent films and early talkies. But such movies also feature female sleuths; in Alfred Hitchcock's *The Lady Vanishes* (1938), for example, high-spirited Iris Henderson initiates the search, investigates as an equal with her handsome traveling companion, foils a faux brain surgeon, and fights off Nazis before rescuing doddery old Miss Froy, who herself turns out to be a foreign-office spy.[1]

While amateur-sleuth mysteries were sidelined in the 1940s by noirs, top directors continued to be drawn to the genre. Hitchcock brought it back into play with *Rear Window* (1954), in which a photographer (James Stewart), immobilized by a broken leg, uses his camera to detect a murder in the opposite block of apartments. Francis Ford Coppola transformed the genre into a vehicle for ambiguity with *The Conversation* (1974), in which a surveillance specialist (Gene Hackman) tries to detect a crime but cannot quite manage to do so. David Lynch's *Blue Velvet* (1986) again reworked the genre with a droll parody in which the amateur sleuth, this time a snoopy young man (Kyle MacLachlan), uncovers a crime—and with it the whole dark underside of existence, including body parts, sadomasochism, and the earthworms of decay.

With noirs, crime became integral to daily (especially nocturnal) life and crime investigation a mere stopgap against corruption that threatened from all sides. Indeed, noir private eyes such as Sam Spade (Humphrey Bogart) of *The Maltese Falcon* (1941), Philip Marlowe (Dick Powell) of *Murder, My Sweet* (1944), and Mike Hammer (Ralph Meeker) of *Kiss Me Deadly* (1955) are themselves part of the problem: mercenary, snarling misogynists, low-life antitheses of the gentlemanly Victorian sleuth. These private eyes may catch their criminals, but they are incapable of restoring lawful order, partly because it bores them. Noir detectives embody tensions between good and evil, the attractive and the repellent, and the best they can do is to throw up temporary barriers against lawlessness.[2]

Noir detectives' legacies to later cop heroes include these ambiguities, ambivalences, and fallibilities as well as their contempt for aristocratic bad guys and disdain for women. Moreover, while few noir detectives are as flamboyantly attractive as later cop heroes, their films nonetheless inaugurate the tradition of eroticizing the detective's body and demonstrating its capacity for enduring (perhaps even desiring) terrific punishment. Noirs took a character—the detective—and began to turn him into spectacle. He became, not just a mystery-

solver but a body to stare at and be impressed by, the human equivalent of earlier films' crowd scenes and outsized stage sets, someone
offered up for our delectation. The action-cop heroes of the 1980s
and 1990s were direct descendants.

An official investigator occasionally played a major role even in
silent films. Such was the case in *The Lodger* (1927), a Hitchcock film
that, like many of his later works, focuses on a golden-haired beauty
in danger of being hacked to pieces. Here the threat is experienced
by Daisy, a blond showgirl, and emanates from the Avenger, an
unidentified killer who claims a fair-haired victim each Tuesday. We
worry about a police inspector who declares himself too fond of fair-
haired girls and starts cozying up to Daisy. But we also worry about
a mysterious stranger who, swathed in scarves, comes to Daisy's
house (number 13) in search of lodging. The Lodger reacts badly to
the pictures of blond women in his rented room and, despite his un-
explained anguish, makes eyes at Daisy. The Inspector, declaring
that he will put a rope around the Avenger's neck and a ring around
Daisy's finger, breaks into the Lodger's locked bureau, where he discovers a map marked with the locations of the murders and a photo
of the Avenger's first victim. But the Lodger, when he is arrested, reveals that he himself has been hunting the Avenger because that first
victim was his sister. The Inspector saves the Lodger from a lynch
mob; his men capture the real Avenger; and the Lodger marries
Daisy. Here, then, an official investigator is a central character, and
even though he doesn't get the girl, he does save her.

Evolution of the Cop Film

Despite this early availability of the cop-hero figure, the police drama
did not emerge as a distinct generic form until 1971, when Dirty Harry
strolled onto the scene. One factor retarding its development was a
problem in characterization: Filmmakers found it difficult to make
official good guys entertaining, and it was much easier to deliver adventure, illicit sex, and mayhem by concentrating on lawbreakers.
Another hindrance was the popularity of Westerns and noirs, both
of which featured a central, law-restoring character with a gun.
There was little need for police heroes as long as cinema could rely
on lonesome sheriffs and private eyes. Then, too, for more than a century police officers had low status in American society. To become a
cop required little more than an eighth-grade education and male

anatomy, and the police worked long hours for low pay and minimal respect. Their standing began to rise, however, with the 1967 publication of a multivolume report by the President's Commission on Law Enforcement and Administration of Justice, a work that sought to redefine policing as a profession requiring advanced education, technical skills, and scientific training.[3] This report helped make the new genre possible.

Before *Dirty Harry* ushered in the cop film genre, most order-maintenance characters fit one of three stereotypes: dopey patrolman, tough federal agent, or cool private investigator. Silent movies often depict patrolmen as ludicrous oafs, men who can be counted on to slip on a banana peel and hold a letter upside down. Buster Keaton's *Cops* (1922) shows hordes of uniformed officers running first in one direction, then another, like a flock of birds, while Mack Sennett's Keystone cops became symbols of madcap ineptitude. Gangster films of the 1930s, elaborating this image, portrayed the patrolman as a stupid "flatfoot" or "gumshoe"—coarse, Irish, and corruptible. This stereotype (almost the opposite of what became the Dirty Harry ideal) continued to turn up in later decades, informing, for instance, the characterization of McCluskey, the crooked police lieutenant in *The Godfather* (1972). A sleazy Irishman who solicits payoffs and pummels helpless citizens, McCluskey (Sterling Hayden) is dining with a mobster when Michael Corleone, in his maiden kill, blows his brains out.

This unflattering image was upgraded by a new cop figure, the tough federal agent, who made his film debut in the 1930s. Professional and straightlaced, the federal officer was created to solve a dilemma posed by Hollywood's recent release of a string of gangster and prison films in which hoodlums were heroes. When Catholic bishops and other moralists condemned these films, Hollywood responded with a new series of movies—*Let 'Em Have It* (1935), *Show Them No Mercy* (1935), *You Can't Get Away with It* (1936)—in which the forces of law and order triumph. These mainly featured the G- or government-men of the Federal Bureau of Investigation, whose publicity-conscious director, J. Edgar Hoover, encouraged positive propaganda from Hollywood. A problem remained, however: While the movie feds were competent, most were still much less engaging than the bad guys. The problem was partially solved in *"G" Men* (1935), starring James Cagney as a crime fighter who began life on the wrong ide of the tracks. Raised by a mobster who finances his education, Cagney becomes a lawyer; but when no clients knock on his door and a G-man friend is killed, he joins the FBI. Thanks to his familiarity with mobsters' ways, he is able to outshine the other agents. Cagney's engaging, street-fighter character could have rescued "*G*" *Men* from the usual woodenness had the film not gone on to preach about the FBI's need for expanded enforcement powers.[4]

The obstacle of the boring good guy was finally overcome by noirs, which devised a third image for the crime-buster, that of the cool private investigator: sexy, debonair, and a whole lot smarter than everyone else. Humphrey Bogart became the archetypal private detective, living dangerously in the borderland between criminality and lawfulness. Even David Bannion, the cop hero of the noir *The Big Heat* (1953), becomes admirable when his wife is blown up by a car bomb meant for him, undergoing a transformation from devoted family man into hell-bent vigilante. When Bannion (Glenn Ford) refuses to bow to mob pressure, his crooked boss demands his badge, thus furthering Bannion's transformation into a marginal figure with whom we can identify. Moving into the underworld, the former police officer befriends a gun moll whose face has been scalded and scarred by the ultimate bad guy (Lee Marvin). Neither sinner nor saint, the noir hero was a bit of both.[5]

Dirty Harry

Several factors worked together in the 1950s and 1960s to release the cop film genre from its chrysalis. The precursor genres featuring men with guns—the Western and the noir—were running out of gas. "There was a need," writes Richard Schickel, "to find a contemporary place for hard loners—traditional males, if you will—to live plausibly. And the most readily available wilderness, the concrete wilderness, suddenly seemed more interesting and dangerous than ever" due to rising rates of urban disorder and street crime.[6] The new medium of television had introduced the police series, with *Dragnet* (1951 to 1959) and *Hawaii Five-O* (1968 to 1980) demonstrating the enormous drawing power of police action episodes. And even though the 1967 President's Commission report brought new respectability to policing, police overreactions to student protests and urban riots forced both the public and police to rethink the role of law enforcement.

A key transitional event occurred when veteran director Don Siegel paired up with actor Clint Eastwood to make *Coogan's Bluff* (1968).[7] Picking up on the Western's heroic lawman, *Coogan's Bluff* follows not a police officer but something close: a sheriff. Moreover, this sheriff tracks a killer from Arizona to New York City, thus anticipating the union of the Western with the city-centered noir that was about to produce a new genre. *Coogan's Bluff* itself is an embarrassing film, awkward and offensive, but it is significant as a forerunner. The cop film was taking shape.

Dirty Harry appeared in the wake of tumultuous events. The assassinations of Martin Luther King Jr., Robert Kennedy, and Malcolm X made people wonder whether the police were in control. When police officers killed peaceful demonstrators at Kent State University, fought with protesters during the 1968 Democratic National Convention, and struggled for five days with gay men outside New York's Stonewall Inn, many people wondered whether they were *out* of control. Critics across the nation reproached the police, who had indeed accumulated a sorry record of brutality. About 1970, however, public opinion began swinging back toward law-and-order positions. Clint Eastwood himself was conservative, as was his Dirty Harry character.[8] With perfect timing, the movie caught public attitudes toward the police just as they began reversing themselves.

The film portrays Harry ("Well, I'm all broken up about that man's rights") Callahan as the ideal cop. Brave and uncomplaining, he is willing to sacrifice his life in the line of duty. But if Harry does die, the film informs us, it will be because bleeding-heart liberals have tied cops' hands, making it impossible for them to keep criminals off the streets. Unwilling to let obvious offenders escape, Harry sometimes has to play dirty, breaking the rules to keep the peace. *Dirty Harry's* adulation of the police and its liberal-bashing contributed to the movie's success, as did Eastwood's sardonic manner and tough-guy talk. But the movie's apparent enthusiasm for vigilante justice enraged the critics.[9]

The second film in the series, *Magnum Force* (1973), addresses the critics' objections in two ways. First, it presents a group of *really* bad cops to contrast with Harry and demonstrate that he is in fact a model of restraint. These are neofascist traffic cops who speed around on motorcycles shooting scantily dressed white girls and black men. Second, *Magnum Force* cleans up Harry's own act. Now he follows the rules even when he despises them, managing nonetheless to vanquish the vigilante traffic cops as well as the usual criminals.[10]

Crucial to the *Dirty Harry* films' success was the ease with which they shifted the familiar character of the gunslinger to an urban po-

Figure 4.1. One of the first cop movies, *Dirty Harry* (1971) can also be considered a law film due to its central theme: the conflict between the aims of crime control on the one hand and the observance of due process on the other. Photo used by permission of Photofest.

lice setting. Without missing a beat, the Siegel-Eastwood team rescued the superannuated but still compelling hero of Westerns from genre decay by transferring him laterally, character intact, into the cop flick. In an essay on the Western hero, Robert Warshow speaks of the gunslinger's melancholy, seriousness, and "moral clarity," of his "personal nobility," modesty, and reluctance to impose himself.[11] These traits are equally characteristic of Eastwood's cop hero, with his sense of limitation and constrained diffidence. Warshow's West-

erner "appears to be unemployed," a "man of leisure"; although Harry
Callahan works for a living, his civilian clothing and scorn for superior officers indicate that he, too, is a freelancer. Much as the Westerner's horse signifies physical freedom, Callahan's car signifies his
freedom to roam the city, which turns out to offer as many spectacles
as the wide-open spaces. With little more than a change of outfit,
then, the Westerner migrated to the cop film, enabling viewers to
switch genre allegiances without bidding farewell to the gunslinger's
essential character. Eastwood, who had starred in a number of Westerns, was the ideal actor for making this transition.

The ease of this character migration illuminates not only the success of the *Dirty Harry* films but also the nature of cop films more generally. "One of the greatest obstacles to any fruitful theory of genre,"
writes film theorist Robin Wood, "has been the tendency to treat the
genres as discrete. . . . At best, they represent different strategies for
dealing with the same ideological tensions."[12] When it first appeared,
the cop film was less a unique new form than a new "strategy" for
analyzing the nature of heroism and the hero's relationship to society. Like the Westerner, Harry Callahan patrols a border between
barbarity and society, abandon and self-control, what John Cawelti
in another context calls the "frontier between savagery and civiliza-
tion."[13] That frontier is both geographical and psychological, a line
that must be drawn within the city and within the hero himself.

After Dirty Harry

A flood of cop films followed immediately on *Dirty Harry*'s release.
The French Connection (also 1971) starred Gene Hackman as Popeye
Doyle, another half-wild police officer, and set a new standard for the
urban car chase with its scene of high-speed pursuit under New
York's Third Avenue "el." *Serpico* (1973) featured Al Pacino, fresh
from his triumph in *The Godfather*, in the true story of a New York
City cop who ratted on crooked officers and suffered grim consequences. By portraying Serpico as an eccentric who, by virtue of being
a good guy in an evil department, is himself a bit of an outlaw, Pacino manages the difficult feat of making an official hero appealing.
With additions such as *Fuzz* (1972), *Cleopatra Jones* (1973), and *The
Black Marble* (1979), the new genre was off and running. Sometimes
it stumbled, as with *The Onion Field* (1979), a movie that begins dramatically with the kidnapping and shooting of two police officers

but then loses its way by following the story into the courts and prison. The blaxploitation detective films (*Shaft* [1971], *Shaft's Big Score* [1972], and *Shaft in Africa* [1973]) probed in a direction that eventually proved to be a dead end.[14] Even the missteps, however, were part of the process through which the new genre figured out what it could and could not do well.

Boldest of the new cop movies was *Cruising* (1980), the story of an undercover officer investigating a series of slasher murders of gay men. Starring Al Pacino as the New York City cop who learns about not only homosexuality but also his own attitude toward it, the movie precipitated furious protests against its lurid views of life in a gay subculture.[15] However, Pacino's cruiser is both plausible and attractive; and at the end, with his girlfriend cross-dressing in the next room and the movie hinting that he himself may have become a slasher, the cop searches his reflection in the mirror as if questioning his sexual identity.

Also innovative is *Night Falls on Manhattan* (1997), the fifth in director Sidney Lumet's cycle of films about the inescapable moral dilemmas of policing. (The earlier four were *Serpico, The Offence* [1973], *Prince of the City* [1981], and *Q & A* [1990].) Lumet traces his interest in police corruption to childhood: "When I was a kid we'd be pitching pennies and the cops would come along, break us up and keep the pennies.")[16] In *Night Falls* the lead figure (played by Andy Garcia) is a former cop turned prosecutor who must choose between protecting a criminal and safeguarding his own father, a detective whose corruption he has uncovered. Like *Cruising, Night Falls* finds a creative solution to the old problem of how to focus on an official hero without boring the audience. It gives him a moral dilemma to struggle with while he cleans up the department.

The cop film genre began subdividing into types. One variety is the rogue cop movie, in which the lead officer will do anything to destroy his or her opponent. Direct descendants of *Dirty Harry* and *The French Connection,* with *The Big Heat* a distant ancestor, rogue cop movies include *Ten to Midnight* (1983), *Cop* (1988), *One Good Cop* (1991), *Insomnia* (both the 1997 Norwegian version and the 2002 Al Pacino remake), and *The Negotiator* (1998). A second type is the corrupt cop movie, in which the lead officer misuses his or her position for personal gain. This category includes *An Innocent Man* (1989); *Internal Affairs* (1990); *Romeo Is Bleeding* (1993); the high-spirited *Unlawful Entry* (1992), in which Ray Liotta plays the bad guy with Cagney-

esque gusto; and *L. A. Confidential*. The corrupt cop category also includes *Cop Land* (1997), in which a pack of venal officers is eventually done in by an internal affairs investigator (Robert De Niro) and
a lumpish local cop (Sylvester Stallone, transformed from action hero
into a character so thick in mind and body that, as reviewer Anthony
Lane put it, "he's like a brick wall walking into himself").[17]

Other types that appeared with some frequency were the cop comedy, the honest cop film, and the woman cop picture. Cop comedies
such as the *Police Academy* series (1984 and following), the *Beverly
Hills Cop* series (1984, 1987, 1994), the *Naked Gun* series (1988, 1991,
1994), and *The Hard Way* (1991) make themselves acceptable by paro-
dying not police officers but other cop films. The honest cop movie,
which has seldom improved on *Serpico,* includes such variations as
Prince of the City, Witness (1985), and *The Untouchables* (1987). *Deep
Cover* (1992), starring Laurence Fishburn as an undercover agent who
embraces his drug dealer role a bit too enthusiastically, blends the
honest cop with the corrupt cop film. Hollywood started including
women cops in police movies in the 1970s, but for a long time these
women ended up in bed with their partners (as in *The Black Marble*),
or had to take orders from other cops and even civilians (*Above the
Law* [1988]), or got shot for their efforts to enter male territory (*The
Enforcer*).[18] With the exception of *Black Widow* (1987), it was not until
the 1990s that films such as *Blue Steel* (1990), *Silence of the Lambs*
(1991), *Point of No Return* (1993), *Copycat* (1995), and *Fargo* (1996)
began featuring women cops as heroes in their own right.

Most successful of all were the cop action films that dominated the
screen in the 1980s and 1990s, especially the *Lethal Weapon* (1987,
1989, 1992, 1998) and *Die Hard* (1988, 1990, 1995) series. These overlap with buddy-cop films, another high-voltage type that tends to
feature odd-couple partnerships (*48 Hrs.* [1982], *Colors* [1988], *New
Jack City* [1991]).[19] Most cop action revolves around a white male police officer who can get along with neither his significant other, his
boss, nor his partner and whose problem-solving skills are limited to
throwing punches and firing guns. In *Heroes in Hard Times,* Neal
King argues that these are essentially political films, expressions of rage
and righteousness by white guys who feel themselves losing ground
through affirmative action and national economic decline.

> Working-class community protectors—cops, for short—blow through
> racial guilt, sexual hostility, and class resentment with a wise-cracking

defiance and a lot of firepower. By pitting themselves against the rich, racist, and woman-hating criminal class, cops stand tall at the centers of their stories. Hard times give them opportunities to retake the center stage they feel they've lost. While on that stage, with all eyes fixed upon them, heroes . . . stake out a white guy turf on which they can star as the most qualified, while they punish the evil around and within them.[20]

That almost anyone can identify with the action heroes' sense of hard times helps explain the phenomenal appeal of their pictures.

Cop Films and Masculinities

Cop films serve as a medium for the definition of masculinity, participating in the construction and reconstruction of gender on the national and even international level, influencing how we react to men and how we ourselves "do" gender when we dress, walk, and talk. Since the early 1970s, cop films have repeatedly raised the gender-related question: "What makes a good police officer?" Sometimes they do this explicitly, as when, in *RoboCop* (1987), the bad guy, having captured the good cop, sneers, "You a good cop? Hot shot? Sure you are. Why you got to be some kind of a *great* cop to come in here by yourself." More often, cop films raise the question of what makes a good police officer indirectly, through character and plot. Specific responses to the question vary, but their general definitions tend to be the same: The good police officer is an ideal man. To identify one, cop films tell us, look for the other.

Earlier films, too, had raised this issue about the nature of the ideal crime investigator, and they, too, tended to respond with traditional definitions of masculinity, picturing the ideal man as fearless, heterosexual, independent, unemotional, and superhumanly powerful. That is, they tended to draw on and reinforce dominant notions of masculinity. Recently, however, movies have started to break with convention, offering new images showing that the ideal cop or private detective can be nonwhite, female, and a quite ordinary (though of course heroic) person.

Traditional Masculinities

Like many noirs, *Kiss Me Deadly* focuses on a private detective, in this case Mike Hammer, the hero of a popular novel series by Mickey Spillane. Mike's masculinity is initially defined by his tough-guy talk, the surly banter with which he figuratively hammers the other characters. The film opens on a terrified woman running down a lonely road at night; after almost hitting her with his automobile, Mike's first words are, "You almost wrecked my car. Well? Get in." But the woman is more amused than offended by this churlish gallantry, and the audience, taking its cue from her, settles in to enjoy Mike's outrageous surliness.

Another aspect of Mike's masculinity (as his surname hints) is sexuality. He is a "bedroom dick," we learn, a private investigator who specializes in proving infidelity in divorce cases, and his secretary, Velda, would happily be his sexual slave. But while women throw themselves at Mike, he reacts with indifference. His job is not to seduce but to save them.

Appearing shortly after World War II, *Kiss Me Deadly* offered escape into unregimented glamour for young men returning from combat and settling down to more humdrum lives. Mike does not live in one of the cookie-cutter housing developments where many GIs were raising their families but an elegant apartment with a rolling bar and high-tech answering machine. Drawing on the stylish masculinity of 1930s films,[21] the movie portrays a detective untrammeled by wife, kids, or regular job, roaming the city at will, driving classy sports cars and rescuing nearly nude blonds at night to the velvety tones of Nat King Cole. The film's opening—the woman running, the credits zooming, the car swerving—bespeaks an existence of excitement and speed.

To underscore Mike's masculinity, *Kiss Me Deadly* contrasts him with two groups of other men, police officers and menial laborers. Neither has much to do with the plot; rather, they function as foils, their deficiencies highlighting Mike's virtues. Mike easily fools police officers at a roadblock, and he has no use for the hectoring feds who solicit his help. But he befriends slow-witted or simply square working-class men, some of them childish immigrants, others simply saps who eat dinner with their families.

In the world of *Kiss Me Deadly*, then, Mike towers above everyone else in intellect and sophistication. He can enter any building, detect the tiniest clue, solve the most impenetrable mystery. Fearless, clever, sexy, and cool, Mike can win almost any fight and persuade almost anyone to do his bidding; even policemen grudgingly admire him. Tireless and unflappable, Mike is never at a loss for a wisecrack. Moreover, beneath that hard shell he is all heart—the man women long for and other men dream to be.

Mike Hammer is only one type of noir hero, as Frank Krutnik points out in his study of noir and masculinity; and Mike's body—beefier than that of, say, Bogart—is only one type of noir-hero physique. But noir's insistence on displaying a tough-guy personality—gutsy, indomitable, aloof—in a tough-guy body of some sort, points toward the future of masculinity among crime-film heroes. In particular, it foreshadows the spectacles of masculinity staged by cop action films, with their skillful satisfaction of scopophiliac desires, their cultivation of viewer enjoyment of hard-bodied heroes who banter their way through beatings. Film scholars differ in their interpretations of detection films' obsession with masculinity, with Krutnik, for example, arguing that in noirs it betokens an underlying anxiety about manliness.[22] But the wisecracks, not to mention the cigarettes dangling from heroes' lips during fistfights, to me suggest a supreme confidence in male identity and sexuality. Indeed, part of the pleasure of watching a noir or cop action film is the protagonist's unshakeable poise and, well, cocksureness.

Which returns us to the *Dirty Harrys*: Nearly twenty years after the release of *Kiss Me Deadly, Magnum Force* used much the same strategies to define the ideal man. *Magnum Force,* as noted earlier, formed part of an ongoing political debate over the nature of good policing—its goals, its limits, and its relationship to law. This debate, which drives the plot, is also presented as a quarrel within Harry Callahan, a conflict between the neofascist tendencies attributed to his character after the first *Dirty Harry* film and the respect for law he claims in *Magnum Force.* The film takes its title from Harry's gun, the symbol of his virility. As the credits roll, a huge black handgun, a .44 Magnum, points leftward; when the credits end, it turns toward us, an emblem of both police power and phallic potency. From then on, guns and flashlights repeatedly point our way, threatening to go off. Harry, it goes without saying, is the best shot of all.

Harry Callahan, like Mike Hammer before him, attracts women like flies but brushes them off, preoccupied with more important matters. Of the three women in *Magnum Force,* two make passes at Harry. The death-squad cops, too, are mad about Harry and his big gun. Harry professes indifference: "If the rest of you could shoot like them, I wouldn't care if the whole damn department was queer." But the film *does* care, defining good men as straight, bad ones as homosexual.[23]

In Harry Callahan's case, as in that of Mike Hammer, impudence and caustic wit ("Do you feel lucky?"; "Go ahead, make my day") are intrinsic to masculinity, evidence of imperturbable self-possession. But Eastwood's long, erect body even better expresses the controlled manhood of the action hero. Moreover, the *Dirty Harry*s go beyond *Kiss Me Deadly* and other noirs in the camera's willingness to ogle the hero's body and put it on display. With bigger budgets and better technology, the *Dirty Harry*s are also able to trump noirs in establishing the hero's dominance over the city, tracking Harry with cameras mounted on cranes and helicopters as he traverses San Francisco, using his movements to demark boundaries between lawfulness and violation. An example of this boundary-setting camera work can be found in the series' first film, when the villain Scorpio, careening through the city on a stolen school bus, looks out the window to see, on a distant bridge, the figure of Harry, calmly waiting for him. But throughout the series, Harry's urban trajectories lay down lines that bad guys should not presume to cross. His disciplining of the city, like his disciplining of himself, is part of his masculinity.

Masculinities and Race

That the lead characters of *Kiss Me Deadly* and *Magnum Force* are white is so obvious and predictable that we may take it for granted (especially if we are white), hardly realizing that race enters into cinematic definitions of both the good police officer and the perfect man. Nonetheless, on the ideological level, cop films have traditionally defined whiteness as a preferred status. They do not make the point explicitly, of course, and moviemakers may well deliver the message unconsciously (and indeed may be dismayed to recognize it in their work). But movies are full of meanings that are not explicitly articulated, including messages about race.[24]

For example, if there are no African American characters at all in a movie, people of color may be more aware than whites of watching what critic Anna Everett calls a "segregated" film—one from which people like themselves are excluded; even if whites recognize the exclusion, it will have different meanings for them. Moreover, watching "integrated" films—movies with some African American actors and characters—people of color may be more conscious than whites of the racial hierarchy in which members of their group seldom qualify as the hero. (Again, even if whites are conscious of the hierarchy, it will have different implications for them.) In addition, because one of the pleasures of watching a police movie is identification with the hero, people of color may forfeit some of that pleasure when the hero is white. One subtextual message in many movies is that whites are "privileged or ideal spectators."[25]

Traditionally, the subtexts of cop films assumed or implied black inferiority. In *Kiss Me Deadly,* the highest-status black person, Nat King Cole, is present merely as a disembodied voice singing "Rather Have the Blues" on Mike's car radio. The black bartender and black singer at Pigalle, a bar Mike frequents, function only as props, to create an atmosphere and show that Mike is hip; they, too, are dehumanized. Eddie, the black gym manager, providing comic relief with his oversized cigar, petty criminality, and cowardice, is less a character than a personification of Sambo-like foolishness. Moreover, Mike does not even acknowledge the presence of a black man in the dead woman's apartment, packing her belongings. These messages of black inconsequence, like *Kiss Me Deadly*'s parallel messages about ethnicity, elevate both Mike and Anglo-Saxon whiteness.

Kiss Me Deadly appeared on the verge of the Civil Rights movement; but two decades later, *Magnum Force* carried similar messages about race. Harry's African American sidekick, Early Smith (Felton Perry), exists mainly to demonstrate that Harry is not racist and that he is an excellent mentor, a good "father" to Early, in contrast to Briggs, the bad "father" of the vigilante cops. Indeed, Harry saves Early's life. But Early is also a foil: Less mature than Harry, weaker, and more squeamish, he merely watches during an airport scene in which Harry rescues a hijacked plane. While Harry detects a bomb in his own mailbox, saving himself and neighbors from destruction, the less-alert Early dies when his mailbox bomb explodes. Early exists to make points about Harry, not as a character in his own right.

The most explicit sex scene in *Magnum Force* involves an African American pimp who rapes an African American prostitute and then beats her to death. Here the film draws on the long-term association of blackness with sexual savagery. The scene, which has no relevance to the plot, exists to imply that whites are more civilized than blacks and to offer an opportunity for voyeurism to viewers who might be offended by the rape of a white woman.

For anyone who belongs to groups that movies subtextually denigrate, spectatorship requires what W. E. B. Du Bois called a "double consciousness": One is forced to identify simultaneously with one's oppressor and one's own group.[26] To experience the pleasures of film, one must to some degree negate oneself. Thus, spectatorship re-creates social hierarchies.

Cop action films seem to thumb their collective nose at political correctness, insisting on the whiteness of their heroes and nonwhiteness (at least much of the time) of their sidekicks.[27] However, while acknowledging the centrality of race in cop action, Neal King argues that such movies are not simply racist. Their working-class heroes ("louts") would not have such a sense of losing ground were they not white males in a profession that until recently excluded everyone else. But they realize, King maintains, that their true enemy is rich white men (or surrogates in the form of Japanese businessmen or hippie-nazi-queers), and cop heroes eventually apologize to sidekicks whom they may have earlier insulted, bonding with them so completely that, as in the penultimate scene of *Lethal Weapon,* black and white partners draw their guns in unison. Moreover, King continues, the heroes come to feel guilty about their racism, which is why they volunteer for so much punishment before the final showdown. In this interpretation, what cop action heroes patrol is not the city but the boundaries of whiteness; in a sense, they learn to police themselves. "The fun," King concludes, "comes in watching the white guys figure out how to get along in a changing world, and watching everyone else learn how to deal with [these] buffoons."[28]

While King's argument may be overly psychoanalytical for these simple action heroes, it usefully forestalls hasty conclusions about the meanings of race in cop action. The genre, King points out, forces viewers to examine racial tensions and to listen as a range of nonwhite characters argue back against the protagonists' white male authority.[29]

A new set of detection films with black male leads avoids the head-on collisions of cop action, conducting race discussions more civilly. *Devil in a Blue Dress* (1995) turns noir traditions inside out, most overtly by featuring a black private eye, Ezekiel ("Easy") Rawlins (Denzel Washington). While nostalgically re-creating a black suburb of the post–World War II period, the movie exposes the era's overt racism. Mouse (Don Cheadle), the knee-jerk assassin, provides comic relief and a sharp contrast to Easy's more mature and complicated character, but instead of laughing at Mouse, the film dwells affectionately on his gold tooth, natty clothes, and harebrained violence.

Other recent films, too, try to counterbalance earlier, raced definitions of the Good Cop. *Shoot to Kill* (1988) features Sidney Poitier

Figure 4.2. *Seven* (1995) blends two genres, the cop and the serial killer film, while at the same time invoking a much earlier narrative tradition, that of the medieval morality play. It was the first major cop film to depict a black officer as more skillful than his white buddy. Photo used by permission of Photofest.

as an aging cop who teams up with a younger, more active civilian (Tom Berenger) to traipse through the Pacific Northwest in search of a killer. *Seven* (1995) gives us—at last—a police movie in which the black cop (Morgan Freeman) is not only the hero but also a better officer than his younger WASP partner (Brad Pitt). In *Enemy of the State* (1998), Will Smith stars as a lawyer forced to investigate a surveillance conspiracy, while *The Bone Collector* (1999) and *Man on Fire* (2004) both star Denzel Washington in coplike roles.

Revising Traditional Masculinities

As these examples indicate, late twentieth-century police films began to comment critically on earlier cinematic conventions of masculinity. While they continued to pose the question of what constitutes good policing, some police films now answered it differently and more inclusively.

One sign of this trend was the release of *RoboCop*, a parody of the Eastwoodian supercop who feels nothing, fears nothing, and shoots everything in sight. RoboCop talks tough, but his wisecracks are computer-programmed. Like Harry, he has a bigger gun than other officers and (in a scene that specifically cites *Magnum Force*) beats them all at target practice; however, the mindless RoboCop keeps shooting till the target is destroyed. Confronting definitional issues head-on, *RoboCop* poses this question: If we could build a mechanical police officer—invulnerable to bullets, programmed to detect all bad guys, and equipped to wipe them out without pause—would *this* be the ideal cop? The movie explores the issue through a character that is a cross between an (almost) dead police officer named Murphy (Peter Weller) and a robotic shell. Half-human and half-machine, Robo-Cop realizes the perfect-cop dream of earlier police films. True, he is absurdly violent, but his vigilantism has almost rid Detroit of crime.

Just as he is about to kill Detroit's number one bad guy, Clarence Boddeker, however, RoboCop gets a message from his internal computer: UPHOLD THE LAW. Like Harry Callahan before him, Robo-Cop suddenly becomes admirable because he does *not* take the law into his own hands. Soon we are given yet another reason for respect: In a final battle with the evil enforcement-droid ED-209, RoboCop wins because his partial humanity makes him more intelligent. At the film's end, he dismantles his metal frame, renouncing invulnerability and returning to ordinary manhood. Murphy's search for identity, and the film's search for the perfect officer, is complete.

RoboCop's gender critique halts abruptly, however, when it turns to femininity. Reflecting the then-recent entry of women into policing, the film gives Murphy a female buddy, Ann Lewis (Nancy Allen). Yet it takes the male's point of view, asking how women cops affect male officers' sense of masculinity. At their first encounter, Lewis and Murphy verbally tussle over who will drive the squad car, an argument he settles by slipping behind the wheel. Later we see Lewis bringing Murphy coffee, an act that is supposed to show that she has risen above petty concerns about servitude but actually suggests the opposite. Lewis is invariably—and cheerfully—subservient.

Lewis is also less competent than Murphy. When she catches a member of Boddeker's gang who is urinating, she glances down, enabling the man to disarm her; thus, moments later she cannot protect Murphy from Boddeker's gunfire. This scene implies that women's entry into policing can spell death for their partners—just what opponents of female officers were predicting.

Internal Affairs, starring Andy Garcia as the new guy in the internal affairs division of the Los Angeles Police Department and Richard

Gere as the low-down, manipulative cop who is his quarry, shows a greater awareness of and sophistication about gender issues. Yet it is unable to move beyond a deep ambivalence toward female cops, represented here, in a fine performance by Laurie Metcalf, by Garcia's partner. Metcalf's character outranks Garcia's, and he both respects her superior skills and values her as a friend. But at the same time, *Internal Affairs* has Garcia give her orders and describe her as a "dyke." Gere shoots her in the end, and the film closes without revealing whether she is going to live, another sign, perhaps, of its ambivalence toward female cops.

Director Jonathan Demme's *Silence of the Lambs* goes further in questioning traditional ideas about what it means to be a good police officer. Clarice Starling (Jodie Foster) is exactly what her names suggests: clear, sterling, and bright. Her character incorporates some traits of earlier male police heroes; for example, although men find her attractive, Clarice shuns romance to focus on her work. Her only real competition as hero is Hannibal ("the Cannibal") Lecter (Anthony Hopkins), and he is "pure psychopath," evil to her good. Like male officers, Clarice does not drop her eyes when others stare but returns looks with a steady gaze. This insistence on her right to look, moreover, does not bring doom, as a mere female glance does in *RoboCop*.

While Clarice Starling's character echoes that of earlier police heroes, however, it also creates a new model. Clarice does not talk tough or insult others. She is not a know-it-all ("I want to learn from you," she tells Hannibal). Nor is she unfeeling; in fact, the film centers around her attempt to come to grips with the death of her father, her need for a good parent, and her compassion for unfortunates. Although Clarice is as impassive as Harry Callahan in the face of horrors, she can also cry.

Like many male cop film heroes, Clarice has an African American sidekick, in this case another agent-in-training. Ardelia is a less important character than Clarice, but she is not given negative traits to contrast with Clarice's positive ones. The two women sleuth together (in nightgowns, no less!—shades of Nancy Drew), cooperating to solve the mystery of the killer's identity.[30]

Devil in a Blue Dress poses yet another sort of challenge to traditional cinematic definitions of the good police officer. While the film's central theme is racism, this is also a movie about breaking free of dysfunctional concepts of masculinity and being a good man. Through the character of Easy Rawlins, it shows that the ideal man can be tough and sensitive at the same time. Whereas the hardbitten detective of traditional noirs is a static character, perfectly formed from the start, Easy's character develops as he learns how to outsmart his enemies. At the start of the film he is penniless and unemployed; at the end he plans to become a private investigator. In the final scene we see Easy surrounded not by the sports cars and guns that have long signified masculinity but children and families. It is a domestic scene, a representation of an aspect of life—ordinary, relaxed, community life—that earlier police films rigorously excluded.

Detection movies have also started questioning the heterosexism that lies at the heart of dominant definitions of the real man and good cop, and revision is taking place in the genre where one might least expect it: cop action films. Cop action is saturated with sexuality—displays of half-naked male bodies, spurting blood, baseball bats and battering rams and machine guns, slashed thighs, orgasmic pain, beatific smiles, heads caught in crotch holds, tangles of thrashing male limbs, constant "fuck you"s, anal rape jokes ("I never forget an asshole," Sergeant Martin Riggs [Mel Gibson] announces in *Lethal Weapon*; "I'm going to catch them and fuck them"), and endless sadomasochism. Moreover, these films overflow with intense buddy love—and it is love between men who, although they don't make a big deal of it, cannot help but notice that the other is impossibly attractive. What are we to make of all this sexuality and adoration?

Again, *Heroes in Hard Times* proves useful. Refusing to label action heroes as straight, gay, or bisexual, King concludes that, irrespective of what their sexual preferences may be when they are with their wives and girlfriends, cop action heroes when they are with each other enjoy sex through beatings, rippings, and sexualized banter.

> If Martin of *Lethal Weapon 2* says that he will fuck a man's ass, later takes it in the thigh with a large knife, rams the blade back into his opponent's chest, and then drops a trailer on him with a happy smile, then maybe that's the sort of fucking Martin likes to do. Next, a criminal shoots Martin many times, and sidekick Roger blows that criminal away. Roger cradles the wounded Martin in his arms; the two seem happy as the sidekick gently strokes his bleeding hero and they joke about the danger of smoking cigarettes. They giggle as Martin tells Roger what a beautiful man he is and asks him for a kiss.

King concludes:

> This is their sexuality. This is what they want. This is how they live and die hard. The payoff scenes for which people know this genre leave

straight gentleness behind and give over to the wilder side of physical play: the wrenching, sodomite trauma to manly bodies that bring these movies to their collective climax.[31]

Cop action films, then, open up space for a sexuality that is neither straight nor queer nor bisexual but intense, playful, and powerful. King terms it "sodomite slaughter."

Film theory validates itself to the extent that it illuminates movies themselves. King's sodomite-slaughter thesis brings a new level of intelligibility to the viewing of cop action, even when a specific film is less drenched in sexual content than a *Die Hard* or *Lethal Weapon*. John Woo's *The Killer* (1989), about the relationship between a hit man named Jeffrey (Chow Yun-Fat) and a police inspector named Eddie Li (Danny Lee), is a case in point. As Eddie hunts Jeffrey down, he studies evidence of his quarry's choices and values; the more he learns, the more admiring he becomes ("He's no ordinary assassin"), especially as he realizes that Jeffrey in fact cares deeply about justice. In their first encounter, the two men can't take their eyes off one another (partly because they are pointing revolvers at one another's temples). Circumstances (love of the same woman, hatred of a common enemy) push them into partnership and—there is no better way to put it—they fall in love. The latent eroticism of their connection, their wild romanticism, and their fantasies of oneness make *The Killer* primarily the story of a perfect, tragic love—although it is also a Hong Kong action film in which the bodies pile up and cars explode. The love is one we cannot name, since "sodomite slaughter" hardly applies to a film in which the touching is always chaste,[32] no one shouts "fuck you," and even the shooters wear suits and ties. But at least we can recognize the narrative for what it is: a story of ardent, doomed love.

Cops in Postmodernist and Critical Films

Postmodernist and alternative-tradition films comment, albeit in very different ways, on both conventional cop film heroes and the politically correct protagonists of more recent detection movies. Making fun of cop film traditions, postmodernist films parody their earnestness and mock their idols. *Reservoir Dogs* (1992) clowns around with two coplike characters, one of them Mr. Orange (Tim Roth), an undercover officer whom the robbers think is their accomplice. Wounded in an early scene, Mr. Orange spends most of the movie on the floor

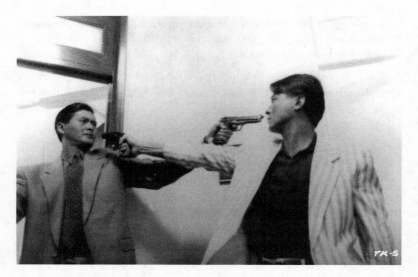

Figure 4.3. John Woo's *The Killer* (1989) pairs a police officer with an assassin, but like the more traditional cop-buddy film, this film, too, explores an intense male friendship, one here made all the more pleasurable by the potential lethality of its embrace. Photo used by permission of Photofest.

bleeding to death from a stomach wound. That his agony seems to occur in real time, taking as long as the movie itself, creates tension between the viewers' expectation that someone will call an ambulance and the criminals' outlandish indifference. Even Mr. White (Harvey Keitel), the sole character concerned about Mr. Orange's plight, refuses to call a doctor and spends a lot of time on the floor with Orange, locked in a sticky embrace that pokes fun at the male bonding of cop action films. The second coplike character is a security guard whom we see tied to a chair and brutalized by the "stone-cold psychopath" Mr. Blonde, who performs a courtship dance, cuts off the guard's ear, and inquires, "Was that as good for you as it was for me?" Writer-director Quentin Tarantino shows no reverence whatsoever for traditional cop heroes, dicing and sending them up with glee.

Another postmodernist movie, *Fargo,* satirizes both the action cop protagonist and the trend toward culturally sensitive cop heroes through the character of Marge Gunderson, who is not only female but also hugely pregnant. Banal and bland, obsessed by food, and devoted to a dolt, Marge nonetheless catches the killer, reacting matter-of-factly to what he is doing to his accomplice in the wood chipper. The writer-director team of Ethan and Joel Coen takes the potentially boring, goody-two-shoes character of Marge and, through deft lampooning of cop film traditions, makes her memorable.

Alternative-tradition films, on the other hand, give us unredeemable cops, lost souls doomed to wander forever in a maze of cynicism. *To Live and Die in L.A.* (1985) begins with an older secret service agent being shot to death under ambiguous circumstances; we cannot tell whether he was part of a counterfeiting scheme. His younger partner sets out to avenge the death but, pursuing that end through illegal means, moves ever deeper into the heart of darkness. *His* new buddy is shocked ("Why don't you just go blow his [a suspect's] brains out?" he asks sarcastically; "That's what you want to do, isn't it?"). But the avenger has already decided that "I can do whatever I want," and so he does, until he himself is killed. At that point the new partner takes over as the bad cop, starting a fresh cycle of brutality and betrayal.

State of Grace (1990), another critical film, stars Sean Penn as an undercover cop who returns to his old New York City haunts and links up with former gang friends. His assignment grows increasingly difficult as he becomes divided between his loyalty to his old criminal companions and to the cops with whom he secretly works. Eventually crushed by the strain of this double life, he tries to quit the force but cannot. Without resolving the issue of torn loyalties, the movie ends by killing nearly everyone off during a hyperviolent shoot-out in a bar. Penn's character survives but seems destined for a life of sorrow and despondency.

Movies in the alternative or critical tradition gravitate toward the character of the corrupt police officer, demonstrating that there is no such thing as a good cop (*Bad Lieutenant* [1992], *Q & A*, *Romeo Is Bleeding*). By implication, they also suggest that there is no such thing as a good man. In both respects they differ from the noir tradition in which they have their origins. Noirs expose a murky world in which everyone is tinged with sin and despair, but their private eyes are nonetheless admirable, wise guys who can solve the mystery and get the girl. Alternative-tradition police films, on the other hand, have no heroes. When postmodernist films deny us heroes, they do so in order to comment on other movies—to burlesque crime movie traditions. But alternative-tradition films aim at negating the very idea of the hero.

Thus, detection films continue to evolve in a variety of directions, adapting to new environments, extending into previously undiscovered niches, incorporating the latest cultural trends, cross-fertilizing with other genres. This vigorous multiplication can madden the tidy taxonomist, but it is a sign of the genre's vitality, and by examining the subtypes we can come to appreciate the genre's amoeba-like adaptability.

Notes

1. Other films of the period with female sleuths include *The Thin Man* (1934) and its five sequels, all of them featuring the mystery-solving couple played by Myrna Loy and William Powell; Hitchcock's *Rebecca* (1940), with Joan Fontaine as the young second wife who must solve the mystery of her predecessor's identity; and *Nancy Drew, Reporter* (1939), based on a popular book series about a girl detective. For a useful analysis of masculinity in some of these movies, see Todd 2005.
2. See, especially, Greenfield, Osborn, and Robson 2001b.
3. President's Commission on Law Enforcement and Administration of Justice 1967.
4. The straightlaced cop figure turns up again in *L. A. Confidential* (1997) in the character of Exley (Guy Pearce), the prim, bespectacled young cop who takes himself too seriously.
5. This aspect of noir tradition was carried into the 1960s by the James Bond series, featuring a hero who, like noir protagonists, was both naughty and nice.
6. Schickel 1996: 258.
7. In the same year, 1968, Siegel also released *Madigan,* another urban police film, and director Peter Yates released *Bullitt,* a prototypical cop film starring Steve McQueen.
8. Paul Newman, a liberal, and Frank Sinatra turned down the Dirty Harry role before it was accepted by the more conservative Eastwood.
9. Carlos Clarens (1980: 303) writes: "*Dirty Harry* was reviewed in the *New York Times* and the *New Yorker* as a violation of civil rights . . . and attacked as excessively violent by practically everybody." For quotes from the reviews, including those by the *New Yorker*'s Pauline Kael, who was deeply offended by the film, see Schickel 1996.
10. The other *Dirty Harry* sequels are *The Enforcer* (1976), *Sudden Impact* (1983), and *The Dead Pool* (1988).
11. Warshow 1974b.
12. Wood 1992: 478.
13. Cawelti, as quoted in Maltby 1995: 121.
14. The Internet Movie Database lists 193 blaxploitation movies and indicates that the genre had a lengthy run. However, the blaxploitation film's popularity reached its peak in the 1970s. George (1994: 63) holds that *Rocky* (1976), by showing Hollywood "that the black action crowd can be attracted by films with prominent black second bananas," dealt "a crucial death blow to the already sagging blaxploitation genre." Also see Reid 1995.

15. The history of the film and gays' objections to it are outlined by Russo (1987), who calls *Cruising*'s release "the last straw in a long stream of Hollywood horrors" about gay life (239). Compare Willis (1997), who argues that *Cruising* is "not so much homophobic as intent on targeting and aggravating homophobic fantasies that the spectator may harbor" (233 n. 27).
16. Lewine 1997: CY4.
17. Lane 1997: 78.
18. For more examples, see Hale 1998.
19. For analyses of buddy films, see Brown 1993 and Fuchs 1993.
20. King 1999: 2.
21. See Todd 2005.
22. Krutnik 1991: part 3. The debates are summarized by King 1999.
23. *Magnum Force* again tweaks homosexuals in a scene in which a fey neighbor flirts madly with Harry.
24. Ames 1992; Dyer 1997.
25. Everett 1995–96: 28.
26. Du Bois 1997 (1903): 49. The psychiatrist Franz Fanon (1968) referred to this experience as having a "colonized" mind.
27. King (1999: 42) reports that in the 193 cop action movies he studied, 80 percent of the heroes were white, compared to 40 percent of the sidekicks.
28. King 1999: 16.
29. Christopher Ames (1992) makes related points about cop action films, noting that the genre's interracial buddy teams reverse the nineteenth-century racist formula that pits the civilized white man against the dark-skinned savage. The white cop of *Lethal Weapon* and other cop action movies is the more savage of the two, and the black partner is sometimes portrayed as not only more civilized but also in need of remasculinization by his wilder colleague. Ames, like King, recognizes the strong homoerotic undercurrents of cop action movies that feature buddies, speaking of such partnerships as "idyllic anti-marriages" (a concept he borrows from Leslie Fielder) in the tradition of *Huck Finn* and *Moby Dick*.
30. While *Silence of the Lambs* rejects many of the gender and racial assumptions of earlier cop films, it reforges links between criminality and homosexuality. The character of Buffalo Bill is little more than a collection of clichés about gay men: He communicates with his current victim in faggy baby talk and he hates women even while trying to become one. In our fullest view of him, Buffalo Bill is in drag, a nipple pierced by a ring, dancing nude. *Silence of the Lambs* has shaken off other biases but continues to denigrate homosexuality.
31. King 1999: 177.
32. Chaste but not lacking sexuality, as in the sacramental church scene when Eddie pours gunpowder into Jeffrey's wound while Jeffrey bites down on something hard, in this case a stick.

5 | Criminal Law Films

> Nick Romano is guilty, but so are we, and so is that precious thing called society. . . . Knock on any door, and you may find Nick Romano.
>
> —Defense lawyer in *Knock on Any Door*

It used to be easy to define law films: They were dramas featuring a heroic, white male lawyer who solved the mystery and settled other dilemmas in the course of a trial. But changes in taste, in attitudes toward law, and in understandings of the nature of law itself have eroded this traditional definition.[1] For better or worse, contemporary audiences have little patience for lengthy courtroom debates and behind-the-scenes glimpses of the lives of virtuous country lawyers. Thus, movies today tend to embed a short trial scene in a longer adventure story that also offers bedroom action and gun battles. Moreover, responding to lawyers' declining status and to increasing public skepticism about the efficacy of legal systems, contemporary films seldom depict lawyers as heroes on the grand scale or courts as places where fundamental social and moral issues are settled. Finally, scholars have realized that there is a large group of movies, including *Rashomon* (1950), *Do the Right Thing* (1989), *Falling Down* (1993), *Eye of God* (1997), and *Mystic River* (2003), that comment on legal issues without referring to lawyers or law, and that these films not only provide information on popular attitudes toward law but themselves constitute legal discourses. One result has been a probing debate among law-and-film scholars over how to define the law film. While as yet inconclusive, this debate has produced a new awareness of the legal subtexts of films long held to be "about" something else.

This chapter begins by discussing traditional courtroom dramas: their stock figures, typical plots, and central themes. Next, to see what happened to courtroom dramas over time, it identifies their main lines of development since the 1930s and the social factors that contributed to their decline. The chapter's final section turns to films that steer clear of traditional legal settings and characters but nonetheless comment extensively on the nature of law and justice. These include movies that self-consciously enter the legal fray to themselves become part of the struggle to define law. Throughout I will be using the term *law films* to denote both movies that include a criminal trial and those that comment on criminal law and its processes outside of court settings.[2]

Traditional Courtroom Dramas

Courtroom dramas set up a tension between two sorts of law: immutable natural law or justice, on the one hand, and fallible man-made law, on the other. They let us know what justice would consist of in the current case and then use that ideal as a template for what should happen.[3] At the same time, they show us how, in the current case, man-made law fails (or is about to fail) to reach that goal, and they proceed to play with the discrepancy between the actual and the ideal. Courtroom films usually include an *injustice figure*, the person responsible for creating or maintaining the gap between justice and man-made law.

Most courtroom films also include a *justice figure*, a hero who tries to move man-made law ever closer to the ideal until it matches the justice template. The film's resolution occurs when man-made law becomes identical to the underlying pattern. The justice figure is usually (but not always) a lawyer; and in a few courtroom dramas, the position of the justice figure is held by several characters at once. In *Marked Woman* (1937), for example, a "clip joint hostess" (Bette Davis) and the district attorney (Humphrey Bogart) work together to convict an organized crime boss who has been taking over New York City's nightclubs. On rare occasions, movies with important courtroom scenes have no justice figure at all. *A Place in the Sun* (1951), *The Postman Always Rings Twice* (1946), and *The Wrong Man* (1956) lack justice figures, and, significantly, they also have no clear-cut villains, absences that flow from their bleak views of the world as a place where people either create their own tragedies or are struck down randomly by fate.[4]

In standard courtroom movies, the closing of the gap between law and justice occurs in the trial scene, where the triumph of the good lawyer over the unsavory one signals resolution of the film's dilemma. However, many courtroom films include other or additional signs of resolution and success. Some conclude with a return to the setting of the first scene, a demonstration that the original equilibrium has been restored. Courtroom films in which injustice has driven happy couples apart end with a scene of reunion. In Alfred Hitchcock's *The Paradine Case* (1947), for instance, the lawyer (Gregory Peck) and his wife reunite after an estrangement caused by his all-too-impassioned defense of a beautiful woman. Similarly, in *The Young Philadelphians* (1959), after successfully defending an old friend against a false first-degree murder charge, the lawyer (Paul Newman) leaves the court-room hand in hand with his long-lost love, heading, no doubt, for the altar.[5] Varying this pattern, *Marked Woman* brings the potential couple (the clip joint hostess and the DA) together after the trial but has them recognize that they are divided by huge differences in so-cial class. And so, saying farewell forever outside the courthouse, they drift apart in the foggy night.

Yet another device that courtroom films use to resolve their plots is to show, at the end, that good personal relationships parallel good legal relationships: Everyone eventually recognizes and happily ac-cepts the rule of a wise father/judge. These movies, which are full of confusions over authority and legitimacy and of breakdowns in pre-viously strong relationships, often conclude with a good father or fa-ther figure (who may also be a judge) settling the case and restoring order.

While many trial films are purely fictitious, emphasizing that "any resemblance to persons living or dead is purely coincidental," others are based on actual cases. *Ghosts of Mississippi* (1996) recounts efforts to bring to justice the killer of civil rights hero Medgar Evers. *Judg-ment at Nuremberg* (1961), one of the best-known of all courtroom movies, incorporates details of both actual World War II war-crimes trials and the broader political context in the United States and Ger-many. *M* (1931), *I Want to Live!* (1958),[6] *Compulsion* (1959), and *In the Name of the Father* (1993) also build on actual trials. In turn, court films feed back into society, becoming touchstones, commonplace ref-erents, and even rallying points for reforms. The name of Atticus Finch, the heroic lawyer of *To Kill a Mockingbird* (1962), is invoked fre-quently during awards ceremonies at bar association dinners, and *In the Name of the Father*, director Jim Sheridan's compelling account of a 1970s frame-up of Irish men and women by the British government, became a reference point for people around the world as they evalu-ated Ireland's political violence. The trial documentaries *Brother's Keeper* (1992), *Paradise Lost: The Child Murders at Robin Hood Hills* (1996), and *Paradise Lost 2: Revelations* (2000) aim explicitly at inspir-ing legal change.[7]

The Grand Theme

Nearly all courtroom films focus on a single theme: the difficulty of achieving justice. While they take up and explore a wide range of subsidiary issues, their overriding point is that as a goal, justice is elusive, demanding, and often more ambiguous than it first appears. Courtroom films sound this theme in various ways, some through stories of false convictions, others by demonstrating the difficulty of identifying the true culprit, and yet others by emphasizing systematic faults in the criminal justice process. Movies of this type also voice various opinions about the complexities of justice: Some condemn courts for delays while others praise their patient deliberations; some despise lawyers while others glorify them. Many show justice officials triumphing after a long struggle with injustice; others openly mock trial procedures. But few fail to stress that justice is an exacting goal, reached only through arduous quests and multiple sacrifices.[8]

To illustrate this theme, a number of courtroom films depict miscarriages of justice. *Trial by Jury* (1994) shows a single mom who dutifully accepts a jury assignment only to deliberately derail the trial when the mobster-defendant has his goons threaten her kid. In *The Juror* (1996), justice is again thwarted when an insidious gangster (Alec Baldwin) intimidates a juror (Demi Moore) into voting "not guilty" in a mob trial. To some extent, justice is reclaimed after the trial, when the juror guns down the gangster, but justice is easily perverted, the movie shows, during the trial itself. In *Jagged Edge* (1985), too, a trial fails to convict the guilty person (in this case through mistaken acquittal), and justice is achieved only later, when the ungrateful killer goes after his defense attorney and she shoots him in self-defense. (*The Letter* [1940] traces a similar pattern.) A particularly silly variation on this idea is rung by *The Star Chamber* (1983), featuring Michael Douglas as a vigilante judge. He and his judicial colleagues, unhappy about cases in which civil rights laws have forced the release of obvious offenders, hire killers to execute these criminals on the streets.

Other films demonstrate how justice can miscarry by telling of false or unfair convictions. *Call Northside 777* (1948), the story of two Chicago men convicted of killing a police officer, shows a newspaper reporter (Jimmy Stewart) becoming convinced of the men's innocence and surmounting immense obstacles to persuade the pardons board to release them. *Call Northside 777* argues that it is impossible for an innocent man to prove what was actually going on at a crime scene, especially after eleven years behind bars. *I Want To Live!, In the Name of the Father,* and *True Believer* (1989) also center on false convictions, while *Murder in the First* (1995) is built on the unassailable premise that three years in one of Alcatraz's "dark" cells is a disproportionate punishment for stealing five dollars to feed a starving child.

Without arguing that justice fails, a number of movies simply stress its burdens and complexities. *The Accused* (1988) probes the guilt of bystanders to a rape, and *Marked Woman* explores witness intimidation (the thugs carve up the clip joint hostess's face and kill her kid sister). With a poignancy all the more vivid for the fact that it is a documentary, *Brother's Keeper* demonstrates that an elderly, retarded man cannot possibly defend himself against a false molestation charge. The innocent defendant in *They Won't Believe Me* (1947), despairing of a fair trial, commits suicide shortly before the jury exonerates him. *A Few Good Men* (1992) and *The Rainmaker* (1997) also emphasize the elusiveness of justice.

Trial films are particularly fond of the insanity defense as a tool for depicting the hazards of determining guilt. *Compulsion* asks viewers to decide whether young men who killed as a "true test of the superior intellect" were, though legally sane, so mentally ill as to warrant excuse from the death penalty. Fritz Lang's *M* poses the issue informally, through a scene in which the entire underworld of a German city assembles in an abandoned distillery to try the child rapist and murderer whom they have captured. The criminals resist turning Hans Beckert over to the police for fear that he will once again plead insanity and that psychiatrists will eventually again release him, just as they did before his current crime cycle began. The underworld leader, assuring Beckert that "everything will be done according to the rule of law," instructs one of the other criminals to serve as defense attorney. Before the mob of "jurors," Beckert mounts his own insanity defense: "I can't help it, . . . this evil thing inside me"; it pursues him through the "endless streets," just as he pursues his victims. Although *M* concludes with formal justice, it never resolves the issue it has so powerfully raised of whether insanity should exonerate an offender who commits crimes of this gravity.

Some trial films use a whodunit-style mystery to indicate the limitations of court processes. *Reversal of Fortune* (1990), based on the trial

Figure 5.1. Hans Beckert (Peter Lorre), the sex psycho of Fritz Lang's *M* (1931), discovers that he has been branded a murderer. Later he is put on trial by criminals, who have little sympathy for his mental illness defense. Photo used by permission of Photofest.

of Claus von Bulow for attempting to kill his wealthy wife, ends (as did the von Bulow trial itself) with a not-guilty finding but lingering suspicions that the outcome depended more on the quality of the lawyering than the innocence of the defendant. In *Presumed Innocent* (1990) and *Primal Fear* (1996), trials again fail to uncover the culprit.

Scrutinizing the intricacies of criminal law, courtroom films reach a wide range of conclusions about legal processes, from adulation to contempt. Many find the law majestic. *The Ox-Bow Incident* (1943), a film about lynching, is one of these. Two outsiders (one of them Henry Fonda) are passing through an isolated western town when they become witnesses to mob violence. Local ranchers capture three other travelers, quickly "try" them for a recent murder, and hang them from a tree limb. These travelers have hardly been "finished" with bullets when the sheriff gallops up to announce that the man whom they thought had been murdered is not dead after all. Depressed and repentant, the lynchers troop into the local bar and listen while Fonda reads a last-minute letter from one of the condemned men to his wife. "Law is a lot more than words you put in a book," the letter explains with an equanimity astonishing under the circumstances. "It's everything people ever have found out about justice and what's right and wrong. It's the very conscience of humanity."

Equally intoxicated with the law is *To Kill a Mockingbird,* another film about lynching (a topic that lends itself to admiration for legal processes).[9] Atticus Finch, a progressive lawyer in a backward town in Georgia, takes on the defense of a black man accused of raping a local white girl. As local rednecks gather for a lynching, Atticus protects the defendant by posting himself outside the jail. At trial, justice itself is thwarted by the defendant's conviction, but the justice figure of Atticus grows in stature until, visually, he fills the entire courthouse, an upward-looking camera framing his head with the "colored" gallery as with a crown. *A Time to Kill* (1996) returns to the topic of a black man accused of violence in a southern town; with four lawyers, it makes a louder (if less persuasive) case for lawyers as searchers for truth and justice.[10] Law is again elevated by movies in which a trial reveals the true villain (as in *Young Mr. Lincoln* [1939] and *The Paradine Case*) or a heroic lawyer argues eloquently for the cause of justice (as in *Inherit the Wind* [1960], *Judgment at Nuremberg,* and *True Believer*). *Twelve Angry Men* (1957), confining its action entirely to the claustrophobic room in which a murder-trial jury is sequestered, at first seems like an attack on criminal law, for few jurors take the process seriously. One wants to hurry to a guilty verdict so he can go to a baseball game; another concludes that the defendant is probably guilty because he is a foreigner. But *Twelve Angry Men* in fact mounts a powerful argument for the jury system, in which a lone but courageous individual can assure justice. The system may not be perfect, the film tells us, but it works well in the end, and it is a microcosm of the democratic process, in which the search for consensus eventually leads to wise decisions.

Counterbalancing such enthusiasm is a set of films that portray the law and lawyers negatively. It includes *The Letter,* in which a woman is mistakenly acquitted of murder. At trial, her lawyer knows she is guilty but helps her purchase the letter which, if allowed into evidence, would incriminate her. She is punished only later, outside the court system, by a vindictive widow. Another example is the first version of *The Postman Always Rings Twice,* with its double-crossing prosecutor and despicable defense attorney. During Cora's trial for her life, these lawyers play legal games with one another; they are less adversaries than friendly competitors who exclude Frank and Cora from the proceedings.[11]

The Lady from Shanghai (1947) goes after lawyers tooth and nail: The trial judge is an elderly cipher; the defense attorney is disabled, sexually impotent, and obnoxious; jurors pick their teeth during the trial; and the trial itself becomes a farce. In both the first version of *The Postman Always Rings Twice* and *The Lady from Shanghai,* the morally negative lawyers are Jewish, reinforcing what film scholar Anthony Chase identifies as one of movies' main negative lawyer archetypes, the New York shyster.[12] This archetype is reinforced by the second version of *Postman,* in which the manipulative defense lawyer is named, emphatically, Katz.

Thus, courtroom films sometimes locate the obstacles to justice in society itself, while at other times they blame the legal system and its all-too-fallible practitioners. In the long run, however, they usually show the impediments being overcome. The actual malefactor is revealed, the intimidated juror gets revenge, the falsely convicted are released from prison, and a hero emerges from the rubble of bigotry and inequity. This was the usual pattern, at any rate, until about 1980, when (as the next section shows) courtroom movies began accenting not so much the difficulty as the impossibility of achieving justice.

The Evolution of Courtroom Movies

While the lines of development are neither steady nor clear-cut, it is possible to discern three phases in the evolution of courtroom films: an experimental period that began in the 1930s and bore fruit in the 1940s and early1950s with "law noirs"; a heroic period that began in the mid-1950s and petered out in the early 1960s; and a period of depletion, 1970 into the present, during which trial movies have tried but often failed to meet the challenges posed by new cinematic and political circumstances.

The 1930s to the Mid-1950s: Experimentation and the Law Noirs

The 1930s were a time of experimentation, a decade during which directors searched for ways of depicting legal struggles that would be simultaneously persuasive and entertaining. The start of the decade saw the release of *Manhattan Melodrama* (1934), a movie that pits a good lawyer against a criminal by following actress Myrna Loy's character as she first tries to reform her gangster boyfriend, Blackie (Clark Gable), and then becomes the wife of a crusading district attorney, Jim (William Powell). Although the two men have been best friends since childhood, Jim prosecutes Blackie and eventually, having become the state's governor, decides to deny commutation of Blackie's death sentence. At this point *Manhattan Melodrama* runs into a problem: Blackie is such an engaging villain, and he goes to the electric chair with such debonair aplomb, that Jim seems dour and rigid in comparison. He wins the legal battle but loses the moral one.

The end of the decade saw the release of *Young Mr. Lincoln,* the most heroic of all heroic-lawyer movies. Law itself is dignified by Lincoln's attraction to it, and the film reveres the future president as not only a superb lawyer but also a perfect American. Featuring Henry Fonda as a lanky Lincoln look-alike, the film anticipates *To Kill a Mockingbird* with a scene in which the attorney blocks the door to the jail where his defendants are being held, holding an angry crowd at bay. The trial becomes the movie's most dramatic moment as Lincoln adroitly unmasks the true killer. But in *Young Mr. Lincoln,* as in *Manhattan Melodrama,* the hero needs a more loathsome opponent. Justice is less a struggle than a foregone conclusion.

Yet another approach to the courtroom film was explored by *Fury,* a protonoir released in 1936. The most bitter courtroom film in Hollywood history,[13] *Fury* stars Spencer Tracy as Joe Wilson, a young man who is mistakenly arrested and imprisoned on kidnapping charges. A lynch mob gathers outside his jail and sets it on fire—the first instance of fury. With his fiancée Katherine looking on, Joe appears at his cell's window, seemingly in flames; and presumably his body is destroyed in the subsequent explosion. Joe lives, however, and plots revenge against the would-be lynchers, who are brought to trial en masse for his murder. Keeping even Katherine in the dark about his survival, Joe plans to sit back and allow all the defendants to be convicted and executed—the second instance of fury—relenting only because he cannot bear the thought of life without Katherine. At the most dramatic moment, Joe interrupts the trial and reveals himself. Sparing the defendants brings him no joy, however; Joe remains deeply resentful, and the criminal justice system stands condemned for a second failure to do justice. If *Fury* leaves a sour aftertaste, it is because injustice goes unpunished and the justice figure, Joe, fights solely for himself, not for a larger cause.

After this decade of experimentation, the courtroom genre hit its stride in the 1940s with the cycle of cynical and stylistically expressionistic films that movie scholar Norman Rosenberg has deftly labeled *law noirs*. Law noirs, Rosenberg writes, present a "baleful view of lawyers" and "portray people, some entirely innocent and others not-so-innocent, trapped in a highly fallible legal system." Unlike more traditional Hollywood fare, law noirs "raise doubts about the ability of the trial process to achieve satisfactory closure."[14] (Their cynicism about the legal system and generally jaded view of humanity make law noirs important forerunners of the alternative-convention or critical crime films that later created their own cinematic tradition.) The cycle begins with *The Letter,* which throws criminality against a background of colonialist racism, and with *Stranger on the Third Floor* (also 1940); in both justice is achieved only outside the court system. These were followed by *The Postman Always Rings Twice, They Won't Believe Me, Call Northside 777,* and *The Lady from Shanghai. Knock on Any Door* (1949) guards against the good-guy hero appearing square through casting and characterization: The defense attorney is played by Humphrey Bogart and given a background—childhood in the slums—that enables him to match the bad guy punch for punch. The cycle extends into the 1950s with a late law noir, Hitchcock's *The Wrong Man,* the story of a family ruined by a mistaken arrest.[15]

From the 1930s into the 1950s, courtroom dramas attracted outstanding directors, including John Ford (*Young Mr. Lincoln*), Alfred Hitchcock (*The Wrong Man, The Paradine Case*), Fritz Lang (*M, Fury, Scarlet Street* [1945], and *Beyond a Reasonable Doubt* [1956]), Nicholas Ray (*Knock on Any Door*), George Stevens (*A Place in the Sun*), Orson Welles (*The Lady from Shanghai*), and William Wyler (*The Letter*). Visually intriguing, these films use the strange camera angles and striking black-and-white patterns for which noirs in general are admired. Law noirs make justice figures engaging by turning them into outsiders of one sort or another—the journalist who cleans up the courts' mess in *Call Northside 777*, the murderous Malaysian widow in *The Letter*, the tough-guy attorney in *Knock on Any Door*. In addition, they give these justice figures worthy opponents, goliaths of injustice that sometimes turn out to be the criminal justice system itself. Thus, viewers can have it both ways, identifying with outsiders to the justice system who end up as saviors of law and order.

The Mid-1950s through the 1960s: The Heroic Tradition

Courtroom drama took a turn toward the right in 1957 with *Twelve Angry Men*, first in a series of films to conclude that justice can be achieved through the courts. *Witness for the Prosecution* (1957), *Anatomy of a Murder* (1959), *Inherit the Wind*, *Judgment at Nuremberg*, and *To Kill a Mockingbird* went on to portray lawyers as men who labor heroically within the system to ensure that man-made law coincides with the justice ideal. Rooted in *Young Mr. Lincoln* and *The Ox-Bow Incident*, with their admiration for law, these movies became the classics of courtroom dramas, the outstanding representatives of the genre's golden age.

In their generally uncritical perspective on the judicial system, these classics are products of their times, reflections of a society that was wealthier, more secure, and less chaotic than the America of the Great Depression and World War II years. Like the best-selling novels on which a number of them are based, the courtroom classics present trials in mythic terms, as battles of good against evil; their courts are hallowed halls, places where the truth, after a titanic contest, emerges victorious. Turning lawyers into cultural heroes, the classic courtroom movies picture them as professional wizards and guardians of the country's sacred traditions.

The classic courtroom films are also cinematically traditional. They use standard devices such as close-ups of nervous witnesses and dramatic outbursts by onlookers, punctuated by the hammer of a judge's gavel. Compared to law noirs, their photography is straightforward and somewhat static. They are, to be sure, cinematically skillful, as in the framing of Atticus Finch's head during *To Kill a Mockingbird*'s trial scenes or Sidney Lumet's subtle shifts of lenses and camera angles during *Twelve Angry Men*.[16] But their camera work is less dramatic than that of law noirs, and less radical—one might almost say more respectful.

Reverence for the law runs strong in *Witness for the Prosecution*, starring Charles Laughton as an aging English barrister who, defying his nurse's instructions, decides to defend an accused murderer. Director Billy Wilder's courtroom is a large, grand place, full of tradition and great men. Bewigged and fiendishly clever, Laughton wins a not-guilty verdict from the jury, only to discover that the defendant did in fact commit the murder. "Vole, you have made a mockery of English law," the barrister admonishes, charging his client with a sin that is clearly much worse than murder. When Vole is stabbed by his common-law wife (Marlene Dietrich), whom he has also double-crossed, Laughton vows to defend *her*, and *Witness for the Prosecution* ends with him charging off to the next contest, revitalized by the struggle for justice.

Judgment at Nuremberg places a judge in the hero's role. Portraying the post–World War II trial of men who themselves served as judges during the Nazi regime, it concentrates, uniquely, on what one character describes as "crimes committed in the name of the law." The key issue is whether judges are fundamentally responsible to man-made law or to a superior natural law. Is it true, as one defense attorney argues, that "a judge does not make the laws; he carries out the laws of his country," or must judges answer to a higher kind of law, justice itself? The film responds to this question primarily through the character of the presiding justice, Judge Dan Haywood (Spencer Tracy), depicting him as a self-deprecating man with a sense of humor who seeks to understand how the wisest judges in Germany could have participated in the Nazi regime. Haywood goes out of his way to be fair.

Judge Haywood's counterpart is the chief figure on trial (Burt Lancaster), a jurist famous for having "dedicated his life to justice—to the concept of justice." Although at first this German judge refuses to participate in the trial, he comes to accept his responsibility for the failures of the Nazi regime, admitting that he and the other defendants knew that the people they sentenced were transported to concentration camps. In effect, this injustice figure condemns himself for choosing man-made over natural law.

In *Judgment at Nuremberg*, as in *Twelve Angry Men* and *Witness for the Prosecution*, a solitary figure's moral courage carries the day.

Judge Haywood convicts the defendants and, despite international pressure for leniency, sentences them to life imprisonment. He bases his decision on belief in a moral law that transcends man-made laws and must be followed by all human beings. The very first time a Nazi judge condemned an innocent man, Haywood declares, he transgressed this moral law.

The tension between public hunger for swift justice and the right to a fair trial, already addressed in *To Kill a Mockingbird*, was further explored in *Inherit the Wind*, a reenactment of the "monkey trial" case of 1925, in which fundamentalist William Jennings Bryan squared off against liberal Clarence Darrow to argue that religious beliefs should dictate how science is taught in the schools. Spencer Tracy plays Drummond, the Darrow character who defends a local teacher facing criminal charges for informing his students about evolution. The prosecuting attorney (Frederick March) is a demagogic religious conservative, and the trial takes place in Hillsboro, "the buckle on the Bible belt." With small-town bigotry and self-righteousness wafting through the courtroom along with the fetid southern heat, the teacher's chances for a fair trial seem nil. Drummond's arguments on behalf of freedom of thought chip away at Hillsboro's prejudices, however, and the teacher, though convicted, is merely fined. Tracy's monumental performance as Drummond, slaying the dragon of biblical literalism, makes this one of the most satisfying of all trial films.

Anatomy of a Murder, concerning an army lieutenant accused of killing a man who may or may not have raped the lieutenant's wife, is less dramatic in presentation, at least from today's perspective. (At the time of its release, audiences may have found it racy, for it was one of the first movies to deal explicitly with rape and extramarital affairs, and the lawyer played by James Stewart, breaking with all previous standards of decorum, presents a pair of torn panties in evidence.) Nonetheless, Stewart's portrait of a homespun attorney, simple yet crafty, reinforces the archetype of the heroic, all-American lawyer. This Lincolnesque figure triumphs through honesty, brilliance, and perseverance, and his victory is only slightly diminished by the surprise ending.

While not themselves classics, other films of the period contributed to the heroic tradition. In *The Young Philadelphians*, Paul Newman plays the tax lawyer as all-around guy: friend to construction workers and wealthy old ladies alike, and savior of the Main Line elite when they fall to bickering over their fortunes. *Compulsion* features a holy trinity of lawyers—the judge, prosecutor, and defense attorney—who labor mightily to achieve justice for the ungrateful young killers. Particularly through the impassioned rhetoric of the defense attorney (Darrow again, this time played by Orson Welles), *Compulsion* portrays law as impartial, awesome, even godlike—quite the opposite of the self-indulgent youths.

A few films of the period hung back from the stampede to glorify law and lawyers. *A Place in the Sun* presents an enigma, a man who did indeed plan to kill his pregnant fiancée but is genuinely uncertain about his responsibility for the boating accident in which she drowned. Thus, the menacing and vengeful prosecutor (Raymond Burr) somewhat misses the mark in demanding the death penalty, and as the young man (Montgomery Clift) walks to his execution, we wonder whether this is justice or legalistic brutality. In *The Caine Mutiny* (1954), the defendants are celebrating their courtroom victory over Captain Queeg when their defense attorney (José Ferrer) tongue-lashes them for the mutiny: Had they supported the captain in his hour of need, the mutiny would have been unnecessary; and although the sailors have been legally exonerated for their rebellion, the attorney assures them that they are not morally innocent. *I Want to Live!* goes even further, showing that criminal justice officials framed an innocent woman (Susan Hayward) and knowingly sent her to the gas chamber. Based on the actual case of Barbara Graham, executed at San Quentin in the 1950s, this film is narrated by a journalist who repents of his sensationalist reporting of the case and decides to expose the miscarriage of justice.[17] Aside from these three movies, however, few midcentury films bucked the trend toward adulation of the law.

From the 1970s to the Present: Depletion of the Genre

As if pausing for rest after their heroic exertions, court films made few appearances between 1962 (*To Kill a Mockingbird*) and 1979 (*And Justice for All*).[18] During the hiatus, massive changes occurred in the movie industry, the judicial system, and the country's attitudes toward authority. Cinematically, films became more reliant on action and violence. Color film became the rule, forcing cinematographers to work in what was in some respects a new medium. Criminal law underwent a civil rights revolution, with new requirements for Miranda warnings, appointed counsel, and (in serious cases) automatic appeals. Social protest movements and frustration with government, both by-products of Watergate and the war in Vietnam, made veneration for the law seem naive, while the entry of women and people of color into law schools exposed the prejudices behind white male images of the ideal lawyer. Justice and injustice had to be reconceptualized.

Situated at the nexus of these aesthetic, legal, and social changes, courtroom dramas released after the 1962–79 hiatus had trouble finding their footing. *And Justice for All,* for instance, is an awkward, uncertain film. Starring Al Pacino as a rebellious young defense lawyer, the film spends much of its energy criticizing the adversary system for being more concerned with wins and losses than with truth. Vignettes in which justice goes awry show that the guilty may go free and the innocent be incarcerated. *And Justice for All* succeeds mainly in its gritty portrayal of state courts as, not dignified halls of justice, but corridors crowded with deal-making cynics. *The Onion Field* (1979) and *The Star Chamber* are similarly jaded in their view of justice and equally uneven cinematically, but in these movies the legal material is less central, edged out by psychopaths and action sequences. In such posthiatus court films, we see less a continuation of earlier traditions than stumbling efforts to rewrite their formulas. Filmmakers were in fact redesigning the genre, struggling to create new justice and injustice figures and to find fresh ways to depict the gaps between natural and man-made law.[19]

A series of woman-lawyer movies revived trial films in the mid-1980s. It began, spectacularly, with *Jagged Edge,* the tale of a corporate lawyer who reluctantly agrees to defend a man accused of the gruesome knife murder of his heiress wife. Glenn Close plays the lawyer, Teddy Barnes, who has an affair with her client, Jack Forrester (Jeff Bridges), before discovering that he actually is the killer. Masked and clad in black, Jack comes after Teddy as she lies in bed—a repeat of the wife's death scene. But this time, the intended victim is prepared.

Jagged Edge set off a debate over whether Teddy Barnes and the woman lawyers of subsequent trial films represent successful professionals or failed females, women who violate their true nature by straying from the kitchen. In a well-reasoned law review article, Carolyn Lisa Miller argues that *Jagged Edge* in fact transforms Teddy Barnes "from powerful attorney to powerless woman, resituating her in her 'proper' role." The film pivots on "the power of men to violently reshape or destroy female identity," Miller continues, noting that we never learn Teddy's full "female" name or why she has a man's nickname. From the start, *Jagged Edge* protects the killer by concealing his identity; and "by assuming his point-of-view in the [wife murder] scene, [it] adopts his identity as its own."[20] The movie shows Teddy breaking her professional code of ethics by becoming involved with Jack, and in court, when this relationship is revealed, she becomes a stereotypical hysterical woman.

Two of the next three woman-attorney films share *Jagged Edge*'s assumptions about the incompatibility of the statuses of "attorney" and "woman." *Suspect* (1987), starring Cher as Riley, a hard-working attorney, implies that Riley is destroying her femininity through over-exertion. Angst-ridden and dateless, she revives only when she has an affair with a juror in a case she is defending. Thus committing an ethical violation that could lead to disbarment, Riley places her need for a man before her career. With a similar lack of professionalism, in *Physical Evidence* (1989) a defense lawyer (Theresa Russell) falls in love with her client (Burt Reynolds).[21] *The Accused* is one of the few 1980s courtroom dramas to present a woman criminal lawyer (Kelly McGillis) who is a true justice figure, strong, competent, and capable of concentrating on her work even with men around.[22]

Courtroom dramas proliferated in the 1990s, but as the numbers went up, quality fell. Although filmmakers continued using trial scenes to create suspense, they now seldom structured an entire movie to build toward a climax in a trial scene.[23] Instead, trials scenes were now enmeshed in a fabric of other, more animated sequences; they had become episodes in a thriller. Echoing actual trials of the period (such as those of O. J. Simpson and the assailants of Rodney King), courtroom films of the 1990s showed legal processes going astray. Many films began with the assumption that the system was broken beyond repair.

Presumed Innocent, based on a best seller by attorney Scott Turow, features Harrison Ford as Rusty Sabich, a criminal lawyer indicted for killing a female colleague with whom he had an affair. The plot-line conceals Sabich's guilt or innocence until the climax. Although he is ultimately exonerated, the judicial system is portrayed as a hollow shell of its former nobility. The trappings remain—the ornate courtrooms, the legal formalities—but beneath the veneer, something is rotting. The bad smell emanates in part from the judge, who pushes for Sabich's acquittal in order to conceal his own malfeasance.[24]

The judicial system blunders again in *Primal Fear,* in which lawyer Martin Vail (Richard Gere) defends a choirboy who murdered a priest. When the audience learns that the accused was molested by the priest and suffers from multiple personality disorder, it roots for the outcome Vail ultimately secures—not guilty by reason of insanity. However, Vail learns in the final scene that the choirboy faked his psychosis and is in fact a sadistic killer. At this point, there is nothing Vail can do. He and the entire system have been duped. So, in a sense, have viewers, for we have been kept in the dark by the film, much as Vail was kept ignorant by his client.

Trial films of the 1990s showed little sustained interest in the social issues that engrossed earlier courtroom dramas. They feigned interest in equality with multiethnic and multiracial casts (a Hispanic defense attorney in *Presumed Innocent,* a female African American judge in *Body of Evidence* [1992]), but they said little about ethnic or racial injustice. While they sprinkled female attorneys across their courtrooms, they seemed less gripped by gender issues than by a desire to include shots of libidinous lawyers undressing. The gap between man-made law and true justice became a plot gimmick. There are, of course, exceptions to both the generally poor quality of 1990s courtroom films and their tendency to sexualize women attorneys. One of the best films of the decade, *In the Name* of *the Father,* opens with a dazzling spectacle of Irish commoners battling English police, and although it alternates trial scenes with action sequences, it keeps track of its themes. That the defense lawyer is a woman is incidental here, and her sexuality is no more at issue than is Atticus Finch's in *To Kill a Mockingbird.*

Significantly, the director of *In the Name of the Father,* Jim Sheridan, is an Irishman, and his production company is located in Dublin. The film draws its energy from the agonized political and legal situation that it depicts. Other outstanding 1990s films about law were generated by the political and legal situation in Sicily, a land traumatized by the 1992 assassination of anti-Mafia Judge Giovanni Falcone and his colleague Paolo Borsellino. Sicily remains mortally divided by the decades-long struggle between Mafia and anti-Mafia forces, a split that takes a terrible toll in terms of lives, criminal activity, and legal corruption but that has also inspired a number of remarkable films. Two of these were written and directed by Gianni Amelio: *Open Doors* (1990), about a judge struggling against Fascism in 1930s Sicily, and *The Stolen Children* (1992), about a cop who finds he must break the law to help the two children he is assigned to transport to Sicily. Two others were made by Ricky Tagnozzi: *The Es-*

cort (1993), which focuses on a Sicilian judge, his bodyguards, and their fight against the Mafia; and *Excellent Cadavers* (1999), a biography of Judge Falcone. Another film based on the judge's life has been made by Giuseppe Ferrara (*Giovanni Falcone* [1993]), while Marco Tullio Giordana's remarkable *I cento passi* (2000) is based on the true story of a young man who took on the Mafia. Like *In the Name of the Father,* these Italian films have a vitality and sense of emergency that derive from involvement in legal issues of pressing national significance.

The disappointing quality of most of Hollywood's late twentieth-century courtroom films stemmed less from their negativity about the law than from their mindless reliance on shopworn conventions and depleted traditions. In fact, they did not say much at all.[25] Lacking anger or other signs of conviction, they seem to be written by computers programmed to reproduce formulas. Their usual theme—the impossibility of achieving justice—cannot be persuasively conveyed through camera tricks, manipulative scripts, and recycled plots. It is no wonder that Hollywood's courtroom dramas were gradually replaced by law films that raised actual issues of justice and responsibility, albeit in noncourt settings.

Law Films without Lawyers

The current lively debate over the best way to define law films has broad implications, not only for this chapter and this book but also for understandings of the nature of law itself and the relationships between films and society. The key issue may at first sound pedantic: Should we define law films narrowly, so as to limit the category to films with trials, lawyers, and issues that might be settled in a law court? If not, where do we set the boundaries? (In the language of film studies, the problem is one of deciding how far to go beyond the traditional genre boundaries of the courtroom film.)[26] The significance of the issue becomes clearer if we look at the way it is posed by Anthony Chase's book *Movies on Trial:* "Where do films tell us (or show us) that law is to be found?" Bypassing distracting side issues, Chase frames the issue as one about not containment (Where do we draw the line?) but removing constraints: What can we learn from films about the nature of law and where law is made and operates? Related is Chase's second key question: "How does cinema . . . unmask or reveal the true relationship between law and justice, between equality and the legal system?"[27] Chase proposes to define law films as movies that depict "lawyers and clients, officials and citizens, courts or other institutions (for example: legislatures, corporations, newspapers, police departments) grappling with legal issues and conflicts, cases, and statutes, or the politics of the rule of law itself."[28] This is the definition I will use for the rest of this chapter, although I will limit the discussion to criminal law films.

Chase's formulation opens up the cinematic territory of law films to movies that discuss criminal law but cannot be squeezed into the "courtroom" category; at the same time, it provides enough of a tether to prevent us from straying beyond the legal terrain.[29] To return to the "boxes" metaphor introduced in the first chapter: Chase's solution encourages us to move films from one box or category to another—to shift them, for example, out of the "cop film" box and into one labeled "law films," as I will be doing in a moment with *Dirty Harry* (1971). This doesn't mean that a movie "really" belongs in one category rather than another; instead it shows that the act of shifting films among categories enables us to discover new meanings and previously overlooked relationships between crime films and society. In what follows, I discuss criminal law films that address three issues: the tension between the goals of crime control and due process, the special problems of defendants with mental retardation, and vigilantism. These are far from the only issues that have inspired good law films, but they provide useful starting points for analyzing law movies without lawyers.

Law films often gravitate toward the ongoing and unresolvable tension in the criminal justice process between the need for crime control, on the one hand, and the desire to protect individuals' rights, on the other. In his classic study of *The Limits of the Criminal Sanction,* Herbert Packer speaks of this tension as the "normative antinomy at the heart of the criminal law,"[30] a persistent struggle between two models or value systems. The crime control model, aimed primarily at identifying and immobilizing criminals, stresses efficiency and begins with the premise that an arrested person is likely to be guilty. The due process model, aimed primarily at protecting rights and ensuring fairness, insists on procedural correctness at all cost, even if this means the criminal goes free. Packer's point was not to argue for one model over the other but rather to show that the two oscillate and compete in their influence over the criminal justice process, giving rise to partisan political struggles. Indeed, nearly all public debates over criminal justice policy can be seen as aspects of the unending tension between the crime control model and the due process model.

Movies, it turns out, are deeply interested in this ideological competition over the criminal justice process. *Dirty Harry,* for instance, although it can be considered a cop or vigilante or serial killer movie, can also be viewed as a law film that argues, vehemently, for giving crime control priority over due process. It begins by trying to establish the need for more conservative policies, maintaining that during the ultraliberal 1960s, criminals were given so many rights that long-haired serial killers wearing peace symbols are now roaming the streets, killing young women while snarling "I have a right to a lawyer." "The law is crazy," officer Harry Callahan declares in amazement on learning that the district attorney will free Scorpio because Harry has violated the serial killer's fourth amendment rights. The DA, the namby-pamby liberal mayor, and criminal-rights court decisions all play into the psycho's hands—forcing a selfless, fearless, dedicated cop like Harry to play "dirty."

Implicit comments on the tension between crime control and due process can again be found in *Minority Report* (2002), Steven Spielberg's movie about a futuristic "precogs" or prior-cognition system that can detect murders before they occur. (In the film's immediate background lay the results of DNA tests demonstrating that many prisoners, including some on death row, were in fact innocent of the crimes for which they had been convicted; thus Spielberg's concern here for the quality of seemingly scientific evidence and for protecting the rights even of those who seem most guilty.) The science of *Minority Report* is oddly dependent on pickling (the three precogs deliver their predictions from a bathlike solution in which they float perpetually, and people convicted of contemplating murder spend eternity preserved in a kind of pickle-jar panopticon), but the film's justice system is exactly what the crime control model calls for: efficient, tough, and excellent at preventing crime. That this system of justice before trial—indeed, even before the crime is committed—leaves a lot to be desired becomes clear when John Anderton (Tom Cruise), head of the precogs system, is himself accused of committing an upcoming murder. Instantly recognizing the system's potential for totalitarian thought control, Anderton switches to the due process position and starts to run. Other cop films that can also be seen as law films due to their concern with the push-and-pull between crime control needs and defendants' rights include *To Live and Die in L.A.* (1985), *RoboCop* (1987), *The Star Chamber,* and *The Thin Blue Line* (1988).

People with mental retardation or related disabilities are depicted fairly frequently on the big screen, often by prominent stars (Lon Chaney Jr. in the 1939 version of *Of Mice and Men* and John Malkovich in its 1992 version; Dustin Hoffman in *Rain Man* [1988]; Sean Penn in *I Am Sam* [2001]; Tom Hanks in *Forrest Gump* [1994]; Juliette Lewis in *The Other Sister* [1999]). Few of these films are interested in law; but those that examine the special problems of mentally retarded defendants do spill over into the law film category. The issues here include criminal responsibility: To what degree are mentally handicapped defendants responsible for their actions, especially if they have been manipulated by others? There are also processing issues, for people with mental retardation may have difficulty negotiating the criminal justice system, and they can be pressured into making false confessions.

Some of these issues are laid out in *Sling Blade* (1996), Billy Bob Thornton's film about a mentally retarded man named Karl released from the mental hospital where he had been sent decades earlier for butchering his mother and her lover due to a misunderstanding. Sharing his perspective, we learn how difficult it can be to comprehend the world and do the right thing. But our broader point of view also enables us to watch Karl, whose scary appearance forces us to think through our stereotypes of "criminal" and "dangerous." A similar legal subtext can be found in *The Green Mile* (1999), which is concerned in part with the story of John Coffey (Michael Clarke Duncan), an innocent but mentally slow prisoner whose execution we get to watch in excruciating detail. A huge black man, John Coffey, too, fits stereotypes of "criminal" and "dangerous" but is actually, we learn, a kind of Christ figure, innocent and forgiving, a healer and not a killer; he even helps the executioner (played by Tom Hanks) get through his sorry task. Had he been better able to defend himself, Coffey would certainly have avoided the electric chair at the end of that green corridor.

While these two examples are marred by sentimentality and easy ironies, *Monster* (2003) makes similar points about the legal problems of people with limited intelligence more cleanly. Based on the biography of Aileen Wuornos, a mentally and emotionally handicapped prostitute, *Monster* tells the story through her eyes, showing that at least some of her crimes were committed in self-defense and that she had a history of emotional and physical abuse. But because she lacked the sophistication to raise these issues in her defense, the media were able to turn her into a monstrous serial killer, an image that dominated Wuornos's legal battles until her execution. Moreover, as Nick Broomfield shows in his documentaries on Wuornos (*Aileen Wuornos: The Selling of a Serial Killer* [1992] and *Aileen: Life and Death of a Serial Killer* [2003]), she became easy prey for an unscrupulous lawyer and people seeking to profit from her story. With similar integrity, *Let Him Have It* (1991) tells the true story of Derek Bentley, brain damaged during the London blitz, easily led into crime by smarter boys, and incapable of defending himself. *Let Him Have It* does have a courtroom scene, but what it says about the needs of people with mental retardation in criminal trials goes far beyond Derek's confusion before the bench. It locates Derek's trial and execution in the context of the profound social changes experienced by England in the aftermath of World War II, especially the emergence of a youth culture that threatened ruling-class values and privileges.

Vigilante movies debate the strength and purpose of law, with most of them arguing that we need more law, either to control the vigilantes or to make up for weaknesses of law that engender vigilantism in the first place. In addition, these films identify the people who, in the filmmakers' opinion, most threaten the law, be they the vigilantes themselves or the criminals whom the vigilantes set out to control. A surprising number of these films smile on vigilante activities.[31] *Death Wish* (1974), first in the popular series of vigilante films that made actor Charles Bronson famous, portrays a politically liberal New York City architect who is soft on crime until criminals murder his wife and rape his daughter. At that point, Paul Kersey goes on a killing spree to cleanse the city of the scum who prey on innocents— a vigilante action that the film endorses. Vigilantism is again endorsed (albeit with less conviction) by *Man on Fire* (2004), starring Denzel Washington as the bodyguard of a girl named Pita in a wealthy Mexico City family. When Pita is kidnapped, the bodyguard sets out to rescue her and avenge the crime. *Boondock Saints* (1999) similarly cheers on two Irish lads called by God to clean up crime in Boston. *Magnum Force,* on the other hand, condemns vigilantism in the form of rogue cops who roar about on their motorcycles, shooting promiscuous women and criminal men whom the liberal courts have foolishly freed. Two other films probe the psychology of vigilantism: *Death*

and the Maiden (1994), in which the wife of a judge in an unidentified South American country unexpectedly comes face to face with a
man whom she believes tortured and raped her as an official in the
former fascist regime; and *Falling Down* (1993) in which a middle-
aged failure comes unglued and lashes out against all the forces that
seem to be conspiring to make men like himself miserable. But all
vigilante films, irrespective of their psychological acuity, spell out
the motives of those who take law into their own hands, thus consti-
tuting, collectively, one of the strongest critical discourses in popular culture on law.

Justice without the Pretense of a Blindfold

All criminal law movies, whether or not they include courtroom scenes,
have the potential to shape viewers' ideas about the nature of legality, either by virtue of what they actually say or through what they
omit. A film such as *Judgment at Nuremberg* encourages us to think of
judges as mature gents, kindly, thoughtful, and selflessly dedicated
to the ideal of fairness. Conversely, the long-term absence of female
lawyers on the silver screen, and later depictions of them as barely
competent, reinforced the notion that men make the best lawyers. Even
when law movies are primarily concerned with extralegal matters, as
in the case of *Rashomon* (1950) and *Runaway Jury* (2003), they are still
capable of affecting public opinion about such matters as the reliabil-
ity of eyewitness testimony and the optimal role for jury consultants.

However, some law movies, usually those aimed at improving legal
processes or exposing injustices, make explicit statements about the
nature of law and aim at actually participating in the making of law.
Let Him Have It, the Derek Bentley film, was part of a forty-five year
campaign to clear his name and show that, in executing him, British
law made a terrible mistake. Bentley, despite his mental incapacities,
was hanged at the age of 19 for a murder committed by someone else
and that he in fact had tried to prevent. The campaign to clear him,
led by his sister Iris, succeeded in 1998 in winning a pardon that not
only overturned Bentley's conviction but placed the blame for the
miscarriage of justice squarely on the shoulders of then Lord Chief
Justice Rayner Goddard.

Other recent films that have been made explicitly to participate in
and, hopefully, change law include *The Official Story* (1985), aimed at
imposing legal responsibility on former members of an Argentinian

Figure 5.2. An example of the law film that spends little time in the court-room, *Capturing the Friedmans* (2003) reflects the confusions of contempo-rary life and the difficulty of finding ultimate truths. It forces viewers to ac-cept the impossibility of certainty about guilt and innocence. Photo used by permission of Photofest.

fascist regime; *Capturing the Friedmans* (2003), a documentary about the micropolitics of child abuse prosecutions; and the two made-for-tv documentaries *Paradise Lost: The Child Murders at Robin Hood Hills* (1996) and *Paradise Lost 2: Revelations* (2000), made as part of a cam-paign to reverse the convictions of three youngsters convicted of grisly Arkansas killings. Such films have an overtly political purpose: to become part of law by contributing to its improvement. Most of the Italian films mentioned earlier, and nearly all political crime movies, share this purpose. These films constitute an aspect of law. Forming a strand in public discourses about legal matters, they become part of the struggle to define law and achieve justice.

Like all films, law movies reflect what is happening in the larger so-ciety. In its early days, cinema reflected a vision or ideology of law as a stately, impartial process, one fittingly symbolized by the figure of justice balancing her scales while blindfolded. As this belief system faded, movies kept pace, depicting law as vulnerable to mistake, ma-nipulation, and outright corruption, and steadily reducing the length of courtroom scenes. At same time, public opinion began to embrace a postmodernist awareness of power as a struggle among many constituencies and discourses, and of law as the contested product of political jousting. In this newer view, law exists not just in law books but also at multiple sites and in thousands of debates, including those of popular culture. Movies, as one vehicle for those discourses, enable us to participate in the construction of law and reconceptualizations of justice.

Notes

For his contributions to an earlier version of this chapter, I owe special thanks to Alex Hahn.

1. On changes in understandings of the nature of law itself, see Freeman 2005b.
2. For a somewhat different approach to "patterns of courtroom justice," but one that, like this chapter, tries to reach comprehensive conclusions, see Silbey 2001.
3. Robert C. Post (1987) makes a related point in his article "On the Popular Image of the Lawyer." Post distinguishes between two images of law in popular culture, writing that "the concept of 'law' itself has assumed a double meaning. Law is on the one hand the positive enactments of the state. Law in this sense is technical, ambiguous, and complex. It can almost always be circumvented. . . . Lawyers stand accused of breaking a different kind of law, the law which is associated with justice and with our values as a community" (383).
4. The second version of *The Postman Always Rings Twice* (1981) becomes flaccid partly because it lacks the legal framework of the first. Scriptwriter David Mamet retains some courtroom material from the first version; but without the opening scene, in which Frank is delivered into the movie by the DA, and the last one, in which the DA leads him off to execution, the other material becomes incoherent.
5. For other examples, see *The Wrong Man* and *Manhattan Melodrama* (1934).
6. While *I Want to Live!* is usually discussed as a prison and death penalty film, it includes a pivotal trial scene.
7. With regard to procedural reform, Director Fritz Lang claimed that his film *Fury* (1936) influenced the way evidence was presented in subsequent trials. When Peter Bogdanovich asked Lang why he had used films in *Fury*'s courtroom sequences, Lang replied: "I didn't know very much about procedure in an American trial, so M-G-M gave me a few experts and all of them were opposed to showing the films in court [the courtroom scene]. . . . I took the liberty of doing it, and afterwards, in many actual cases, it was permitted in court" (Bogdanovich 1967: 29). If *Fury* did in fact lead to the use of filmed materials as evidence in actual trials, this is an example of film affecting real-life legal practices.
8. Carol Clover (2000) argues that trial movies equate the audience with a jury, turning the movie theater into a courtroom. She doesn't mention *Rashomon*

(1950; discussed in chapter 8, this volume), but surely it is one of the best examples of this equation.

9. In this case, the lynch mob is after a black man, but in other films of the period, the target is white. Directors and script writers would have preferred to depict lynchings more honestly, showing that blacks were the usual victims. However, they were prevented from doing so, either by studio heads (see Bogdanovich 1967: 32 for L. B. Mayer's censorship of *Fury*) or the Production Code Administration (see Maltby 1995: 369–70).

10. Although *A Time to Kill* condemns the Ku Klux Klan vigilantes who come after the black man, Carl Lee Hailey, it supports Hailey's own vigilante actions (he is on trial for shooting two white men for raping his daughter). Thus, it ends up making a provigilante statement.

11. However, the defense attorney does manage to have Cora sentenced to probation, even though she was charged with killing her husband, and later both lawyers are rehabilitated as characters, an inconsistency not explained in the film.

12. Chase 1986: 284, 293 n. 38.

13. *Fury*'s bitterness, critics speculate, may have derived from the background of its director, Fritz Lang, who had recently fled Nazi Germany for the United States. Indeed, there may be "a parallel between the gradual and menacing growth of hatred in [*Fury*'s] crowd lusting for a lynching, and the Hitler terror" (L. Eisner, as quoted in Chase 1986: 297 n. 44).

14. Rosenberg 1996: 282.

15. Hitchcock's *The Paradine Case,* although it has courtroom scenes and dates from the 1940s, does not fit the law noir category due to its lack of sense of corruption and its upper-class setting and characters. In fact, *The Paradine Case* is as much a mystery as a courtroom film.

16. In his autobiographical *Making Movies,* Lumet describes the "lens plot" of *Twelve Angry Men:* "As the picture unfolded, I wanted the [jury] room to seem smaller and smaller." Thus, he slowly shifted to longer lenses, at the same time lowering the camera from above eye level to eye level in the second third of the film and below eye level in the third. These changes increased the sense of claustrophobia and tension. "On the final shot, an exterior that showed the jurors leaving the courtroom, I used a wide-angle lens" and "raised the camera to the highest above-eye-level position," thus releasing the built-up tension (1995: 81).

17. In an unusual combination, the journalist's character thus functions as both an injustice figure and a justice figure.

18. One exception was Orson Welles's *The Trial* (1963), a film that closely follows Franz Kafka's hallucinatory novel and bears little resemblance to any other courtroom movie. Another exception was *Madame X* (1966), a Lana Turner vehicle that may be the worst trial film ever made.

19. See also Berets 1996.

20. Miller 1994: 212, 212 n. 32, 213.

21. *Nuts* (1987), a trial film centered around a female character who is not an attorney but a high-priced call girl accused of murder, avoids the female-lawyer gender stereotyping of other courtroom films of this period, but only

by substituting another negative stereotype, that of the hysteric—the "nut" of the title.

22. Another exception, discussed later, appears in *In the Name of the Father*. For a fuller analysis of female attorney movies, see the first edition of this book and Bailey, Pollock, and Schroeder 1998.

23. An exception is *A Few Good Men*, a film that takes place mainly in the court-room and has little or no "action." Successful at the box office, *A Few Good Men* won over audiences through dialogue and exposition—a rare feat in the 1990s.

24. On the general decline of the lawyer's status in film, see Asimow 1996.

25. Compare Asimow 2005.

26. On this debate, see Greenfield and Osborn 1999; Greenfield, Osborn, and Robson 2001a; and Chase 2002. A useful overview of related issues can be found in Robson 2005.

27. Chase 2002: xiii.

28. Chase 2002: 170.

29. Some of the discussions in Black 1999, with its completely unbounded def-inition of law films, exemplify such straying.

30. Packer 1968: 153.

31. An exception can be found in *Of Mice and Men*, which, although not pri-marily a vigilante film, is remarkable for the vigor with which it condemns vigilantism in its two lynch mob scenes.

||6|| Prison and Execution Films

> This is hell, and I'm going to give you the guided tour.
> —The evil warden in *Lock Up*

The prison film genre took shape during the days of silent cinema; toward the end of that period, studios were releasing one or two movies about prison life each year.[1] Ranging from stories of jailbreaks and inmate reformation through melodramas about unjust convictions and hangings, these silent films created a cinematic vocabulary that was incorporated by talkies in the 1930s and could still be found, almost unaltered, in the 1990s success *The Shawshank Redemption* (1994).[2] Movies of this type are essentially fantasies, films that purport to reveal the brutal realities of incarceration while actually offering viewers escape from the miseries of daily life through adventure and heroism. Presenting tales in which justice is miraculously restored after long periods of harsh oppression, prison movies enable us to believe, if only briefly, in a world where long-suffering virtue is rewarded. But in recent decades, a few filmmakers have begun producing movies that critique the traditional fantasy formulas or bypass them entirely, an indication that, after close to one hundred years, the prison film may be on the verge of transformation.

Characteristics of the Genre

Certain stock characters, plots, and themes turn up over and over again in traditional prison films.[3]

The Cast

The Big House (1930), one of the first prison films with a sound track, revolves around three convicts: Butch, an older, hardened criminal who is experienced in the ways of the prison; Kent, a yellow-bellied snitch; and Morgan, the handsome, middle-class hero who never squeals and is a loyal friend. It turns out that Morgan did nothing worse than commit forgery—once. He escapes long enough to fall in love with Kent's sister, only to be recaptured and returned, brokenhearted. When a riot breaks out, Butch and Kent die, but Morgan halts the violence single-handedly, an act for which he is rewarded with his freedom. At the movie's close he leaves prison to marry Kent's sister and live "abroad," where he can start over as an honest man. Two other characters also play important roles in *The Big House:* the warden, who is wise, tough, and fair ("If you've got grievances," he tells the prisoners, "come to me. . . . I'm running this show, and I'm ready for you"); and a "rat," who sneaks around gathering information for the administration.

These same character types show up in a second prison film of the early 1930s, Howard Hawks's *The Criminal Code* (1931), which tells the tale of a fine young man who is mistakenly convicted of manslaughter and sentenced to ten years in the penitentiary. In prison Bob bonds with other prisoners, including Gallway (Boris Karloff), a hardened criminal plotting a revenge murder. One buddy plans an escape, only to be thwarted by a stool pigeon. "The years go on," we are told by an intertitle, "drab—empty—hopeless years," and indeed we do find that six years of hard labor in the prison's jute mill have broken Bob spiritually and physically. Fortunately, the prison doctor realizes that Bob "isn't a criminal at all." "There is something there worth saving," he informs the warden, "and it is almost gone." The kindly warden reassigns Bob to work at his house, where the young man and the warden's daughter fall in love. When Bob is erroneously blamed for a murder, he refuses to break the criminal code by squealing, even though this refusal may lead to the gallows. But the warden's daughter saves him, they embrace, and Bob is behind bars no longer.

Ingredients of these and other early prison films became staples of the genre: convict buddies, a paternalistic warden, a cruel assistant warden or guard, a craven snitch, a bloodthirsty convict, and the young hero, who is either absolutely innocent or at most guilty of a minor offense that does not warrant prison. Some movies vary the secondary characters: In *Murder in the First* (1995), for instance, the buddy is not a fellow prisoner but a lawyer (Christian Slater) who helps a prisoner (Kevin Bacon) close down the dungeons at Alcatraz. Few, however, tamper with the essential innocence of the lead character, with whom viewers must be able to identify. In *Each Dawn I Die* (1939), the hero (James Cagney) is a crusading journalist, framed for manslaughter by crooked politicians. *Birdman of Alcatraz* (1962) stars Burt Lancaster as the convict with a heart of gold. In *Cool Hand*

Figure 6.1. Convicts played by George Raft and James Cagney plot in *Each Dawn I Die* (1939). The attraction of prison films lies partly in their depiction of close male friendships and heroic revolts, partly in their offer of access to the secret world of convict life. Photo used by permission of Photofest.

Luke (1967), a petty offender (Paul Newman) sacrifices himself to save his chain-gang buddies from a cruel overseer; and in *Mrs. Soffel* (1984), a prisoner (Mel Gibson) and his brother escape from the jail where they are waiting to be hanged, even though they are, by their own account, "innocent as snow."

Only the character of the warden changes significantly over the years, as the sympathetic father figure of early talking films becomes a heartless brute. By 1984, the release date of *Mrs. Soffel*, the warden has evolved into a despicable bully—fat, cruel, and insensitive; by 1995, the release date of *Murder in the First*, the jailer (Gary Oldman) begins his day by slashing prisoners with his razor; and in the 2001 offering *The Last Castle*, the warden (James Gandolfini) personally shoots his inmate rival for the convicts' allegiance in front of the entire prison population. *Brubaker* (1980), a film in which Robert Redford plays a heroic warden, is no more than a partial exception to the rule of the steadily worsening warden, for Brubaker's mission is to reform a penitentiary where his predecessor raked in bribes and encouraged convicts to rape and maim one another.

The Shawshank Redemption includes character types that have hardly changed since the 1930s: the innocent hero; the experienced convict buddy; the malevolent warden; and a knot of nasty prisoners who try to harm the hero. The degree to which these characters are crucial to prison films is suggested by the way they turn up in a different but related type of prison film: titillation movies with titles such as *Blond Bait* (1956), *Caged Heat* (1974),[4] and *Slammer Girls* (1987). These babes-behind-bars films, too, feature innocent inmates with confidants and treacherous enemy prisoners; if the superintendent is kindly, there will be a butchy and sadistic assistant superintendent to take up the traditional role.[5]

Stock Plots

The major incident of a traditional prison film is usually a riot or escape, with much of the preceding footage devoted to the planning for this event. *The Big House,* for example, culminates in a spectacular riot during which armored tanks roll into the prison (and right over the camera), while the central concern of Jules Dassin's *Brute Force* (1947) is an unsuccessful jailbreak led by Burt Lancaster's character. In these movies, escapes tend to be coupled with revenge on the bad guys, as in the case of *Midnight Express* (1978), the story of a clean-cut American youth who is caught smuggling hashish out of Turkey and sentenced to life in an incredibly brutal Turkish prison. His parents fail to gain his release, and his buddies languish and die, but he finally escapes, killing the most bestial guard on his way out. In *Escape from Alcatraz* (1979), the flight of Clint Eastwood's character is itself retaliation against the hard-hearted warden, who will lose his post. Eddie, the hero of *Mrs. Soffel,* manages not only to escape from death row but also to take his brother and the warden's wife with him, and although Henri Young, the central figure of *Murder in the First,* remains in custody, he triggers investigations that close Alcatraz's dungeons and lead to the arrest of the depraved jailer. When the main character of *The Shawshank Redemption* escapes, he also cleans out the warden's bank accounts, arranges for the arrest of the ruthless guard, and blows the whistle on the warden's kickback scheme—one of the most fulsome revenge sequences in prison movie history. In all these films, good triumphs over evil and the moral order is restored.

Riot (1969), starring Jim Brown and Gene Hackman as the cons Culley and Red, sounded the breaking-loose theme in ways that uncannily anticipated the two most deadly riots in U.S. prison history. The film's riot starts when inmates in the punishment wing, including Culley (who is unfairly being sent to solitary by a racist "bull") and Red (a natural leader), take advantage of a sudden opportunity to jump the guards. From the punishment wing the disturbance spreads throughout the prison. Some inmates present their demands at the front gate while others dig a tunnel under the wall to the rear. The tunnelers reach daylight just as officials retake the yard, and all are killed except Culley, who escapes.

Two years later, when New York State inmates took over Attica prison, they, too, seized an unexpected opportunity to jump a guard, and as on-the-scene footage shows, the state regained control by stationing officers on the walls with rifles aimed down at the yard almost exactly as they had been posed in *Riot*. Nine years later, when inmates at the Santa Fe, New Mexico, penitentiary rampaged, they got drunk on home brew and butchered one another much as inmates in the film had. These parallels between art and life, film and history, occurred because *Riot*'s filmmakers went out of their way to accurately reproduce prison conditions. Although the movie has fictional elements, it was filmed entirely on the grounds of the Arizona State Prison, with the institution's warden and inmates playing themselves, and it purports to have been based on an actual escape attempt. Thus do fiction and reality intertwine, with fiction sometimes foreshadowing reality.

Not only stock plots but also stock scenes show up in prison films across the generations. *The Big House,* seemingly enchanted by the cinematic vistas its camera was discovering, depicted roach-racing in the yard, maggots in the food, knives passed from hand to hand under the mess-hall table, dungeons, tossed cells, and shifty-eyed plotting during the chapel services—scenes that became leitmotifs of this film type. Convicts in *Each Dawn I Die* use the weekly movie as an occasion to knock off their enemies, as they do again half a century later in *In the Name of the Father* (1993). When Paul Newman's character joins the chain gang in *Cool Hand Luke,* he busts rocks in a tradition that began with *The Whipping Boss* (1922) and was perpetuated by *I Am a Fugitive from a Chain Gang* (1932). Graphic scenes of life behind bars became de rigueur, one of the elements audiences expected to find in prison movies.

Stock Themes

Nearly all prison films dwell on the theme of rebellion against injustice. Innocents, we find, are being punished, not only by incarceration but also by diabolic officers and sadistic fellow convicts, a point these films drive home with obligatory scenes of brutalization. To restore justice, the prisoners sometimes take matters into own hands (*Cool Hand Luke, Escape from Alcatraz, Midnight Express, Papillon* [1973], *Riot, Riot in Cell Block 11* [1954]). At other times, someone comes to their rescue, as in *The Last Detail* (1973), a going-to-prison film in which the agents of justice are the petty officers who escort a naive young sailor from their naval base to a northern prison. During their week-long journey, the older men (Jack Nicholson and Otis Young) befriend the sailor (Randy Quaid) and, appalled by his approaching fate (eight years behind bars for snitching $40), decide to initiate him in the pleasures of life. The following week of adventure and perfect companionship is their way of settling accounts in advance and thus helping Quaid's character through the years of incarceration. In *Murder in the First,* the agent of justice is the buddy figure, the young lawyer who helps Henri Young shut down the dungeons and records his story for posterity. The central concern of traditional prison films, then, has been oppression, transgression, and the restoration of a natural order of justice.

A second and related theme is that of control. These movies pose questions about who controls whom and what being under someone else's control implies for prisoners' manhood. For example, Luke, in *Cool Hand Luke,* repeatedly baits the guards, controlling them psychologically even though he knows he'll be punished in the long run. He does so because he hopes his tactics will help the other convicts regain self-control and throw off the guards' false authority, maintained with chains and dogs. In short, Luke restores his buddies' manliness. Manliness also surfaces as an issue in *Riot,* in which the racist guard, affronted by Culley's dignity, attempts to humiliate him.

In many films, prison becomes a metaphor for the state or some other oppressor that controls and limits the hero, sapping his potential. Imprisonment in *American Me* (1992), the movie about Chicano gangs in East Los Angeles, comes to stand for the self-destructive violence with which gang members enchain their own communities. *Brubaker*'s prison becomes a symbol of a political system that tolerates corruption among warden and guards. ("Henry, stop the digging," warns one of the system's representatives, referring to Brubaker's literal and figurative unearthing of skeletons.) And when *Cool Hand Luke*'s hero explains to his mother that "I just can't seem to find no elbow room," he indicts not only incarceration but all the establishment forces that restrain youthful nonconformity.[6]

A third prison film theme concerns the gap between appearance and reality. At first, appearances fool both the heroes and the viewers who perceive through their eyes. The apparently worst convicts, such as Butch in *The Big House,* turn out to be sweethearts once you get to know them, a principle summarized by the title of another prison film, *Angels with Dirty Faces* (1938). In the latter, the juvenile delinquents who revere the local hoodlum are actually cherubs behind their tough exteriors, and most angelic of all is the hoodlum himself (James Cagney), who pretends cowardice on the way to execution so the kids will stop admiring him and go straight. On the other hand, prison movies are full of hidden enemies; one never knows where danger lies. Friends turn out to be cowards, the shower room is full of rapists, and the officer who seems helpful really plans to shoot you. These films are prone to somersault reversals, revelations, and ham-handed ironies. In the Sylvester Stallone vehicle *Lock Up* (1989), as in *Brute Force* and many other prison movies, the prisoner is the good man, the warden evil incarnate.

The Attractions of Prison Films

"What we need to ask" about genre, film theorist Robin Wood advises, "is less what than why."[7] Applied to prison films, Wood's question becomes: Why has this genre, despite its formulaic characters, plots, and themes, flourished from the 1930s into the present, resilient and often fresh in its reconceptualizations? The answer has four parts. It lies in the opportunities prison movies offer us, first, to identify with a perfect man; second, to participate in perfect friendships; third, to fantasize about sex and rebellion; and fourth, to acquire insider information about the apparent realities of prison life.

Identification with a Perfect Man

Traditional prison films invite us to identify with heroes, even superheroes. In *Papillon,* the central character (played by Steve McQueen) is sent to a prison on Devil's Island, where he endures lengthy periods in solitary, hard labor in swamps, and encounters with terrifying lepers before he, and he alone, devises a way to escape.[8] His buddy (Dustin Hoffman), though equally smart, cannot keep up with these superhuman feats of fortitude. *Cool Hand Luke*'s main character defies savage overseers and survives a string of escapades only to be betrayed by a fellow convict and shot to death. The film stages his death as a crucifixion, however, comparing Luke's willingness to die for others to that of Jesus. Leads in other prison films tend to utter lines such as "I could run the whole show from solitary," and sometimes they do, as in *American Me*. In *Bad Boys* (1983), Sean Penn's character beats up all the bullies in juvie hall, and when his archenemy, Paco, comes at him with a knife, he not only wins but also refrains from killing Paco, thereby exhibiting the moral superiority of the true hero.

Sassy and truculent, the heroes of prison movies remain defiant even in the face of threats or inducements that would sway an ordinary mortal. "You think I'm a stoolie?" asks Barbara ("Babs") Graham in *I Want to Live!* (1958), one of the few prison films to focus on a woman.[9] Sneering at officials' attempts to bribe her, even though her life is at stake, Babs (Susan Hayward) refuses with a vehement "NO DICE!" Plucky till the end, she insists on listening to jazz in her cell the night before execution and on dressing up for her trip to the gas chamber.

The supermen of standard prison films are perfect partly because they embody old-fashioned gender ideals, proving that there are still real men, men who can lead without pettiness or manipulation and who can walk through the yard (as *Shawshank*'s narrator remarks admiringly of lead character Andy Dufresne) as if they were out for a stroll, unruffled and unafraid.[10] These men know how to avenge a slight; they emerge unbroken from months or years in solitary confinement (decades, in the case of Sean Connery's character in *The Rock* [1996]); they are true to themselves and their ideals. They demonstrate that the old-fashioned tough-guy ideal is intact and available, even (or perhaps especially) in prison.[11] Movie prisons, no matter how appalling their conditions, are a comforting sort of world, ruled as they are by men who are a little more godlike than the rest of us.

Participation in Perfect Friendships

A second source of prison films' enduring popularity lies in the opportunities they offer to participate vicariously in perfect friend-

Figure 6.2. Susan Hayward, playing the real-life Barbara Graham, is escorted to the gas chamber in *I Want to Live* (1958), one of the few prison films to focus on a woman. Like many prison movies, this one is based on a true story of injustice. Photo used by permission of Photofest.

ships. These movies are full of ideal companions, buddies more loyal and true than any on the outside. Like Christian martyrs, death row prisoners in *The Last Mile* (1932) help one another through the ordeal of execution; when they overpower the guards, one convict willingly dies so another can be set free. In *Bad Boys,* Sean Penn's character bonds with a Jewish kid who teaches him the ropes and helps him plot the big escape. *Mrs. Soffel*'s buddies are brothers; the buddies in *Sleepers* (1996) are the guys who as kids were sentenced to reform school and are now joined in their quest for justice by their old mentor, Father Bobby (Robert De Niro), who lies for them on the witness stand.[12] Confinement somehow rewards prisoners with friendships deeper, purer, and more enduring than those experienced by law-abiding citizens. As viewers, we participate in these heroic relationships.[13]

Prison film friendships gain strength from their single-sex settings. These movies relentlessly exclude women. When a woman does appear, she is near death (as in *Cool Hand Luke*), merely part of the scenery (as in *Papillon*), killed off quickly (as in *The Shawshank Redemption*), or banished for her treachery (as in *Murder in the First*). Closed off from the distractions of female companionship, these all-male worlds promote solidarity.

Fantasies of Sex and Rebellion

A third answer to our variation on Robin Wood's "why" question—why are the formulas of traditional prison films attractive?—lies in the films' encouragement of fantasies about sex and rebellion. The babes-behind-bars subgenre is the type of prison film most obviously concerned with sexual stimulation. Movies of this type appeal to aficionados of cult and pornography films, especially pornography of the chains-and-whips variety. Featuring young women who tend to remove their bras before riots and mannish, sadistic officers, these films are fixated on the sexual implications of an all-female society, usually from the viewpoint of a heterosexual male who enjoys watching pin-ups in action.[14]

Less obviously, prison films with male inmates often have a homo-erotic subtext in which the buddy gets both a perfect friend and a lover. This message remains subtextual, and in fact traditional prison films are somewhat homophobic insofar as they characterize rapists and other bad guys as homosexuals.[15] This homophobia is a strategy to underscore the hero's heterosexuality and relieve viewers from any worry they might have about admiring a man who is gay. At the same time, however, prison movies hint at physical intimacy between the hero and his best pal. Robin Wood discusses this type of hint in an essay titled "From Buddies to Lovers," in which he writes (of a different group of movies) that "in all these films the emotional center, the emotional charge, is in the male/male relationship, which is patently what the films are *about*."[16] In traditional prison films, too, the male-male relationship is frequently central to the movie's meaning.

In *Kiss of the Spider Woman* (1985), that relationship becomes overtly gay as the two prisoners merge and assume aspects of one another's personalities. The relationship is almost explicitly gay in *Lock Up*, in which Donald Sutherland's warden cannot take his eyes off Sylvester Stallone's body and expresses his homoerotic attraction through sadistic punishments. Voyeurism is again a strong theme in *Cool Hand Luke,* in which convicts call the most perverted guard, a man who hides behind reflector sunglasses, "the Man with No Eyes."[17] In fact, he seldom takes his eyes off the half-naked convicts, vigilantly watching for a new occasion to connect with their bodies through punishment.

The gay subtext occasionally involves a biracial couple. There are traces of an erotic attachment in *Escape from Alcatraz* between Clint Eastwood's character and his black buddy, and an even stronger bond develops in *The Defiant Ones* (1958) between the escaped convicts played by Tony Curtis and Sidney Poitier, who are literally chained together and compare their condition to a marriage. At the end of *The Shawshank Redemption,* when former prisoners Andy Dufresne (Tim Robbins) and Red (Morgan Freeman) reunite on a beach in a warm embrace, with the promise of living happily ever after, we witness a relationship that can be understood to include sexuality.[18]

Traditional prison films, then, are open to various interpretations and are somewhat more flexible than they may initially appear. Their heroes—masculine ideals who can be considered heterosexual, "surreptitiously gay" (Wood's term),[19] or both—appeal to the sexual fantasies of a range of audiences.

Prison films further encourage sexual reveries through their concern with issues of domination and submission, entrapment and escape, control and powerlessness. Their preoccupation with punishment, cruelty, sadism, hidden enemies, and violation speaks in undertones of sadomasochism to those who might be listening.

Fostering daydreams of rebellion, on one level prison movies invite us to participate in the mythic ritual of killing the old king (or father, or warden) and ushering in a new and more just social order. Few traditional prison films fail to indict the state and its officials, casting them as brutal oppressors. Much as we learn to sympathize with the convicts, we learn to despise the officials who torment them. These films legitimate fantasies of seizing power.

Prison films often portray inmates as helpless children, at the mercy of all-powerful parents in the guise of rigid officials. In a few cases, such as the 1947 version of *Kiss of Death,* one of these officials turns out to be benign, a good parent who helps the hero go straight. But in the majority of prison movies, officials are repressive, and in some cases they actually push the convicts deeper into criminality (*I Am a Fugitive from a Chain Gang, Murder in the First*). How could it be wrong to resist such curs? Through the heroes, viewers vicariously participate in rebellion against unjust authority and the establishment of a new order that recognizes and honors true worth.

Claims to Authenticity

A fourth and final source of pleasure in prison films lies in their claims of authenticity. The genre offers the inside scoop, a window onto the inaccessible but riveting world of the prison. About half of all traditional prison movies assert that they are "based on a true story" or are "fictionalized accounts of an actual event." *Brubaker* relates occurrences in the life of Tom Murton, a reform warden who did in fact find unmarked convict graves at the Arkansas penitentiary and the remains of prisoners apparently killed by officials. *Riot in Cell Block 11* derives from the experience of the producer, who had spent time behind bars for shooting his wife's lover,[20] while *The Executioner's Song* (1982) reproduces the final days and execution of Gary Gilmore. Other films that claim to be based on actual circumstances include *American Me, Birdman of Alcatraz, Dead Man Walking* (1995), *Escape from Alcatraz, I Am a Fugitive from a Chain Gang, I Want to Live!, Midnight Express, Mrs. Soffel, Murder in the First, Papillon, Riot, Sleepers,* and *Weeds* (1987). In addition, some were filmed at actual prisons: *Riot in Cell Block 11* at California's Folsom prison, *An Innocent Man* (1989) at the Nevada Penitentiary, *The Last Castle* at the Tennessee State Prison, and scenes in both *Bad Boys* and *Natural Born Killers* (1994) at Illinois's Stateville prison. No other genre so loudly proclaims its verisimilitude.[21]

Partly due to these claims, prison movies form an influential source of information (and misinformation) on what goes on behind bars. They teach viewers how inmates (or purported inmates) talk, contributing such argot terms as *bulls, fish, hole, house, screw,* and *shiv* to the national vocabulary. Howard Hawks professed to have used prisoners as script consultants for *The Criminal Code.* "I got together with ten convicts and said, 'How should this end?' and they told me in no uncertain terms. They had a great deal to do with the formation of many scenes."[22] Through these movies we gain access to otherwise inaccessible details about prison drug smuggling, inmate therapy sessions, parole board hearings, and life on a chain gang, receiving what the evil warden of *Lock Up* calls "a guided tour" of "hell." When the tour ends, we are nearly as hip as the hero.

Notwithstanding their assertions of authenticity, however, traditional prison movies are incapable of providing a true picture of life behind bars. Key elements such as the centrality of riots and escapes, the focus on a heroic figure who has been unjustly incarcerated, and the romanticization of life behind bars preclude concentration on what inmate accounts tell us are the central facts of incarceration: boredom and distasteful companions. Inmates watch prison movies not to glean more information about incarceration but for the same reason the rest of us turn to them: to escape into a dream world where those who suffer are saved and indeed rewarded with awe and respect.

The genre's artificiality is perhaps most apparent in its inability to accommodate gender differences. Until recently, if one wanted to see a film about women in prison, there were only two choices: *I Want to Live!* and soft pornography. The choices have now been nominally broadened by *Point of No Return* (1993), a Pygmalion story featuring Bridget Fonda,[23] and *The Last Dance* (1996), starring Sharon Stone as the prisoner who walks that final mile. However, *Point of No Return* merely repeats the formula in which an older man (here Gabriel Byrne) saves a young woman by reforming her (here transforming a drug addict into a killer cop), and *The Last Dance* is no more than a clone of a men's prison film, *Dead Man Walking*. Two more late twentieth-century entries, Ashley Judd's *Double Jeopardy* (1999) and Sigourney Weaver's *A Map of the World* (1999), embed prison scenes in broader-scope dramas, while *Brokedown Palace* (1999), the story of two American girls who find themselves in a Thai prison with thirty-three-year sentences for drug smuggling, is a female version of *Midnight Express*.[24] In sum, these films do not in fact develop or sustain a women's point of view on incarceration; rather, they simply substitute women for men in order to broaden the movies' appeal without changing their basic nature.[25]

The great exception to the artificiality of the traditional prison film is the death penalty movie that tells a true story about the execution of an innocent. There is no denying that fictional death penalty movies often devolve into melodrama (*The Last Mile, The Chamber* [1996],

The Green Mile [1999], *Angels with Dirty Faces, The Life of David Gale* [2003]). Moreover, films that memorialize the executions of real-life bad guys (*In Cold Blood* [1967], *The Executioner's Song*), while they may be less corny and even accurate, are seldom impressive. But movies based on actual miscarriages of justice have both the ring of authenticity and power of true tragedy. These include *I Want To Live!*, the story of Barbara Graham's execution in San Quentin's gas chamber; *10 Rillington Place* (1971), an account of the hanging of a young English father for murders committed by his downstairs neighbor; *Breaker Morant* (1980) and *The Story of Women* (1988), both movies about the intentional execution of innocents for political purposes; and *Let Him Have It* (1991), the story of the outcome of extreme judicial bias. Based as they are on historical events, such films are able to offer realistic (if appalling) portrayals of not only executions but also the politics of death penalty sentencing.

New Developments in Prison Films

The limitations of most films in the prison genre—their fantastical depictions of prison life, their unrelenting masculinism, the sentimentality of their fictional death penalty scenes—have led to a search for new ways of depicting incarceration and execution. The majority of such films remain locked in old formulas, but a few moviemakers are sawing away at the chains of tradition.

While the stock figures of early prison films persist as lead characters, the stereotype of the typical convict has undergone transformation. In recent movies, prison populations are blacker and more Hispanic. They are also less gentlemanly; indeed, the cinematic prison yard now holds some real monsters, reflections of the national panic about serial killers and child sex-murderers, characters whom Ray Surette calls "predator icons"[26] The stock inmates of 1930s and 1940s films have been replaced by the embittered racist (Sean Penn's death row inmate, Matthew Poncelet, in *Dead Man Walking*), by the man on death row who actually deserves to be there (Mos Def's character in *Monster's Ball* [2001] and, again, Poncelet in *Dead Man Walking*), and by the bodybuilding member of the Aryan Brotherhood (*American History X* [1998]).

Whereas early- and mid-twentieth-century films assume that rehabilitation is desirable, later prison films reflect the ideological shift away from rehabilitation as a purpose of incarceration and its replacement by the goals of punishment and incapacitation. Paralleling this shift, the cinematic critique of rehabilitation began in the early 1970s, appearing first in *A Clockwork Orange's* (1971) philosophical attack on the presumption of trying to reform others and carried forward by *One Flew Over the Cuckoo's Nest* (1975), which shows how rehabilitation can be used to justify mind-control and lobotomies. The convicts and officials of later prison films leave little room for faith in the malleability of human nature: The nun in *Dead Man Walking* challenges Matthew Poncelet's racism but hardly converts him to multiculturalism, while *Minority Report* (2002), with its vast panopticon of the comatose, depicts the ultimate in incapacitation.

Following the late-twentieth-century trend toward genre fluidity, filmmakers began grafting prison and execution material onto other genres and turning it into episodes in broader narratives. The condemned man in *Monster's Ball* is of interest mainly because his guard falls in love with his wife; the prison in *Silence of the Lambs* (1991) is primarily a showcase for Hannibal Lecter; and *Minority Report,* its spectral prison scenes notwithstanding, is fundamentally a detection film. Although Alcatraz prison is the putative site for most of *The Rock's* action, it has become a museum, and the action concerns a takeover of the old penitentiary by right-wing paramilitaries; the grizzled former prisoner who saves the day seems as much an emblem of nostalgia as the old cell blocks, a gesture of longing toward a cinematic past. In theory, the postmodernist fracturing and resuturing of film genres could have led to more realistic prison movies, but for the most part the opposite has occurred: Combining with science fiction (*Minority Report*), with the film of inspirational uplift (*The Green Mile*), and with the war movie (*The Rock, The Last Castle*), prison films have become more divorced than ever from reality.

But some moviemakers are attempting more radical breaks with the past. Their efforts fuel three specific trends in recent prison films: the formation of an alternative tradition; the emergence of a new sort of prison documentary; and the appearance of films that comment on the genre itself.

Alternative-Tradition Prison Films

Historically, prison films have taken for granted a clear and stable system of morality. The heroes may be criminals, but they are obviously admirable, the bad guys are obviously abominable, and the heroes win. Based on comforting moral verities, standard prison films raise questions about justice in particular cases but do not doubt that justice exists and lies within human reach. Nor do they ask hard questions about the prison system. What they do best is what they do over and over again: set up a situation in which an individual is being punished unfairly and then develop a plotline in which the balance of justice is restored.

Bored with these old formulas and anxious to create movies that do not ideologically justify the prison system, around 1980 moviemakers began producing prison films in the alternative or critical tradition. These movies refuse to present characters who are clearly heroic or villainous. Instead of taking for granted a stable and universal moral system, they assume that living without a moral compass is part of the human condition. These critical films are less uplifting than their traditional counterparts, but they may be more suitable to a society that lacks consensus on basic religious, philosophical, and political issues, and they are certainly more accurate in their depictions of life behind bars.

The first movie to strike out in this new direction, *On the Yard* (1979), has no hero. The character closest to a hero is a loner (played by John Heard), a lifer who seems to be making some progress with his personal problems when he is murdered over a minor debt. From then on the movie forgets him. It reaches no satisfying resolution and makes no effort to make sense of prison brutalities. Gone are the criminal code, the transcendent rebel, the guard whom it is fun to hate. At best, inmates form weak alliances; most of the time, viciousness prevails.

A second alternative-tradition film from 1979, *Short Eyes*, was shot at New York City's high-rise jail, the Men's House of Detention, and is unrelenting in its determination not to prettify the situation. It is so close to documentary that throughout its long introduction, *Short Eyes* resists giving viewers a story line, instead acclimatizing us to the routines and personnel of a particular cell block. The narrative, when it does begin, concerns a middle-class white man who has been arrested for child molestation (and is thus nicknamed "short eyes," prison argot for a person guilty of this crime). His innocence is revealed only after other prisoners have brutally raped and butchered him. For a prison film, *Short Eyes* is as far as a movie can get from the concurrent Hollywood production, *Escape from Alcatraz*.

Prison film tradition is again inverted by *Kiss of the Spider Woman,* which gives viewers not triumphant masculinity but a broken revolutionary and a second prisoner decked out in a silk robe and lipstick who is no leader of men but rather the narrator of a World War II romance. The two become buddies, but what they do together is not manly in the conventional sense: They gently help one another when they weaken, and they end up openly making love. Not brawn but imagination is the central value in *Kiss of the Spider Woman,* and although the movie admires courage, the courage it endorses is distinctly different from the bluster of a James Cagney or the imperviousness of a Clint Eastwood.

A bleaker example of the alternative-tradition prison film can be found in *American Me,* Edward James Olmos's controversial movie about Chicano gangs in Los Angeles. Santana, the lead character (played by Olmos himself), is head of *la Eme* (the Mexican Mafia), the powerful prison gang that extends into the streets. A cross between Latino machismo and American violence, Santana is at once a victim of his culture and its victimizer. Although young men revere him and he longs to help them, Santana merely leads them into an escalating cycle of drugs and violence. Assassinated in prison, he is not even an antihero but rather a nonhero, a failure, an indictment of his culture's loss of traditional values and failure to find new ones. In this empty world, sex is impossible, love cannot save, buddies destroy one another, and savagery rules.

A self-conscious attempt to establish Chicano film, *American Me* documents harrowing passages in Mexican American history. The film, as critic Rob Canfield observes, explores its own "cinematic and cultural lineage as it repositions Latino identities and conflicts in a new light: the urban barrio of the 1990s and the prison institution that has become its new site of struggle. . . .This is a film that spotlights cultural boundaries and unmasks the violence that penetrates the borders of urban Latino masculinity."[27] While *American Me* has been trounced for its negative images of Chicano culture, it is in fact reformist in thrust, a condemnation of violence and Chicano stereotyping. Its reformism differs drastically, however, from that of earlier prison films (*The Criminal Code, The Last Mile, Riot in Cell Block 11*), which aimed at reforming prison management, not society itself. Moreover, while traditional prison films were hopeful, predicated on the idea that prison reform would lead to human reform, *American*

Me harshly denies viewers the illusion of simple solutions. Like *On the Yard* and *Short Eyes,* it grapples with a social problem that cannot be solved in a happily-ever-after ending.[28]

New Prison Documentaries

For decades, there was only one high-quality documentary about prison life: Frederick Wiseman's *Titicut Follies* (1967), a film shot, through a near-miraculous lapse in security, at Massachusetts's institution for criminally insane men. (*Titicut* refers to the road on which the institution is located. *Follies* refers, on the first level, to the amateur-hour show with which the film opens; later it comes to signify the entire institution, with its doomed attempts to "treat" the mentally ill in a prison setting.) This situation improved with the release of *Fourteen Days in May* (1988), a film that stays with a Mississippi prisoner and his family in his final hours before execution, and Errol Morris's *The Thin Blue Line* (1988), the riveting documentary about a prisoner on death row in Texas. *The Thin Blue Line* is less a documentary about prison life than a probe of the evidence used in this particular case and, beyond that, a pioneering investigation of the nature of perception and the creation of meaning. Famed for having led to the prisoner's release, *The Thin Blue Line* also led to a new line of documentaries about prison life and the cases of specific prisoners, including *Through the Wire* (1990), *The Execution Protocol* (1993), *Aileen Wuornos: The Selling of a Serial Killer* (1992), *Aileen: Life and Death of a Serial Killer* (2003), and the quasi-documentary *Dead Man Walking.*

Through the Wire, director Nina Rosenblum's exposé of a federal prison for women convicted of political crimes, takes a cinema-verité approach to its subject matter, using the camera to document the institution's sensory bleakness and debilitating routines. Prison footage is interspersed with shots of the women's families, giving background on their crimes, and with newsreel images of the crimes themselves. *Through the Wire* achieved two close-to-impossible goals: It presented extensive footage of routines in one of the most secure and secretive prisons in the United States; and through this exposure, it forced the prison to close and transfer its three revolutionaries to more humane institutions. *The Execution Protocol* again takes us inside an institution that even most prison officials are unlikely to penetrate: a state-of-the-art lockup designed to hold only men with sentences of death or natural life. Guided by a prisoner anticipating execution in the near future, the tour takes us into the death chamber and observes in minute detail the workings of the lethal injection machine. Most chilling of all, perhaps, are scenes of officials methodically reviewing the protocols for an upcoming execution.

Aileen Wuornos: The Selling of a Serial Killer, one of the most complex of the new prison documentaries, focuses on the death-row inmate known as "America's first female serial killer." Director Nick Broomfield traveled to Florida to interview Wuornos, the former prostitute who had confessed to killing seven male customers. He includes footage of negotiations with the prison officials who repeatedly thwart his efforts to meet with Wuornos, as well as scenes with Wuornos herself, whom he eventually succeeds in interviewing. Broomfield also interviews others involved in her story—a former lover who testified against Wuornos to avoid being charged as her partner-in-crime; a self-proclaimed Christian who "adopted" Wuornos in order to profit from her story; one of Wuornos's johns; and so on. The result is a many-layered tale with multiple views of the woman and her crimes. Wuornos comes to stand for historical truth and the difficulty of discovering it, while the film becomes a paradigm of historical excavation and assemblage, an example of the process of uncovering and reconstructing events. This is a process obscured by Hollywood movies, with their linear narratives, continuity editing, and authoritative presentations of events. Broomfield made a second Wuornos documentary after her execution, *Aileen: Life and Death of a Serial Killer,* and she was again memorialized in *Monster* (also 2003), Patty Jenkins's documentary-like rendering of her life and death.

Broomfield's Wuornos films belong with not only recent prison documentaries but also a group of new documentary films, including *The Thin Blue Line, Paris Is Burning* (1991), and *Shoah* (1985), that borrow fictional techniques while calling attention to themselves as artifacts. These documentaries, film theorist Linda Williams observes, seek "truth" in a new sense: not the objective and definitive truth that older, cinema-verité documentaries sought but a "more contingent, relative, postmodern truth."[29] Although Williams uses other examples, her words apply equally well to *Aileen Wuornos.* The new documentary, she writes, offers "highly expressionistic reenactments of different witnesses' versions" of events, as if to emphasize the circumstantial and constructed nature of knowledge. The new documentary "is acutely aware that the individuals whose lives are caught up in events are not so much self-coherent and consistent identities as they are actors in competing narratives."[30] *Aileen Wuornos* actually catches witnesses in the process of devising and revising their story lines.

The new "anti-verité documentaries," Williams concludes, "attempt to overturn" the older "commitment to realistically record 'life as it is' in favor of a deeper investigation of how it became as it is."[31] Thus, *Aileen Wuornos* gives us the story not of Aileen Wuornos but of the "selling" of Aileen Wuornos as a serial killer and of the filmmaker's involvement in this process. Life and art flow together. Historical truth exists, but we can get at it only by artifice. Some truths are more accurate than others, but none, we learn from *Aileen Wuornos*, can be stripped down to stand naked and free of the interpretive process. This is a lesson that cannot be learned from Hollywood.

Dead Man Walking adheres far more closely to Hollywood traditions. Based on the autobiography of Sister Helen Prejean, a nun who befriended a death-row prisoner at the Louisiana State Penitentiary, it has stars (Susan Sarandon and Sean Penn), and beneath its high-gloss surface, it carefully articulates two sets of values around the poles of the central characters. Yet in some ways, this is a documentary-like film. It is based on actual events. It has no hero—certainly not the prisoner, Matthew Poncelet, with his negativity and repellent racism, and perhaps not even Sister Prejean, whose interest in Matthew offends the victims' families. In any case, there is no trace of heroic masculinity, and for the most part, the film avoids sentimentality in its insistence on the realities of execution.

Dead Man Walking does endorse certain values—the love, non-violence, and self-scrutiny associated with Sister Prejean—but its emphasis falls on value clashes (between Matthew and the nun, and the nun and the victims' families). Sister Prejean is a friend to Matthew, but hardly a buddy. While director Tim Robbins apparently opposes the death penalty, he lays out both sides of the issue. There is no victory of one central character over the other but rather a merging as they learn to understand one another. Toward the end, their images overlap in the glass window that divides them. Like other nontraditional prison films, *Dead Man Walking* does not pit the main convict against the state or society but rather presents that character as an emblem of society's problems. If Santana is insufficiently heroic and Matthew Poncelet is pitiful as well as repellent, this is because their films have outgrown the mythologies of traditional prison movies.

Self-Reflexive Prison Films

A third development in prison films is a trend toward self-reflexivity, with the films exhibiting a self-consciousness about themselves as representations and about the traditions to which they belong. Of course, producers of traditional prison films are fully aware of what they are doing when they use set characters, canned scenes, and other conventions. *The Shawshank Redemption,* for instance, is entirely conscious of prison film traditions and deliberately nostalgic for them. However, *Shawshank* exploits those traditions without irony or other commentary, acting as though it is delivering a story untouched by interpretation or artifice. Hollywood has always submerged its self-consciousness about filmmaking in this way, to give viewers illusions of reality. But recently, some moviemakers have brought that self-consciousness to the surface, speaking to audiences more directly about their craft and what it implies about the relation of movie events to prison actualities.

Weeds, for example, playfully spoofs the authenticity claims of traditional prison movies. The chief character, convict Lee Umstetter (Nick Nolte), writes a play about prison life and produces it in prison, using other inmates as actors. When he and the others are paroled, Umstetter reassembles the troupe and takes his play on the road. One ex-con dies; Umstetter replaces him with an actor (played by actor Joe Mantegna) who *pretends* to be an ex-con (and then plays an ex-con actor). The play, *Weeds,* turns out to be plagiarized—Umstetter cribbed it from the work of the (real) playwright Samuel Beckett. Umstetter revises the play to be more "real" (that is, artificial). Nevertheless, a New York City critic pans the production (now a musical about prison life), writing, "Truth may be stranger than fiction, but it will never be more dramatic." In other words, to become good art, reality must be transformed; and art will convey "truth"—persuasive renderings of the experienced world—only through artifice.

*Weeds'*s playful treatment of art-life relationships continues as the ex-cons take their play into a prison, producing it under the watchful eyes of guards who are "real" in the sense of being outside the play (but "unreal" insofar as they are actors in this movie about a prison in which a play is produced). Inspired by Umstetter's speech on injustice, the prisoner-audience riots, "actually" injuring the ex-con actors, and everyone behaves as though they are acting in a prison movie. *Weeds,* then, presents a paradox: We need artifice for a represented event to seem true, and in movies, we get truth only through art.

Self-reflexivity infuses every frame of Oliver Stone's *Natural Born Killers,* a movie dedicated to probing interrelationships among violence, society, and the media. It lampoons babes-in-prison films with shots of Mallory (Juliette Lewis), alone in her cell, wailing the born-bad blues ("I'm baaad, baaad, all baaad"). The callous, sexually repressed warden of traditional prison films reappears here as a hysteric (Tommy Lee Jones), bragging and fulminating while clutching his crotch. The heroic journalist of films such as *Call Northside 777* (1948) and *I Want to Live!* here transmogrifies into Wayne Gale, a tabloid TV star who helps Mickey and Mallory escape from prison and, when they turn on him, poses for and films his own execution. Prisoners watch themselves riot on closed-circuit TV while Mickey, reborn as the convict-who-runs-the-show-from-solitary, engineers the riot-escape with which *Natural Born Killers,* like traditional prison films, culminates. "Stone wants us to note how the medium alters the message," writes *Newsweek* reviewer David Ansen; "he wants to force us to watch ourselves watching a movie."[32] Wayne Gale's camera becomes the movie's camera, so that we watch ourselves watching a movie being filmed by a camera within the movie. If Stone's directorial self-consciousness ultimately says little about how violent media affect violent crime, it nonetheless says a great deal about the variety and ubiquity of media violence today.

Swoon (1991), writer-director Tom Kalin's version of the Leopold and Loeb case, uses different strategies to reach the same goal as *Natural Born Killers:* exploring issues of representation in movies. Although *Swoon* is every bit as stagy and artificial as Alfred Hitchcock's *Rope* (1948),[33] it is profoundly interested in issues of realism and how a film can accurately re-create the past. Insisting on the representation of aspects of the crime that earlier films repressed or sensationalized (such as Leopold and Loeb's sexual relationship), Kalin's film is in some respects more "accurate," while at the same time it reminds us that it itself is simply a fabrication. Representational issues become thematic through repeated references to the acts of seeing and blinding—glasses lost at the crime scene, subterfuges to elude detection, Leopold's decision to will his eyes to a blind woman—leading viewers to ask what a "full" view might mean in a movie. Like *Natural Born Killers, Swoon* deals with time and history, investigating not only how movies represent crimes but also the history of that representation, and *Swoon,* too, constantly interrupts viewers' habitual expectations about plot and illusion to remind us that what we are seeing is "just" a movie. Both films spoof prison film history (*Swoon* partly through a 1920s-like dance number, "When You Wear a Ball and Chain around Your Ankle"), but *Swoon* concludes by summarizing the past, both its own (the previous versions of the Leopold and Loeb story) and that of Leopold and Loeb themselves. Thus, *Swoon,* a quieter, even elegiac film, is equally reflective about its past.

The United States is now concluding the biggest prison-building spree in all history, a binge that, lasting thirty-five years, led to one of the highest incarceration rates in the world and to huge, impersonal institutions disproportionately filled with people of color. In this context, it is increasingly difficult to escape into a world of Hollywood prisons where the good guys look like movie stars and injustices are ultimately repaired. In the face of the new realities of incarceration, feel-goodism grows obsolete.

Producers of prison movies have two choices. One is to continue making genre movies that, while they may substitute women for men, develop a campy edge, or depict futuristic technologies for immobilizing inmates, essentially repeat the formulas of the past. The other is to create critical movies that turn old conventions inside out, self-reflexive films that explore new possibilities in representation, and documentaries that attempt to depict truths of incarceration and execution.[34] Whether we will continue to have two tracks, one for commercial entertainment and the other for political truth-telling, remains to be seen. The two tracks may eventually merge in some way or—more likely—the second, experimental track will eventually develop coherence as new types of prison films accumulate and acquire a clearer identity.

Notes

1. Querry 1973.
2. For a listing of titles, see Parish 1991.
3. Cheatwood (1998) distinguishes "four distinct eras of prison films" (215), but most of the characteristics he attributes to distinct eras in fact run through them all. Thus, it seems best to subsume chronological developments under the headings of cast and theme.
4. *Caged Heat* was director Jonathan Demme's first film.
5. For an analysis of stock characters and themes in four women-in-prison films, see Morey 1995.

6. Due to this theme of control and release, prison films tend to be preoccupied with boundaries and the crossing of boundaries, including those imposed by law, social class, and race. The boundaries become palpable in *One Flew Over the Cuckoo's Nest* (1975), a quasi-prison film in which a con man (Jack Nicholson) arranges a transfer from the penitentiary to a mental institution, where he breaks the glass in the nurse's station and breaches the hospital's walls before hurling himself against one barrier too many.

7. Wood 1992: 477.

8. *Papillon* was based on the autobiography of a French thief, Henri Charrière.

9. This generalization about the scarcity of women-in-prison films evidently applies better to movies made after 1930 than to those produced during the silent era. Such, at any rate, is the impression gained from Ronald Querry's (1973) annotated filmography of prison films released between 1921 and the early 1970s. Querry mentions *Manslaughter* (1922), a Cecil B. DeMille production about a spoiled rich girl who finds redemption in prison; *Midnight Flower* (1923), in which an incarcerated woman falls in love with a minister; *The Lullaby* (1924), in which a man is hanged and his pregnant wife sent to prison; and so on. The degree to which women were featured in silent-era prison films but erased from later prison movies is a matter that deserves research. Since 1990, filmmakers have made more efforts to produce serious films about women in prison, but with questionable success.

10. The literature on the sociology of prisons helped create these characters by identifying a convict type it labeled "real men" or "right men" and defining them as convicts who "pull their own time" and confront their "captors with neither subservience or aggression" (Sykes 1958: 102). Also see Brown 2003: chaps. 5, 27.

11. Gender is a key concern in babes-in-prison films as well, but the characters of such movies are neither superheroes nor admirable ordinary women but rather sex objects. Thus do movies contribute to the construction of gender, in this case by limiting the number and type of roles available to women.

12. *Sleepers's* Father Bobby character echoes *Angels with Dirty Faces,* another film in which the delinquents' buddy is a priest.

13. In *Cool Hand Luke* the buddy is the admiring fellow convict who at the last moment betrays Luke; in *Papillon,* it is the swindler (Dustin Hoffman) who shares Pappy's adventures; in *Midnight Express,* it is the drugged-out prisoner-companion. *The Last Detail* varies the pattern by pairing the two petty officers who conduct the sailor to prison; befriended by them, the sailor becomes a third buddy, and therein lies his salvation. In *Weeds* (1987), a film about prisoners who stage a play, the buddy is the inmate who is closest to the play's author. There is even a buddy in *Brubaker,* the movie about a reform warden; in this case it is the elderly prisoner who gives the new warden advice. (Unfortunately, he is crucified upside down for this act of friendship.) One of the oddest pairings can be found in *Kiss of Death* (1947), in which the thief who wants to go straight is befriended by the district attorney.

14. But see Herman 2003 and 2005, commenting on the normative lesbian viewpoint of the British television drama *Bad Girls* (1999 and following).

15. In reality, prison rapists usually are heterosexuals.

16. Wood 1986: 228 (emphasis in original). Wood is discussing such films as *Butch Cassidy and the Sundance Kid* (1969), *Easy Rider* (1969), *Midnight Cowboy* (1969), *Thunderbolt and Lightfoot* (1974), and *Scarecrow* (1973). For related arguments, see Fuchs 1993 and Sandell 1996. Steve Neale writes, "Male homosexuality is constantly present as an undercurrent, as a potentially troubling aspect of many films and genres, but one that is dealt with obliquely, symptomatically, and that has to be repressed" (1993: 19).

17. Robert Ray points out that the Man with No Eyes is "clearly derived from *Psycho's* [1960] highway patrolman, looming at the window of Janet Leigh's car" (1985: 304).

18. The relationship certainly would be understood that way if one of the characters were female; and it certainly would *not* be so interpreted if the filmmakers had given Andy a girlfriend in the final scene. However, when Red runs toward him on the beach, Andy is alone. Gutterman (2002: 1523) quotes a wonderfully ambiguous explication of the men's relationship by Morgan Freeman: "It's a love affair. They're not in love with each other—they're friends who are interdependent. Its what *Butch Cassidy and the Sundance Kid* and *Thelma & Louise* were about."

19. Wood 1986: 229.

20. Siegel 1993: 157.

21. The content of true prison stories has a built-in urgency that attracts filmmakers interested in social reform and justifies sympathetic views of prisoners. Few filmmakers know the prison world directly; it comes to them (as to most of the rest of us) through news items and celebrated biographies. Thus, true-life narratives provide access to the otherwise inaccessible social milieu of prisons. Moreover, the real-life incidents that make their way into the news and books are often particularly compelling and sensational stories of injustice and brutality—stories with built-in appeal. Edward Montgomery, a Pulitzer-Prize–winning journalist for the *San Francisco Examiner*, was personally involved in Barbara Graham's case and wrote *I Want to Live!* to clear her name. Edward James Olmos, who wrote, acted in, and directed *American Me,* is a crusader on behalf of Los Angeles's Mexican Americans and created the film to warn his people of the destructiveness of gang violence. Robert Redford, the star of *Brubaker* and *The Last Castle,* has long championed liberal causes.

22. As quoted in Clarens 1980: 50.

23. *Point of No Return* is an American version of *La Femme Nikita* (1990).

24. Brown (2003: 10) points to the colonialist and racist dimensions of films such as *Brokedown Palace, Midnight Express,* and *Papillon,* arguing that such "films provide complex intersections of xenophobic fantasies and colonialist desires" and that they "often fram[e] American penality as more civilized, procedural, and just against the backdrop of exotic spectacle."

25. It is surely no coincidence that *Mrs. Soffel,* the only traditional prison film directed by a woman (Gillian Armstrong), concludes with scenes—sympathetic scenes—of a woman in prison (Mrs. Soffel herself, as played by Diane Keaton). *Prison Stories: Women on the Inside* (1991), an excellent made-for-

TV film, consists of three stories, directed by three women (Donna Deitch, Penelope Spheeris, and Joan Micklin Silver). Didi Herman (2003, 2005) sees hope in the British television prison drama *Bad Girls* with its normative lesbian point of view.

26. Surette 1995.

27. Canfield 1994: 62–63.

28. *Blood In, Blood Out* (also known as *Bound by Honor*) (1993), a long-winded epic that deals with themes similar to those of *American Me,* also exemplifies this alternative tradition in prison films.

In a series of incidents that illustrate the complexities of the relationship between film and society, life and art, the release of *American Me* gave rise to considerable violence. Three of Olmos's consultants were killed, and Olmos himself was threatened, in retaliation for the film's negative portrayal of *la Eme.* When gang members were subsequently tried for these crimes, the letter *M* mysteriously appeared on the judge's bench, despite round-the-clock surveillance of the courtroom by the U.S. Marshall's office. *La Eme* apparently decided that because the movie hurt its image, it would kill the filmmakers—which would be like members of the Kennedy family who disliked the movie *JFK* deciding to kill director Oliver Stone and star Kevin Costner. The retaliation suggests a confusion of film with life and actually confirms the movie's point about *la Eme* and its destructive violence. In this sequence of events, art represented life, and then life reproduced art.

29. Williams 1993: 11.

30. Ibid.: 12.

31. Ibid.: 15.

32. Ansen 1994: 54.

33. *Swoon*'s opening sequence, in which actors/characters move past the camera as if facing an audience from a stage, refers explicitly to *Rope,* which was based on a play and filmed like one.

34. But see Dow 2000, arguing, essentially, that this is impossible.

7 | The Heroes of Crime Films

Let's try to figure out who the bad guy is, all right?
—Mr. Pink in *Reservoir Dogs*

There's something heroic about him. He doesn't look like a killer. He comes across as calm, acts like he had a dream, eyes full of passion.
—Police officer speaking of the assassin he is hunting in John Woo's *The Killer*

Of the many reasons for the popularity of crime films, the most potent lies with the nature of their heroes. Viewers delight in watching characters who can escape from tight spots and outsmart their enemies, all the while tossing down scotch and flipping jibes. Good-guy heroes please us by out-tricking the tricky, facing down psychos, solving impossible mysteries. Bad-guy heroes appeal by being bolder, nastier, crueler, and tougher than we dare to be; by saying what they want, taking what they desire, despising weaklings, and breaking the law with impunity. Both good-guy and bad-guy heroes operate on the basis of austere, unambiguous moral codes that are as bracing as they are simplistic and brutal. When Lily, the elegant racetrack swindler of *The Grifters* (1990), summons a physician to treat her sick son, she advises him, "My son is going to be all right. If not, I'll have you killed." We may smile, but we may also envy, if only a little, the unadorned directness of Lily's approach.

Hollywood gives us more than heroes; it gives us ideas about heroes and the nature of heroism. Why do we revere the powerful instead of the weak (who, after all, struggle more in life)? Why do we admire reckless adventurers more than homemakers, the brash more than the timid? Above all, why do we savor heroes who constantly break the law? Traits glorified by films and other media constitute a kind of ideology of heroism, a set of assumptions about what *admirable* means.

Types of Crime Film Narratives

To build a comprehensive typology of crime film heroes, we need first to create a typology of the kinds of stories that can be found in movies of this type. Eight kinds of narrative (which can also be thought of as patterns in plot development)[1] turn up time and again: the mystery or detective story; the thriller; the caper or heist; the tale of justice violated/justice restored; the disguised Western, in which an outsider saves the victim or threatened community; tales of revenge and vigilantism; chronicles of criminal careers; and the episodic plots of action stories. The types sometimes overlap or combine with one another, but these eight constitute the essential narrative patterns that one finds in the majority of crime films.

In *mystery and detective stories,* the basic pattern is that of the search. These tales have what David Bordwell and Kristin Thompson call "goal-oriented plots," patterns of action to which investigation is key.[2] Mysteries and detective films often mete out clues in small, progressive portions, so that the viewer's process of discovery parallels the investigator's.[3] Sometimes (e.g., *Sea of Love* [1989], *Minority Report* [2002]) they conceal the object of the search, such as the villain's identity, as long as possible. (At these times mysteries and detective films may overlap with thrillers, as in *Rear Window* [1954].) At other times the goal of the search is clear from the start, and the investigator's job is to find the thing that is missing. In mysteries, especially, the crime may have been committed before the film starts (so to speak), so there is minimal violence on screen and lots of puzzling over clues.[4] In both mysteries and detective stories, the search can be for a person (as in *The Limey* [1999]), a thing (as in *The Maltese Falcon* [1941], where the hunted object is a valuable statuette, and *Kiss Me Deadly* [1955], where it turns out to be uranium), or even an intangible, such as the source of corruption in a family (*The Official Story* [1985]) or a police department (*L.A. Confidential* [1997]). Most private investigator and cop films fall into this category, which includes *Bad Day at Black Rock* (1954), *Chinatown* (1974), *Fargo* (1996), *The Long Goodbye* (1973), and *Witness* (1985).

Thrillers toy with us, leading viewers to expect violence at points where it does not occur and bludgeoning us with brutality when we least expect it.[5] These nail-biters frequently involve a chase in which the central character is pursued by a figure who is in some respect horrifying. In one of the classic thrillers, director Charles Laughton's

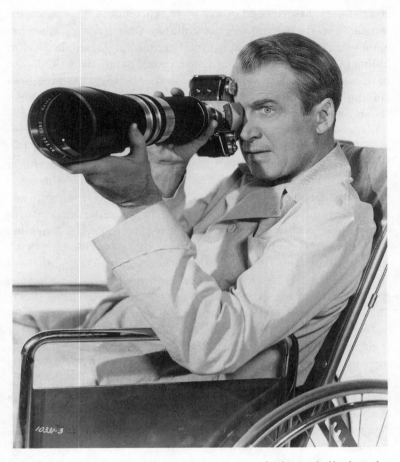

Figure 7.1. Although L. B. Jeffries (James Stewart), the hero of Alfred Hitchcock's *Rear Window* (1954), is immobilized by a leg cast, he is able to uncover a murder and catch the killer. The film combines the detective plot with that of the thriller but can also be read as a psychosexual study. Photo used by permission of Photofest.

Night of the Hunter (1955), the first pursued character is the young widow who has been tricked into a new marriage by a fortune hunter posing as a preacher. Laughton shows us the preacher with a knife, falling on Willa in bed, but then fades to an ice cream shop, where the preacher is moaning to the proprietors about how Willa took off in the night in his old Model T. Suddenly, with no transition, Laughton shocks us with an underwater shot of Willa's body floating among river grasses, hair combed gently by the currents. At that point, the pursued become the widow's two children, who, having stashed her money in a doll, flee the phony preacher. Paddling down the river or hiding in its banks, the children (and viewers) occasionally think they have made it to safety, only to hear, in the distance, the preacher's chilling song, "Leaning on Jesus, leaning on the light that shines above." By the film's end, just a few notes of this song can terrify.

Because thrillers need to repeat shocks to maintain their nightmarish quality, they tend to be episodic. In another classic of this type, *North by Northwest* (1959), director Alfred Hitchcock puts Roger Thornhill (Cary Grant) through a series of frights, starting with being kidnapped, proceeding through a chase by a crop-dusting airplane, and ending with a literal cliff-hanger. Hitchcock understood that audiences love to be scared, and scared at regular intervals. A number of his films fall into the thriller category (*Dial M for Murder* [1954], *Rear Window, Rope* [1948], *Strangers on a Train* [1951], and, above all, *Psycho* [1960]). Thrillers by other directors include *Basic Instinct* (1992), *Fatal Attraction* (1987), *The Firm* (1993), *House of Games* (1987), *The Last Seduction* (1994), and *Marathon Man* (1976).

More leisurely in pace, the *caper* or *heist* film follows a criminal or criminal group planning a complicated, audacious theft that will set them up for life. The first part of a caper movie is usually consumed by scheming, with the leader rounding up the gang and targeting the bank, racetrack, rich Texan, or train that is to be robbed, after which everyone practices with stopwatches and getaway cars. The remainder is devoted to the execution of the crime and, in many cases, the criminals' last-minute failure, although, delightfully, *Bound* (1996), *Ocean's Eleven* (2001), and *Ocean's Twelve* (2004) let their thieves escape at least the worst consequences of their crimes.[6] Less successful but more typical are the thieves in *The Asphalt Jungle* (1950), John Huston's dark and brooding caper in which the hooligan dies unfulfilled, and of Stanley Kubrick's *The Killing* (1956), in which the suitcase full of money flaps open as the gang's leader boards the plane to escape. One of the best of all caper films is Don Siegel's *The Killers* (1964), starring Ronald Reagan as the criminal mastermind, Lee Marvin as the sneering assassin, and Angie Dickinson as the bait, and involving a prodigious number of cars. An ironic variant on the caper, *Reservoir Dogs* (1992) concentrates on the aftermath of a failed caper, during which the robbers squabble over "who the bad guy is."

Justice violated/justice restored movies, in which the main character has been falsely accused or is being unjustly punished, begin with scenes demonstrating the unfairness and emphasizing, through settings of enclosure and oppression, that the injustice is likely to last for a very long time.[7] Through a plot device such as a jailbreak or unexpected discovery of the true villain, the main character finally breaks free of the unjust situation and is recognized (by the audience, at least) as a much maligned, long-suffering hero. Many prison films fall into the justice violated/justice restored category, including *Escape from Alcatraz* (1979), *In the Name of the Father* (1993), *Midnight Express* (1978), and *Papillon* (1973). In execution films such as *I Want to Live!* (1958), release is achieved through the protagonist's death, and the recognition of true virtue comes after the fact, through the filmmakers' and audience's sense of loss. Courtroom films, too, sometimes fall into the justice violated/justice restored category. *Presumed Innocent* (1990), for instance, chronicles the trials of lawyer Rusty Sabich as he defends himself against a false murder charge. Although he is eventually exonerated, he is unable to reveal the identity of the true killer; thus, his relief remains partial, and our admiration rests in part on his sorrowful determination to maintain the secret.

More unusual as a justice violated/justice restored film is *Dolores Claiborne* (1995), the story of a tight-lipped, truculent woman (Kathy Bates) who lives on an island in Maine and is suspected of murdering both her wealthy employer and, years earlier, her own husband. In this case the sense of enclosure is provided by the island setting, the false accusations, and Dolores's inability to speak the truth. Release comes when the investigators discover Dolores's actual devotion to her employer and when her sullen daughter (Jennifer Jason Leigh) realizes that Dolores fought the father to protect the girl from sexual abuse. Dolores Claiborne is redeemed by the recognition that she is the opposite of what she seemed to be.

Although the old-fashioned Western has faded in popularity, its narrative line has migrated to other genres, turning up there as *disguised Westerns:* tales in which a heroic outsider reluctantly consents to clean up some equivalent of Dodge. A number of courtroom films conform to this pattern. *Witness for the Prosecution* (1957), for example, begins by introducing the ailing barrister who seems too feeble to handle a murder case; once persuaded of the defendant's innocence, however, he revives and saves the day (mistakenly, as it turns out, but because we leave him charging off to the next showdown, the error does not diminish his heroism). *Judgment at Nuremberg* (1961), *To Kill a Mockingbird* (1962), and *Sleepers* (1996) also feature outsiders—men different from and better than the majority—who decide to join the fray and in so doing become saviors.

Some police and prison films qualify as disguised Westerns: *Cop Land* (1997), in which Sylvester Stallone's sad-sack cop cleans up a suburban police department full of violent glamour boys; *RoboCop* (1987), in which an outsider to the human species cleans up Detroit; and *Angels with Dirty Faces* (1938),[8] in which the gangster on his way to the death chamber saves the juvenile delinquents. Callie Khouri, the author of *Thelma and Louise* (1991), playfully inverts the disguised Western by creating outsiders who intrude upon an actual Western landscape from the domestic realm (Thelma is a housewife, Louise a waitress) and, in the process of getting even with the bad guys, shoot a few holes in Western movie conventions as well.

Revenge and vigilante movies derive from the Elizabethan revenge play, in which the lead figure (such as Hamlet, prince of Denmark) discovers a violation (of himself, his family, or his country) and retaliates. More immediately, as Will Wright points out, revenge and vigilante plots derive from a variation on the Western in which the outsider who decides to clean up Dodge is less interested in upholding a principle than in settling a personal grudge.[9] As in *Cape Fear* (1962, 1991), *Straw Dogs* (1972), and *The Star Chamber* (1983), revenge and vigilante films tend to feature scenes of stalking.

Murder in the First (1995), in which a brutalized prisoner seeks legal redress, is a revenge film with a courtroom setting, as is *The Accused* (1988), in which the outraged victim demands accountability from the men who cheered while she was raped. Cop films are occasionally cast in the revenge mold: *Sudden Impact* (1983), for instance, deals with a woman who, to avenge herself and her sister for being raped, goes around shooting men. The revenge/vigilante form sometimes combines with other plot types. *Taxi Driver* (1976), for example, merges the vigilante plot (Travis as political assassin) with that of the disguised Western (Travis as New York City's street cleaner), while *Falling Down* (1993) marries the revenge plot, embodied in the trajectory of vigilante D-Fens, with that of the detective story, embodied in the hunt for D-Fens by an about-to-retire police officer. *Natural Born Killers* (1994), too, introduces the revenge plot from

time to time, partly as a narrative device and partly as an explanation for Mickey and Mallory's violence.[10]

Crime films' most common type of narrative is the *chronicle of a criminal career*. Originating with gangster films, this category includes nearly
all examples of that genre, as well as more recent mob movies such as
the *Godfather* series (1972, 1974, 1990), *Goodfellas* (1990), and *Donnie
Brasco* (1997). The category also encompasses many noirs (*Double Indemnity* [1944], *Detour* [1945], *Night and the City* [1950]), crime-spree
couple films (*Gun Crazy* [1949], *Normal Life* [1996]), street gang stories
(*Menace II Society* [1993], *New Jack City* [1991]), and tales of corrupt
cops (*Q & A* [1990], *Romeo Is Bleeding* [1993]). These tales of underworld life, starting with the assumption that criminality is a normal
condition, often do not bother to explain how their characters went
astray but rather begin (sometimes spectacularly) with a violation of
the law. (Caper films, too, focus on criminal acts, but they are concerned with a single major crime, not the protagonist's career.) Sometimes, as in *The Talented Mr. Ripley* (1999) and *Catch Me If You Can*
(2002), the protagonist is an upper-class crook.

The eighth story type, the *action film,* overlaps thematically with
some of the other categories but is distinctive in its narrative quality.

Figure 7.2. *New Jack City* (1991) stars Wesley Snipes as an organized crime
boss. With the advent of movies with all-black or mostly black casts, African
Americans gained access to the culturally valuable image of the outlaw
hero. Photo used by permission of Photofest.

Lacking shapely plots, action films string together a series of episodes, marking transitions with fights and explosions. While they are violent, their violence is deployed less to terrify the audience (as in thrillers) than to create spectacles. Films of this type can be sorted almost endlessly into such subcategories as James Bond movies, the *Die Hards* (1988, 1990, 1995), the *Lethal Weapon* series (1987, 1989, etc.), hostage and takeover movies, airplane films, and so on. Few are fraught with meaning, but the better ones, as Peter Parshall argues in an analysis of *Die Hard,* assume a mythic quality by following an epic hero "into the underworld to battle with dark forces" that represent, among other things, the uncivilized elements in his own nature.[11]

In addition to these eight main types of crime film stories, there are a few minor forms such as the *bildungsroman* or account of the moral development of a central character (*Boyz N the Hood* [1991], A *Place in the Sun* [1951], *A Few Good Men* [1992]).[12] Moreover, some crime films do not fit easily into any narrative category.[13] But the eight categories are sufficiently inclusive and discrete from one another to provide a foundation for analyzing crime films by types of heroes.

Types of Crime Film Heroes

The simplest way to classify crime film heroes is to distinguish between official heroes (or good good guys) on the one hand and outlaw heroes (or bad good guys) on the other. Film scholar Robert B. Ray observes that the official hero is often cast as a farmer, lawyer, politician, or teacher. Stalwarts of their communities, official heroes stand for law and constructive, law-abiding behavior. Crime film examples include the district attorney of *Manhattan Melodrama* (1934), the almost-retired cop of *Falling Down,* and the heroic lawyers of classic courtroom dramas. In contrast, the outlaw hero, whom Ray identifies as a loner—an adventurer, explorer, or gunfighter—stands for "that part of the American imagination valuing self-determination and freedom from entanglements."[14] Individualistic and anarchic, outlaw heroes represent the freedom to do what one wants, including commit crime. Examples include D-Fens, the angry white male of *Falling Down;* the conscienceless femme fatale of *The Last Seduction;* and Michael Corleone, the gangster hero of the *Godfather* series.

In crime films, outlaw heroes far outnumber the official heroes. Moreover, movies often spend much more time developing the characters of outlaw heroes and encouraging viewers to identify with them. These tendencies raise a question: Why do crime films want us to identify with outlaws, and why do we enjoy complying?

To answer this question in depth, we need first to refine our terms. Ray and others who discuss the official hero/outlaw hero distinction are usually referring to American movies in general (or to American movies and novels in general), not to crime films in particular, and certainly not to subdivisions within the crime films category. In speaking more specifically about crime films, it is useful to make finer distinctions before turning to issues raised by outlaw heroes and to oppositional values they embody.

The central challenge faced by the heroes of *mystery and detective stories,* as we have seen, is to solve a puzzle: to discover whodunit and where the perpetrator is hiding. As a direct result of this plot type, these heroes are typically clever, persistent, imaginative, and adept. They would make ideal parent figures if they were older and less distracted by crime, for there is no problem they cannot solve. The heroes of mysteries and detective films are often amateurs or eccentrics (*The Conversation* [1974], *The Lady Vanishes* [1938], *Sudden Fear* [1952]) while those of detective films are more likely to be fighters, but otherwise there are few systematic differences. When the detective is actually a police officer, as in, for example, *Dirty Harry* (1971), his or her immediate ancestor is the lead character of Westerns such as *The Wild Bunch* (1969) that feature "professionals"—heroes who are paid to fight for law and justice.[15]

Thrillers depict their heroes as ordinary people who are suddenly thrust into a nightmarish predicament. These protagonists keep a half step ahead of the horror through acumen, inventiveness, resolve, and dexterity—traits common to heroes of this type—but eventually realize that to escape with their lives, they must trap and kill the beast. Thus, we also admire them for their willingness to face the darkness, to engage in mortal combat (even though violence does not come naturally to them), and to win. Because they are tormented before they triumph, thriller protagonists fall into the category that Carol Clover calls "victim heroes," a type that can accommodate female as well as male heroes.[16] Victim heroes turn up often in psychopath movies.

Among the most engaging of crime film protagonists, the heroes of *capers* are the ones who plan the heist, assemble the team, and keep the vault blueprints in their back pockets. They are heroic because they are ambitious, smart, and superb planners, but more than that, they are admirable for the sheer audacity of their plans, the scale of their greed and presumption. True princes of the underworld, they operate with a regal sense of entitlement, a confidence that they were born to boss their underlings around and commandeer other people's money.

The lead characters in *justice violated/justice restored* films are admirable for their patience, superhuman endurance, and ability to overcome all obstacles (eventually). Sometimes they are victim heroes (as in the case of Dolores Claiborne); more often, they are compromised characters, guilty of something but undeserving of the suffering they currently endure. (Rusty Sabich of *Presumed Innocent* had an extramarital affair with the dead woman; Gerry Conlon of *In the Name of the Father* burglarized houses and was disrespectful to his dad; Barbara Graham of *I Want to Live!* was a floozy.) Capable of growth and change, these heroes tend to become magnanimous and incorruptible.

The leads of *disguised Westerns* are best conceptualized as *outsider heroes,* a term that emphasizes their differentness without implying illegality. These outsider heroes fight for the sake of the group. Unlike the more self-absorbed leads of justice violated/justice restored films, they act on principle, deciding to intervene because it is the right thing to do. Atticus Finch, the rape victim of *The Accused,* and the leads of other disguised Westerns are closely related to the traditional Western hero; like him, they are brave, self-sacrificing, lonely (many are widowed or separated), melancholy, and proud. They, too, are fighters, though they prefer other weapons than guns. (This is true even in *Serpico* [1973] and *Cop Land,* where the outsider heroes are police officers.) More perspicacious than their friends and colleagues, they recognize trouble where others are blind to it, and when they are headed for death, they foresee their fate (e.g., *Cool Hand Luke* [1967]). These heroes have more integrity than the protagonists of any other type of crime film. Pure, like the archetypal Westerner described by Robert Warshow, they value honor and nobility.[17]

Like outsider heroes, the protagonists of *revenge and vigilante movies* are slow to anger; unlike outsider heroes, avengers pursue the bad guys for intensely personal reasons. Patient, calculating, and implacable, avengers may nurse their anger over many years of preparation for the final battle. When the target of their fury is relatively abstract, avengers may commit the act of retaliation repeatedly, turning the plot in the direction of action films. For example, the nurse played by Pam Grier in *Coffy* (1973) is enraged by street drugs, which have crippled her kid sister and led to the death of a friend; her form of retribution consists of shooting drug dealers in her off hours, which she does over and over, from the first scene to the last.

The central characters in *chronicles of criminal careers* are *criminal heroes,* a label that stresses the heroes' break with lawful society and their self-acceptance as offenders. The criminal hero's traits were first defined by gangster movies, which portrayed him (rarely her) as brutal, individualistic, ambitious, and doomed.[18] As Robert Warshow argues, the gangster must ultimately be a failure, not only to absolve viewers who have identified with his earlier successes but also because "the gangster is the 'no' to that great American 'yes' which is stamped so big over our official culture," the pessimistic note at the celebration of success, the dark figure hovering at the edge of one's consciousness.[19]

Over time the criminal-hero category expanded to embrace the shady detectives of film noir, lovers on the lam, cops on the take, and drug lords. It incorporated the tendency, seen in bad-good-guy Westerns such as *The Wild Bunch,* to show morally compromised heroes, hired guns who were less thoroughly heroic than traditional cowboys such as Shane. Today's criminal heroes crave and enjoy power; bolder and more imaginative than ordinary people, they dare to violate boundaries that the rest of us observe. They gamble on being bad, aware of the risks but preferring to die infamous rather than unknown. Doing what we might like to do, they act with a freedom we are afraid to assume. As a result, we admire them, and when they die, we have a sense of loss and waste. The most interesting criminal heroes—Cody Jarrett of *White Heat* (1949), Thelma and Louise, Michael Corleone—destroy themselves either literally or figuratively, thus becoming tragic heroes. We know that they will do themselves in, and it is this knowledge that enables us to enjoy their crimes. An audience, Robert Sklar points out, "can like a bad man who it knows is doomed."[20]

The protagonists of *action crime films,* the final narrative category, are superheroes. Capable of scaling elevator shafts and performing mechanical wonders while hanging beneath a careening bus, of dodging machine-gun bullets and emerging from explosions unsmudged, action heroes are unflappable, invulnerable, and unbelievable. The plots in which they appear leave little time for character development or the exposure of human qualities beyond machismo and sex appeal.

Table 7.1 Crime Film Heroes by Plot Type

Hero type	Plot type
Sleuths	Mysteries and detective stories
Victim heroes	Thrillers
Criminal masterminds	Capers and heist films
Mistreated heroes	Tales of justice violated/justice restored
Outsider heroes	Disguised Westerns
Avengers	Revenge and vigilante stories
Criminal heroes	Chronicles of criminal careers
Superheroes	Action crime movies

Crime films, then, have a wide range of heroes: the sleuths of mysteries and detective stories; the victim heroes who in thrillers slay the dragons and banish nightmares; the criminal masterminds of caper films; the mistreated heroes of justice violated/justice restored movies; the outsider heroes of disguised Westerns; the avengers of revenge and vigilante stories; the criminal heroes of chronicles that follow an offender's career; and the superheroes of action crime films. These hero types are summarized in table 7.1.

The traditional distinction between official heroes and outlaw heroes is not particularly useful in the case of crime films, partly because official heroes are few in number and partly because the outlaw-hero category is so broad that it makes distinctions among crime film heroes difficult. Thus, when analyzing the nature of crime film heroes, it is useful to subdivide the traditional outlaw-hero category as I have done here, distinguishing between *outsider heroes* (the protagonists of disguised Westerns) and *criminal heroes* (the central figures in chronicles of criminal careers). It is in the criminal hero (and at this point I would also include in this group the masterminds of caper or heist films) that one finds crime films' unique contribution to the pantheon of movie protagonists—the hero to whom we are drawn even though (or perhaps because) she or he is harmful. Viewers' manifest fondness for this hero type leads directly to the issue of value conflicts in crime films.

Value Conflicts in Crime Films

Crime films deal with value conflicts that permeate our culture: tensions between selfishness and commitment to others, violation and obedience, freedom and responsibility, promiscuity and fidelity, force and persuasion. Indeed, audiences choose crime films partly because these movies illustrate moral clashes with which people deal on a daily basis. To depict value conflicts, movies sometimes pit an official hero against an outsider or criminal hero (*Manhattan Melodrama, Falling Down*), but more frequently they concentrate on the bad guy, sketchily indicating the opposite set of values through lesser characters (Betsy, the unattainable girlfriend in *Taxi Driver,* for instance, or the feds who chase Cody Jarrett in *White Heat*). In both cases, crime films tend to organize value conflicts around two poles, one represented by the criminal, the other by the good citizen (represented or implied). While crime films differ in the tensions they emphasize, the values associated with the two poles remain fairly consistent across movies, as follows:

the criminal	*the good citizen*
lawlessness	conformity
freedom	constraint
violence	peace
danger	safety
cruelty	kindness
cynicism	idealism
guilt	innocence
autonomy	commitment
integrity	compromise
spontaneity	deliberation
sassy repartee	polite speech
subculture	dominant culture
adventure	routine
courage	timidity
life	spiritual death
youth	age
masculinity	femininity
mean streets	hearth and home
broads	old ladies
strength	weakness
wise guys	saps

Here is one answer to the question "Why do we enjoy identifying with movie criminals?" While neither pole has a monopoly on virtue, it is not hard to tell which is preferable. Moreover, crime films, like other texts that create value oppositions, work a bit like matted seaweed: Lift one strand and you lift them all. For experienced moviegoers, each term in one of the columns implies the others, so that when viewers see wise guys and mean streets, they expect to find broads and guns as well.

Rather than forcing us to choose between the qualities associated with "the criminal" and "the good citizen," the value structure of crime films enables us to shuttle back and forth, to have it both ways. In one common pattern, these movies induce us to identify with the hero till near the film's end, at which point they have the hero shot by a good-citizen type. This turn of events (and others like it) lets viewers off the hook. We can savor the dangers of the streets *and* the safety of the home, the excitement of violence *and* the pleasures of peace. Movies with criminal heroes, then, do not so much reject the law as embody ambivalence about it and, in their conclusions, temporarily lay that ambivalence to rest.

This resolution of value conflicts is what Robert Warshow was thinking of in his seminal essay "The Gangster as Tragic Hero" when he wrote that "the final bullet thrusts him [the gangster] back, makes him, after all, a failure."[21] Like the gangster, Warshow explains, we are all under pressure to succeed, even while we know that our efforts will be undone by death. "The effect of the gangster film is to embody this dilemma in the person of the gangster and resolve it by his death. The dilemma is resolved because it is *his* death, not ours. We are safe."[22] Criminal heroes play out and temporarily alleviate some of our most profound anxieties. We keep coming back to crime films because they enact struggles that divide us as individuals and as a society. Valuing both sides of the struggle, we feel regret when the bad guys are killed, but we also understand that they must be wiped out.

Fabricating Criminal Heroes

How do movies go about turning criminals into heroes? What steps do they take to help us identify with characters who, outside the film, we might cross the street to avoid? Much depends on the persona of the actor, on his or her ability to simultaneously project two contradictory messages (I am despicable, I am delightful), as critics began to discover as early as 1931 with the release of *Public Enemy*. This was one of the first talkies to depict the career of a thoroughly bad man (the mobster Tom Powers, portrayed by James Cagney). Critics of the day understood that Cagney was crucial to the movie's success. One wrote:

> I doubt there is an actor extant who could have done what James Cagney does with the extraordinary character of Tom Powers. . . . He does not hesitate to represent Tom Powers as a complete rat—with a rat's sense of honor, a rat's capacity for human love; and when cornered, a rat's fighting courage. And what is more, although his role is consistently unsympathetic, Mr. Cagney manages to earn for Tom Powers the audience's affection and esteem.[23]

In later bad-guy roles, Cagney again demonstrated this gift for keeping criminal characters charming; it was his greatest asset as a star.

The creation of successful criminal heroes further depends on the fit between the criminal's characteristics and current concepts of glamour; Tom Powers's character, for example, responded to the public's fascination with Al Capone, a figure who stood for business success, lavish consumption, an exhilarating lifestyle, and urban culture as well as rebellion against the law.[24] On the other hand, many heroes of early movies (the good-guy lead in *The Criminal Code* [1931], for instance) seem ridiculous today. The scriptwriter's ability to camouflage flaws and create other characters who, by contrast, make the criminal seem worthy also plays a role, as does the use of setting, camera angles, color, and music. To exemplify the elements involved in the fabrication of criminal heroes, it is useful to examine *Bonnie and Clyde* (1967) in some detail.

Based on the true story of three companions who went on a bank-robbing spree through the Southwest during the Great Depression, *Bonnie and Clyde* adheres in many respects to what is known about the historical figures. (The actors' poses replicate those in photographs of the original Bonnie and Clyde, for instance.) In terms of characterization, however, the film departs radically from the originals. The historical Clyde Barrow was gay, apparently,[25] and at first he traveled with not only Bonnie Parker but also his male lover. Getting rid of the lover, the movie replaces him with the sexually uninspired C. W. Moss and reduces Clyde's homosexuality to impotence. ("I'm no lover boy," Clyde warns when, fifteen minutes after their first encounter, Bonnie jumps him.) Ordinarily, a film would find it difficult to present an impotent man as heroic; in this case, however, Warren Beatty's off-screen reputation as a Don Juan counterbalances Clyde's impotence. Moreover, Clyde in a sense becomes Beatty in the course of the film, developing a love for Bonnie that flowers in sexual success in one of the final scenes. As Richard Maltby observes, "A convincing performance is . . . one in which the character becomes the star persona as the movie progresses."[26] By the end of *Bonnie and Clyde,* the gap between Clyde Barrow and Warren Beatty has closed.

At the time of the movie's release, Faye Dunaway was an unknown, but her extraordinary beauty and svelte coolness did much to glamorize Bonnie Parker; and director Arthur Penn took full advantage of Dunaway's appearance from the first shot, in which her mouth, luscious with lipstick, fills the screen. Dunaway and Beatty both proved adept at expressing contradictory emotions, especially conflicts between their delight in being wicked and their suspicion that robbing banks was not a good idea. Thus, as in the case of Cagney's mob films, in *Bonnie and Clyde* the actors contribute strongly to the iconography of heroism.

This was the right film at the right time, as noted in chapter 1, in that it gave the rebellious youth of the period heroes with whom they could instantly identify. Bonnie was Clyde's equal in crime, and more than his equal in bed, at a time when the budding women's movement was calling for gender and sexual equality. The film explicitly contrasts Bonnie with more traditional women, as personified by Blanche (Estelle Parsons), Clyde's silly, screamy sister-in-law. That the

Figure 7.3. *Bonnie and Clyde* (1967) emphasizes its roots in the real-life story of Depression-era bank robbers while also fashioning new heroes for the 'sixties generation. Some viewers modeled their own behavior on that of the movie characters, in the process illustrating the complex interactions between crime film and society.

film's protagonists stole from banks and did so with guns made them appealing in the 1960s, a period in which some middle-class youths dreamed of leading a violent revolution that would wipe out capitalism. (According to reports, at the Hollywood premiere someone in the audience, in full-throttle identification with the protagonists, angrily shouted out, "Fucking cops!")[27] In an era of ubiquitous peace symbols, Bonnie and Clyde further appealed by occasionally devising alternatives to violence, as when they decide not to shoot the Texas Ranger who almost captures them but rather to pose with him in a photograph that they release to the press. *Bonnie and Clyde* was initially panned by mainstream critics, who deplored its violence ("the most gruesome carnage since Verdun," one wrote),[28] but poor reviews from stuffy authority figures endeared the movie to the younger generation, and in any case it survived to become a box-office marvel and win two Oscars. The social context in which the movie was released, then, contributed to Bonnie and Clyde's stature as heroes, just as in the late twentieth century the aging of baby boomers contributed to the popularity of "mature" actors such as Harrison Ford.

But the key factor in the movie's success was the way viewers empathized with Bonnie and Clyde. That audiences were able to identify with what were, after all, two long-dead punks arose from the scriptwriters' skillful downplaying of the characters' negative traits and emphasis on their virtues. Clyde is a model of gallantry (when he first kills someone, he offers to take Bonnie home so she can avoid a murder charge); they are loyal and sensitive to one another's vulnerabilities; and, when they know death is in on the way, they remain defiant. Brave and inventive (as during the final motel escape), Bonnie and Clyde are also smarter, more sophisticated, and more playful than the other characters.

The screenwriters create foils to make the protagonists shine all the brighter: comic characters such as Blanche, C. W. Moss, and the courting couple, Eugene and Velma, who briefly join the gang; and bad guys such as the bounty-hunting Texas Ranger and C. W.'s hypocrite of a father. Yet other characters exist simply to admire Bonnie and Clyde ("Is that really Bonnie Parker?" whispers a resident of the shantytown where they stop to treat their wounds). Although they are violent, the film does everything it can to dull the sting of their violence: They rob banks, not poor people; they are essentially innocents ("He tried to kill me!" an astonished Clyde reports); they refrain from shooting the bounty hunter who later helps gun them down;

they are killed because they stop to help C. W.'s treacherous father. The bad guys are older, overweight, rednecky, and mean-spirited. In sum, the film carefully structures its value oppositions to ensure that we identify with and relish its criminal heroes.

Mythic elements further enhance the heroes' stature. Bonnie and Clyde are Robin Hoods who steal only from the rich. They are Davids fighting the Goliath of "the laws" who pursue them. Such mythologizing would become cloying if the film did not undercut its own romanticism with a subtext about playacting. Nearly every character is to some extent a ham actor, constantly trying on new roles, mugging for an audience.

For example, at first Bonnie cannot get her tone right, torn as she is between attraction to Clyde and a desire to play the lady. Indulging her posturing, Clyde responds, "I bet you're a movie star." He is loath to have her seem a *cheap* movie star, however, so he instructs her to get rid of a spit curl when he notices a waitress with a similar hairdo. He wants Bonnie to play the role, but he wants her to get it right.

Other members of the Barrow gang and even the cops who pursue them are also poseurs, trying on and discarding new identities like costumes. Blanche, the movie's ultimate in inauthenticity, is never at ease with herself, at first acting with ultrapropriety, as she thinks wives should behave, later parading in riding britches with a whip like a lion-tamer. In one very quick shot, a police officer brags into the camera, "And there I was staring square into the face of death!" Clyde and his brother Buck, awkward with silences, maintain a show of whoopee fun—a tone that the kidnapped couple Eugene and Velma adopt instinctively. Clyde's entire persona turns out to be a show, as we discover during a somber late scene when he weaves an optimistic yarn about the future for Bonnie's mother. The movie, by giving so many examples of playacting (and the list could go on), comments ironically on its own patina of vivacity, the heroic imagery with which it burnishes the gang members' characters.

Arthur Penn's emphasis on playacting underscores his interpretation of Bonnie and Clyde: that they became outlaws to achieve a measure of immortality. Bonnie writes her own "Ballad of Bonnie and Clyde," and Clyde compliments her by remarking, "You made me somebody they're going to remember." They are criminals who construct their own mythology. To highlight the protagonists' awareness of making their own meaning, the filmmakers include several characters who are incapable of artifice, chiefly C. W. Moss, who although he is completely wrapped up in the mythology of Bonnie and Clyde is also bluntly unselfconscious, and Bonnie's mother, the movie's truth-sayer. The opening sequence of old photographs associates the protagonists' posturing with clicks that could come from a gun trigger, a camera shutter, or both, thus framing the film and its violence as a self-conscious construct. As a result, if we notice Penn mythologizing, or if like Bonnie we notice that Clyde has come to believe his own lies, we are unlikely to hold it against them.[29]

Setting, camera angles, color, and music work together to increase the heroic qualities of Bonnie and Clyde. The setting—rural Texas in the early 1930s—distances the story, indicating that we don't need to take the protagonists' criminality too seriously, a point accentuated by the raucous bluegrass music. Until near the end, *Bonnie and Clyde* is suffused with a golden glow, its colors warm, sunny, and benign. This impression of amiability is accented by "Foggy Mountain Breakdown," the Flatt and Scruggs banjo tune that accompanies the chase scenes; high-spirited, fast, exuberant, it forms a musical equivalent to the characters. (Clyde: "You're not going to have a moment's peace." Bonnie: "You promise?") The camera looks up at Bonnie and Clyde, increasing their stature, and close-ups magnify their features to mythic dimensions.

As the end approaches, however, the camera distances itself from the protagonists, helping viewers disengage before the death scene. At the same time, we begin to get some scenes that exclude the main characters and give others' points of view. The dunes scene, in which Bonnie says farewell to her mother and both she and Clyde realize that "we ain't heading to nowhere," uses a blue filter and blurs the images so as to locate Bonnie and Clyde in a melancholy past; during it, many characters wear black. It is followed by a scene in which the couple's car is shot to pieces by "the laws," forecasting their own fate. Bonnie's ballad, too foretells their end ("but it's death for Bonnie and Clyde"). Even while preparing viewers for the slaughter, however, Penn makes sure we will experience a sense of loss: More devoted than ever, the couple become increasingly pure as their enemies grow in malevolence. In the final scene, as Robert Ray points out, "the heroes' white clothes and car and the sudden flight of birds [make] the massacre seem to violate nature itself."[30]

Crime Films without Heroes

A few crime films—usually those that fall in what I have been term-
ing the alternative or critical tradition—have lead characters who are
neither good good guys nor bad good guys but rather no-good bad
guys, men and women devoid of redeeming traits. If we categorize
crime film protagonists according to their degrees of criminality, as
in table 7.2, these no-good bad guys are nonheroes, figures designed
to thwart our thirst for characters better than ourselves. Nonheroes
bring us up short, forcing us to examine our expectations of movies,
refusing to gratify any hope we may have of enjoying fantasies of
heroism. Films in which the protagonist is a nonhero avoid the satisfying resolutions of mainstream movies in order to represent crime
and its consequences naturalistically.

In some cases, we can partially identify with nonhero protagonists. The teenage misfits in *Badlands* (1974) can at first be understood by anyone who has chafed at life's constraints, *Taxi Driver*'s
Travis Bickle by any one who has entertained rescue fantasies, *Monster*'s Aileen Wuornos by any viewer who has felt abused. In other
cases, though, it is nearly impossible to identify with the nonheroes
of alternative-tradition crime films. We watch from an emotional distance as Alex, the hyperviolent delinquent of *A Clockwork Orange*
(1971), rapes and pillages; as Santana, the drug-lord protagonist of
American Me (1992), destroys his community; and as Lily, the swindler
of *The Grifters,* steals from and tries to seduce her own son.

The death of the traditional hero proved advantageous for crime
films, which were able to provide entertaining alternatives with their
endless supply of bad good guys. But alternative-tradition movies
push the evolution of the hero a step further. If bad-good-guy characters invert the traits of the traditional hero, the nonheroes of alter-

Table 7.2 Crime Film Protagonists by Degree of Criminality

Degree of criminality	Type of hero
good good guy	official hero
bad good guy	outlaw hero (antihero*)
	outsider hero
	criminal hero
no-good bad guy	nonhero

*The term *antihero* has traditionally been used to denote a character who re-
verses the traits of the traditional hero without entirely negating the idea of
heroism.

native-tradition movies erase the very idea of heroism, a difference highlighted by a comparison of the two versions of *Scarface.*

The Tony Camonte of the first *Scarface* (1932), modeled on Al Capone and played by Paul Muni in a script by Ben Hecht, remains attractive despite his disfigurement and primitive violence. He is bigger than life, awesome in his greed and boldness, and, accomplishing his aim, he does rise above the dark city's impoverished masses. The Tony Montana of the second *Scarface* (1983), modeled on the first Tony and played by Al Pacino in a script by Oliver Stone, is more difficult to admire. A drug lord who begins as a petty criminal shipped out of Cuba in the 1980 Mariel exodus, Tony Montana seems smaller than life, dwarfed by the crowded first scenes and the huge detention center to which he is initially assigned. This Tony, too, is a risk-taker, and he, too, makes millions from contraband, but he is more repellent. Both Tonys marry a blond bauble, but the second Tony's wife (Michelle Pfeiffer), anorexic and addicted to cocaine, is self-destructive and frightening. The incest theme, suppressed in the first version of the film, here emerges full-blown, foul and repulsive. Whereas the first version begins like a thriller, cool, slick, and mysterious, the second starts with a sweaty, shifty-eyed Tony, lying his head off to immigration officers.

Reviewing the second *Scarface* at the time of its release, critic Vincent Canby noted yet another difference between it and the original— Pacino's Tony ignores a crucial rule of the underworld: "'Don't get high on your own supply.' This is a major switch on the work of Hecht, who might have guffawed at the suggestion that Al Capone, Chicago's most powerful Prohibition gangster, might have been done in by alcoholism." And by the end, Canby continues, Pacino's Tony, incapacitated by and smeared with cocaine, is "close to the brink of parody. . . . It's like watching a Macbeth who is unaware that his pants have split."[31]

To take the measure of the protagonist in the second *Scarface,* it is instructive as well to compare him to *The Godfather*'s Michael Corleone. Michael, unlike Tony, has something to lose: his decency, warmth, and achievements in the straight world. Although he turns to crime, Michael's affection for and loyalty to his family persist for a long time before corruption sets in. Michael loves his children well, if not wisely; Tony longs for children but has none. In contrast to the sumptuous sets and spectacles of *The Godfather*, *Scarface*'s sets are tawdry (even for Tony's *Godfather*-like wedding). Michael gains ever more control, while Tony disintegrates in a coke-induced stupor. With these contrasts, Oliver Stone and director Brian De Palma make a statement about the nature of heroism in the modern world. Early twentieth-century immigrants could use crime as a shortcut to the American dream, but today the dream has become empty, sleazy, and worthless, and crime has lost its glamour. Instead of soaring above the masses, crude yet powerful, today's organized crime figure hops around like a toad, ugly, fearsome, and ultimately ineffective.

Bad Lieutenant (1992), directed by Abel Ferrara[32] and starring Harvey Keitel, further illustrates how alternative-tradition films use nonheroes to make statements about the impossibility of heroism in the late twentieth century. A nameless New York City cop, the lieutenant is at least as bad as the criminals from whom he extorts drugs and money. Drinking, drugging, and gambling himself to death, he ruins his family as well and encourages disrespect for the law. However, he is a Catholic, and when a nun is raped (with a crucifix), the lieutenant wants to avenge her. She thwarts him by refusing to give the rapists' names ("They are good boys. . . . Jesus turned water to wine. . . . I ought to . . . turn hatred to love"). Wailing with pain for the nun and for his own wasted life, the lieutenant collapses in a church. Jesus comes to him; the lieutenant curses and hurls his rosary at the figure but also kisses his bloody feet. This is the lieutenant's hour on the cross, and it is followed by a miracle (Jesus turns into a black woman). The lieutenant then learns the names of the nun's assailants, gives them the $30,000 he desperately needs to pay his gambling debts, puts them on a bus out of town, and is immediately murdered by his creditors. His death causes barely a ripple in the life of the big city.

Bad Lieutenant is as grim as movies get. Those who are meant to uphold the law break it. Society is corrupt, morality dead, and heroism almost nonexistent. *Bad Lieutenant* does imply another set of values— the purity, naïveté, and generosity of the nun, and the redemptive potential of the cop's generosity to the rapists. But it suggests that there is no reason for behaving decently other than faith in God. Like an old-fashioned morality play, this film urges us to make the leap of faith, but it also suggests that such a leap requires a miracle and can lead directly to death.[33]

Risking commercial failure, alternative-tradition crime films do not aim at making viewers feel good; in fact, they can make us feel terrible. If most Hollywood movies center around a likable character who encounters a series of increasingly difficult tests in order to achieve a goal,[34] then alternative-tradition crime movies are those in which a despicable character encounters a series of increasingly difficult tests only to fail them all. But while they reject the comforting mythology of the heroic individual who can hurdle all obstacles, movies in the alternative tradition expand definitions of what movies can and should be.

Notes

1. Bordwell and Thompson 1997: 99.
2. Ibid.: 99–100.
3. Maltby 1995: 299–300.
4. McKenna 1996: 227.
5. Andrew McKenna argues that the chief characteristic of thrillers lies in their "display and exercise of violence," in the way they build up stress by forcing us to wait for the "outbreak of violence" but deferring it until unexpected moments (1996: 226–27).
6. See also the less delightful *Killing Zoe* (1994), where a bank worker saves the safe-cracker and they drive off together in the end. In *The Usual Suspects* (1995), a caper-within-a-caper film, a single member of the gang gets away with the crime.
7. In *Escape from Alcatraz* (1979), the sense of oppression and enclosure is established even before prisoner Frank Morris reaches the island by a nighttime boat ride through a heavy downpour. "We were not allowed to use salt water for our rain effects because of erosion," reports director Don Siegel (1993: 443). "We used large barges filled with thousands of gallons of fresh water." Whatever the water type, the storm creates a mood of inescapable misery typical of films about oppression.
8. That *Angels with Dirty Faces* is a disguised Western is pointed out in Ray 1985: 75.
9. Wright 1975: 157.
10. As Carol Clover points out in her book on horror movies, the revenge theme is not confined to crime films and Westerns, and when the triggering event is sexual violation, "the rape-revenge genre . . . is . . . a premier processing site for the modern debate on sexual violence in life and law" (1992: 151).
11. Parshall 1991: 136. Compare Willis 1997: 20, arguing that the white male action hero is "a figure for masculinity in crisis."
12. Other minor types are the crime-story romance (e.g., *Regeneration* [1915]) and the crime-event history (e.g., *Rosewood* [1997]).
13. These include *The Lady from Shanghai* (1948), *Kiss of the Spider Woman* (1985), *Pulp Fiction* (1994), and *Run Lola Run* (1998). For a different set of categories, this one based on types of violence in movies, see Newman 1998.
14. Ray 1985: 59.
15. Wright 1975: 85–88.
16. Clover 1992.

17. Warshow 1974b.
18. Warshow 1974a.
19. Warshow 1974b: 136.
20. Sklar, as quoted in Maltby 1995: 255.
21. Warshow 1974a: 131.
22. Ibid.: 133, emphasis in original.
23. Robert Sherwood, as quoted in McCabe 1997: 82.
24. Ruth 1996 (esp. p. 2). Similarly, in *Criminals as Heroes,* a book about not movies but American Robin Hoods such as Jesse James and Billy the Kid, Paul Kooistra argues that the fit between "the actual behavior of the men chosen for the Robin Hood role and . . . the particular social context in which they acted out their criminality" is the factor that determines "why a particular criminal is selected from the heap of common thieves and murderers and fashioned into a heroic figure" (1989:10).
25. Older sources describe Clyde as homosexual, and while more recent biographies omit this detail, they are often created out of fantasy rather than fact, overeager participants in the Bonnie and Clyde industry. In any case, director Arthur Penn clearly was familiar with stories of Clyde's initial sexual disinterest in Bonnie Parker.
26. Maltby 1995: 254.
27. Gitlin 1980: 199.
28. *Newsweek*'s reviewer, as quoted in Prince 1998: 19.
29. For other discussions of heroism, myth, and irony in *Bonnie and Clyde,* see Cawelti 1992 and Ray 1985: chap. 9.
30. Ray 1985: 323.
31. Canby 1983.
32. Ferrara also had a hand in writing the script.
33. Whereas *Scarface* and *Bad Lieutenant* have nonhero protagonists, a few crime films have no protagonist at all. One of these is *The Ox-Bow Incident* (1943), the Henry Fonda movie about passersby who witness a lynching. *The Ox-Bow Incident* has several important characters, but the emphasis is spread among them. Although we witness events through the Fonda character, who is the moral center of the story, he does nothing heroic and is mainly a testifier.
34. Maltby 1995: 300.

8 | The Alternative Tradition and Films of Moral Ambiguity

> "I don't understand it. I don't understand it at all."
> —The opening words, spoken by
> the Woodsman, of *Rashomon*

Crime films provide a celluloid rendezvous where audiences engage with major social issues: criminal responsibility, the nature of heroism, the impact of gender and race on legal decisions, and the nature of justice. To treat these issues, mainstream crime films have traditionally relied on a formula whose main ingredients are heroes, villains, and satisfying endings. In these films, justice is achieved—not painlessly but without final frustration. Films in the classic Hollywood tradition, I have argued, characteristically exhibit a double movement, first challenging the status quo with questions, then reassuring us that justice has been served (or will be), that moral dilemmas can be resolved, and that good guys win.

But films in what I have been calling the alternative or critical tradition are different. These films turn their backs on the pleasing heroes and consoling resolutions of mainstream cinema. Critical crime films either try to get by with no hero at all or offer a flawed protagonist, vulnerable and perhaps (as in *Taxi Driver* [1976]) delusional. In them, justice is thwarted or achieved only through roundabout irony. They eschew the double movement that sends us on our way with, if not a song in our hearts, at least a reassurance that the world outside the movie theater remains morally intact. These critical crime films take human evil for granted, assuming that people are fundamentally selfish and justice systems easily corrupted. Even when such films are clear about where right and wrong lie, they may show wrong thriving and virtue being crushed.

This chapter concentrates on a particular type of critical crime movie: the film of moral ambiguity. In the broader domain of critical crime films, viewers often know who the bad guy is (e.g., *Bad Lieutenant* [1992]), but in the subtype of morally ambiguous films, we sometimes don't even know the bad guy's identity. In the former, right and wrong are knowable, though a corrupt criminal justice system may prevent a just outcome; in the latter, however, morality itself is relative or deeply obscure. In critical crime films generally, the bad guy often goes unpunished (e.g., *Chinatown* [1974]); in morally ambiguous films specifically, we may not even know if he or she *should* be punished. Likewise, whereas films in the broader category have identifiable victims, films in the narrower category can be unclear about the victim's identity, or their victims may seem partially responsible for the crime. In films of moral ambiguity, the standards for judgments about guilt and innocence are difficult to discern, perhaps unknowable. And the crimes are likely to be committed by ordinary people—not Mafia godfathers or sultry dames of iconic beauty but nebbishes, nonentities, a bedraggled roadside prostitute or the quiet neighbor across the street. Moreover, the characters' noncriminal decisions—the spur-of-the-moment betrayal, the emotional abandonment of a child—may be judged more harshly than the crime itself. Challenging the moral clarity of Hollywood tradition, directors have been making morally ambiguous crime films for decades. These include some of the best known works of the world's most influential auteur directors. I discuss three classic examples—*Rashomon, Breathless,* and *The Conversation*—before turning to contemporary examples.

Moral Ambiguity in Three Film Classics

Rashomon (1950)

Rashomon, the film that introduced Japanese cinema to the West, tells an apparently simple crime story set in feudal Japan. The first half of the story is clear: A samurai warrior and his wife, the latter veiled and seated on a white horse, thread their way through an ancient forest. They come upon a bandit who ties up the husband and rapes his wife; later, the husband's body is discovered, riddled with stab wounds. But who killed him? The events are related by a series of eyewitnesses—the bandit, the wife, the dead man (speaking through a female medium), and a woodsman—who give conflicting accounts of what happened after the rape. Each account is depicted through flashbacks, sometimes through flashbacks within flashbacks, creating a tangle of narrative lines. This baroque narrative elaboration contrasts sharply with the clarity of the first half of the story, and it contradicts the expectations of steadiness and constraint established by the film's magisterial rhythms, by the mythic flatness and anonymity of its characters, and by their ritualistic (even hackneyed) expressions of emotion. In sum, the visual stylization of *Rashomon* indicates that the material is under tight directorial control while the wildly metasticizing plot line suggests ungovernability.

Director Akira Kurosawa emphasizes the impossibility of reconciling the conflicting accounts. The problem is not only that humans lie; it is also that they may report utterly different versions of the same event when they are telling the truth. There is no such thing as absolute truth, *Rashomon* tells us, even when, as in the cinema, we witness events ourselves.

All commentaries on *Rashomon* emphasize these messages, but when we think of the film as a crime film, another dimension comes to the fore: the fact that all of the narrators are testifying before an invisible court. Speaking right into the camera, they directly address the filmmaker and the film's audience as well. Judge (or Jury), camera, and viewer become one. Thus, the film engages us directly in the impossibility of determining guilt and innocence. The law can summon eyewitnesses, but even truthful eyewitnesses will give contradictory accounts; there are no ultimate criteria for judging responsibility and criminality; law cannot determine the truth. Thus the film is virtually a paradigm for the stance of the critical tradition and moral ambiguity.

Breathless (1960)

Jean-Luc Godard's *Breathless,* one of the most influential films of French New Wave cinema, was revolutionary both in what it showed and how it showed it, demonstrating an extraordinary freedom from Hollywood in content and style. It portrays two young lovers, in Paris in the late 1950s, adrift in an amoral universe, apparently indifferent to life and its loss, guided by their own whims rather than the moral strictures of others.

Michel (Jean-Paul Belmondo) is a gangster and car thief, manipulative, unfeeling, a habitual liar. Directionless and uneducated, he models himself on movie tough guys. At the start of the film, Michel shoots a cop, evidently with no remorse and, in fact, barely noticing what he has done. Patricia (Jean Seberg), an American studying at the Sorbonne, is interested in art and literature; she also does interviews for the *New York Herald Tribune* and hawks the newspaper on the streets. She, too, is directionless, although she has more resources than Michel. When Patricia learns that Michel has killed a cop, she finds the fact mildly interesting and goes on to steal a car under his tutelage. Since he is being hunted for murder, they discuss running away, but instead, on impulse, she phones the police to inform on him. The police find Michel on a street and shoot him. He could shoot back but—"à bout de souffle" (the French title), out of breath and energy—he has too little interest in life to bother. In the final scene Patricia stands over him, expressionless, as he uses his last moments to mug, call her *dègueulasse* (disgusting, a scumbag), and close his own eyes. She, ready as always to improve her French vocabulary, asks what *dègueulasse* means.

While Patricia and Michel seem to be concerned about almost nothing, including their own past and future, they do care about how they look to others and constantly try on new poses to see which ones might fit. At the same time, paradoxically, they are unselfconscious, unbounded. Their reality lies in their appearances, but they are also searching for themselves—and, apparently, finding very little there. They see and don't see simultaneously, as in the image of Michel peering through sunglasses that lack one lens.

With their existential ennui, Michel and Patricia may seem to live in utter moral blankness; yet they are heroically free from tradition, improvising their lives in complete independence. Godard's cinematic style—fresh, spontaneous, authentic, improvisational—echoes theirs. The story is told dispassionately, with a startling lack of moralism. In the background of nearly every scene is Paris, the beautiful, indifferent city. What Michel and Patricia do or do not do is not a matter of importance. And that's what's important here.

Breathless stunned audiences by showing not only that there are no rules but that it is cool not to miss them. For all his homage to earlier noirs, Godard tore up the rules of the traditional crime film, refusing to depict crime as a negative, death as a loss, or betrayal as despicable. Here law and order are bores, distractions from the more important activity of ignoring them. Most radical of all is the image of Patricia: Instead of the 1950s good girl, Godard presents a young woman on her own, starting a career, unconcerned about finding a permanent partner or about the pregnancy that she mentions in passing to Michel. Patricia is not rattled by having her boyfriend shot to death in front of her, any more than she is by her responsibility for his death; as an American student in Paris, her primary responsibility is to learn French. *Breathless* radically revised the rules for crime films and, in so doing, fired the opening shot for a decade in which young people found a moral imperative in ignoring the moral imperatives of others.

The Conversation (1974)

The more we spy, and the more sophisticated our surveillance technology, the less we will know: This is the message of *The Conversation,* the muted psychological drama that Francis Ford Coppola sandwiched between his spectacular first and second *Godfather* films (1972, 1974). Surveillance may encourage us to think that we have detected a crime; but, Coppola tells us in this film that he wrote as well as directed, we will never know for sure, and the discovery can lead to paranoia and despair.

The Conversation centers on the figure of Harry Caul (Gene Hackman), a surveillance specialist hired by an executive to surreptitiously record the executive's wife and a man she meets in a San Francisco park. Secretive, cold, and hypercautious, Harry veils his thoughts and even wears his raincoat to bed.[1] He makes the recording and then spends long hours trying to clarify the sound track, concluding that he may have uncovered a murder plot. Trolling for evidence, he sees or hallucinates a murder in which, in a reversal of his expectations, the couple kill the executive. Meanwhile, Harry himself is being watched: by his own guilt (personified by Martin Stett, the assistant to the executive, played by Harrison Ford) and by other surveillance specialists trying to steal his secrets. Increasingly paranoid, he tears his own apartment apart in the search for a (perhaps nonexistent) bug, dismantling his own sanity in the process.

The roots of *The Conversation* lie in Alfred Hitchcock's *Rear Window* (1954), another surveillance film in which the protagonist searches for a crime, and in Michelangelo Antonioni's *Blowup* (1966), in which a photographer repeatedly enlarges an image, scrutinizing it for evidence of a murder. Coppola's film also grew out of the Watergate scandal: the burglary of the Democratic Party's headquarters by henchmen of President Richard Nixon and the subsequent discovery that Nixon had been secretly recording conversations in the White House. Concerns about surveillance and violations of privacy intensified when the public learned that the FBI had been collecting information on political protesters. This political background helps explain *The Conversation*'s enormous (and paradoxical) mistrust of recording tech-

Figure 8.1. Francis Ford Coppola's *The Conversation* (1974), inspired by discovery of Nixon's secret tapes and the FBI's illegal surveillance program, demonstrates that one can't trust what one sees and hears, even in the movies. It helped establish an alternative to the Hollywood tradition of happy endings and constituted an early example of the film of moral ambiguity. Photo used by permission of Photofest.

nologies. The movie begins with a tracking shot that equates filmmaking and film viewing with surveillance. Later we watch Harry listening to the tape he made in the park, a recording that engulfs Coppola's film, just as it takes over Harry's life.

Harry Caul is one of cinema's least heroic protagonists: rigid, weird, puritanical, obsessive, evasive, and, like a Kafka character, guilty of something he can't quite identify. Moreover, this is one of cinema's most ambiguous crime films: We can't tell *when* there is a crime, or even *if* there is a crime. As viewers, we become involved in the couple's lives, just as Harry does, but we, too, find it difficult to understand the surveillance tape, and gradually we realize that spying may disorient us, just as it disorients Harry. If you watch others, they may watch you, too; and due to the inevitable failure of intelligence data, what they learn about you may well be wrong. Indicting surveillance in modern society, Coppola lectures his audience on the dangers and immorality of snooping.[2] But maybe that is not what he actually is saying: Watching this perfectly ambiguous film, participating in Harry's snooping, we can't tell anything with certainty.

These classic morally ambiguous crime films tell us that accurate perception is difficult, perhaps impossible. They have no clear heroes, villains, or victims. Truth, we learn, depends on one's point of view, and therefore there is no absolute truth. The world is morally indifferent to its inhabitants. We are all bit players in a drama with no clear narrative line and no all-powerful director. Nor can we look to law for answers, for law itself is powerless to distinguish authenticity from pretense, appearance from reality, and guilt from innocence.

Moral Ambiguity in Contemporary Sex Crime Films

Contemporary films of moral ambiguity cover a wide range of subject matters and approaches. *Normal Life* (1996), for example, deals with the difficulties of loving someone who is mentally ill, *Fight Club* (1999) with the attractions of danger, *Run Lola Run* (1998) with the possibility of writing alternative plots for one's own life. *Ghost Dog* (1999) shows a hit man calmly awaiting execution by the mob, *Hard Eight* (1996) explores the ironies of attempting to expiate for past sins, *Eye of God* (1997) grapples with the mystery of a God who would allow innocence to be annihilated, and *Insomnia* (2002) follows a cop whose skills and integrity are impossible to determine. Instead of attempting to cover the full range of such films, I will focus on a subset in which the alternative tradition and its deep interest in moral ambiguity find a tailor-made subject: stories of sex crimes. It is fitting—and perhaps in retrospect even predictable—that alternative-tradition films would be drawn to the exploration of this type of content since sex crimes, their perpetrators, and their victims comprise one of the most morally fraught and obscure areas of criminology, and one of the most complex, controversial, and ambiguous areas of criminal jurisprudence. Moreover, such films are strikingly responsive to current events and emerging social trends, providing a prime example of the reciprocal mirror-relations of crime films and society.

Until recently, directors avoided taking sex crime as their text. The topic was socially taboo, and in any case no one (including criminologists) knew much about it. In addition, the complexity of victim-offender dynamics and relationships in sex crimes did not lend itself to easy distinctions between good and evil. Sometimes a notorious offense would inspire a film, as happened when Fritz Lang based *M* (1931) on the depredations of Peter Kürten, the "Dusseldorf vampire."[3] At other times scriptwriters sneaked sex crime in by a side door, as in the case of *Cape Fear* (1962), in which psychopath Max Cady intends to rape Sam Bowden's daughter, or in *Dolores Claiborne* (1995), which uncovers incest in the daughter's past. But, for the most part, the distasteful nature of the subject combined with ignorance about it worked to keep sex crime off movies' agendas.

Change began in the early 1980s when a moral panic about child sexual abuse by day care workers spread across the United States. Today these cases are generally remembered as the results of mass hysteria, a national witch hunt fueled by faulty investigations and the implantation of false memories in toddlers.[4] But at the time they got people talking about the possibility of sex crime by trusted figures in everyday life, and they stimulated legal debates over issues such as whether children should be required to give evidence in open court. Discussions of sex crimes opened up still further as cases of clergy abuse surfaced, along with evidence of mass cover-ups of child sexual exploitation by Catholic priests. Infamous individual cases further eroded the wall of secrecy that had traditionally protected sex offenders; for example, the tragedy of seven-year-old Megan Kanka, lured into a neighbor's house with the promise of seeing a puppy, only to be raped and murdered, caused national outrage, especially when it was learned that the neighbor had been previously convicted of sex offenses. Similarly, the bizarre sexual predilections of serial killers such as Jeffrey Dahlmer prompted widespread arguments over the legal responsibility of those with psychosexual illnesses. False memories, recovered memories, the exposure of religious leaders as predators, and sex offender registries became favorite issues of the news media. Could movies lag far behind?

This section examines six crime films made since 2000 that use sex crime to comment on the ethical complexities and legal dilemmas of modern life: *Capturing the Friedmans* (2003), *In the Cut* (2003), *L.I.E.* (2001), *Monster* (2003), *Mystic River* (2003), and *The Woodsman* (2004). These films vary considerably among themselves: some deal with adult victims, while some explore evidentiary issues. But, like the films discussed in the previous sections, they share a distaste for analyzing issues in simplistic, black-and-white terms. Eschewing easy divisions between victims and perpetrators, most of them examine the intertwining of guilt and innocence, showing that the offenders may have once been victimized by such crimes, or that the victims themselves behaved ambiguously. Nearly all are concerned with gaps between appearance and reality; those concerned with children in particular ask whether steps taken to protect young people can backfire, causing more harm than good. A few ask if we should try to live with sex offenders in our communities and whether such people are morally responsible or mentally ill. Many of these films use dark palettes, partly because their subject is a somber one, partly because that subject is filled with the murk of moral ambiguity.

The Hazards of Assigning Blame

Mystic River takes place in a Boston neighborhood where the Mystic River flows into the harbor, close to downtown but a world apart, a small, apparently stable, working-class community, Catholic, tough, and standoffish with outsiders. The film opens with a scene of three boys playing. One is kidnapped by two adult men who hold him for several days in a basement and rape him repeatedly. The rest of movie relates how the effects of the original crime ripple through the boys' adult lives and into the next generation.

The teenage daughter of one of these adults, Jimmy Markum (Sean Penn), is brutally killed. She was about to leave him in any case, he discovers, to elope with a neighborhood youth. Jimmy, whose mom-and-pop store is a front for criminal enterprises, suspects that Dave Boyle (Tim Robbins), the character who was raped as a boy, is his daughter's killer. With thuggish friends aptly named the Savage brothers, Jimmy kills Dave at night on the river's edge. The third member of the trio of boyhood playmates, state trooper Sean Devine (Kevin Bacon), investigates the daughter's death, figuring out who really killed her and also discovering that Jimmy killed Dave. However, for the moment at least, he lacks the evidence to bring Jimmy to justice.

Thus, the three central characters fill the roles of criminal, victim, and avenger, although the avenger is unable to function effectively.

The central themes of *Mystic River*—misperception, abandonment, loss of fathers, loss of children, loss of childhood, vengeance—play out against a background of nighttime scenes and constricted interiors. These themes cut across the film's central conundrum, the source of its moral ambiguity: the value conflicts between the small, closed community and the broader society. Change does occur—a Starbucks moves into the neighborhood, for instance—but the solidarity of Jimmy's criminal enterprise, the neighborhood's code of silence, and generations of hardscrabble resentment toward the outer world all work to thwart the police investigation and throw the community back on its own resources. The community's resistance to the outer world is summed up in the final scene by the smile that Jimmy's wife (Laura Linney) bestows on Dave's widow, a chilling, triumphant nod that says, we will let you survive here if you ask no questions and play by our rules. Power and a hunger for justice have met head on, and power has won. The neighborhood defines its own values.

A comparison of *Mystic River* with *To Kill a Mockingbird* (1962) reveals the gulf between critical crime films and those pitched in the mainstream mode, especially when the former reveal irreconcilable value clashes. Both movies depict a small town split by a crime (in *Mockingbird*, false allegations of a crime) against a teenage girl. Both speak passionately of children's need for moral guidance, of parents' hopes for their children, and of crime's corrosion; both show vigilante action against the wrong person; and both have someone associated with the law eventually solving the crime, albeit too late to prevent vigilantism. But *Mockingbird* has a hero—one whose very name, Atticus Finch, has become a synonym for heroism—and a clear victim—the black man whom the would-be lynchers shot—whereas there is no hero at all in *Mystic River* and victimization is diffuse, spreading in widening circles across the community and generations. Although Jimmy Markum is no hero, his vigilante action does not make him a villain either; he remains a sympathetic character, struggling to do the right thing by his daughter. *Mockingbird*, however, has villains one can enjoy hating: the bigots who are all too ready to deny justice to a black man. *Mystic River* turns *Mockingbird* inside out, replacing its bright childhood scenes with gloom, demonstrating that injustice will win.

Released in the same year as *Mystic River, Capturing the Friedmans,* too, meditates on the hazards of assigning blame, but from a totally different angle. Director Andrew Jarecki created his documentary about a Long Island, New York, case of child sexual abuse by using the home videos of the Friedman family, two members of which were accused in the mid-1980s of molesting children who took computer lessons in their home. Arnold Friedman, the father of three boys—previously regarded as an upstanding citizen—was charged with multiple counts of child sexual abuse. He pleaded guilty and was sent to prison, where he died, an apparent suicide. His teenage son Jesse also pleaded guilty, having been advised by his lawyer that conviction was inevitable and a guilty plea would reduce his sentence. (Jesse, who almost certainly was not guilty, served thirteen years.) Jarecki intersperses footage from the home movies that the Friedmans shot obsessively with interviews that he himself shot years later to raise perhaps unanswerable questions about the nature of guilt and justice. It's as though *Rashomon* were remade as a documentary in Great Neck, Long Island.

The central moral ambiguity of *Capturing the Friedmans* concerns Arnold: Was he a great father or a child molester? a model citizen or a mentally ill pervert? We cannot tell, and we will never be able to tell. The answer is probably that he was *both* a great father and a child molester, though it is doubtful that Arnold actually molested children in his Long Island home.[5]

Although one of the earliest films about sexual crime against children, Fritz Lang's *M,* also falls into the alternative tradition, it has little of the moral ambiguity found in *Capturing the Friedmans.* In *M,* the police and the underworld join forces to hunt down a man who rapes and kills children. Hans Beckert is apprehended and brought to some sort of justice. There is no hero here, nor is there a resolution to *M*'s central moral dilemma, since Lang leaves open the question of Beckert's criminal responsibility, portraying him as sick, helpless, and revolted by himself. But if we compare *M* with *Capturing the Friedmans,* we can see that the latter film pushes the alternative tradition much further, raising tougher questions about judgments of wrongdoing. We can't even be sure that Arnold committed a crime, and we don't know what would constitute valid evidence (in this film, even confessions are suspect). While Beckert is a moral monster, Arnold is the neighborhood dad with three kids.

Yet another take on the interlacing of guilt and innocence is to be found in *Monster,* the biography of the prostitute Aileen (Lee) Wuornos, executed in 2002 for a series of highway murders. Wuornos does not at first glance seem promising material for an argument about the hazards of determining culpability, but Patty Jenkins, the film's author and director, manages to dig through the layers of media obfuscation to the bedrock of Wuornos's personality.

That *Monster* succeeds is due in large part to the dramatic skills of Charlize Theron, the actor who portrays Wuornos. Theron is able to express a wide range of emotions—often conflicting emotions—through her face and body. When Lee is hooking, for instance, we see a mixture of distaste, apprehension, and hope play across her countenance. As she becomes more desperate, her mouth grimaces in a confusion of nervous tension, hurt, defiance, and determination. Theron, who gained thirty pounds for the role, came to closely resemble Wuornos herself, hardscrabble and belligerent except when her face lights up with love.

While Jenkins's script stays close to the facts of Wuornos's life, it shapes those facts to make the story palatable, most significantly by portraying Selby, Lee's lover, as a virtual child and casting a small woman, Christina Ricci, for the role. Lee's sense of responsibility emerges in contrast to Selby's infantile dependency; we see Lee making heroic attempts to cope, braving hopeless odds to provide Selby with "a house, cars, the whole fucking shebang" by becoming "a business person, something like that." She buries her own fears to protect Selby, only to be betrayed by Selby in the end.

Wuornos's rage toward and terror of men become understandable when we learn that she was raped at the age of eight and had her first baby when she was thirteen. We see her hideously victimized by a customer before she commences her killing spree; and many of her clients are criminalistic themselves, brutish and repellent. The film does not whitewash Lee's crimes; nor does it show her as anything other than slow-witted, mentally ill, foulmouthed, and socially illiterate. She is also self-deluded ("I'm good with the Lord. . . . Who the fuck knows what God wants? . . . People kill each other every day, and for what, huh? For politics . . . and religion . . . and they're heroes. I'm not a bad person, I'm a real good person"). But her self-hatred counterbalances at least some of her negative traits. And so at the end, as Lee is hurried into the death chamber, we can see her not as a serial killer against whom to lob our hatreds but as a pathetic woman in whom good mixed with evil.

The Guy Next Door

The day care sexual abuse cases and scandals over predatory priests sowed mistrust of the familiar figures to whom parents entrust children and on whom they rely for help. This mistrust fed into the emergence of a new kind of movie bad guy: the neighborhood pervert, camouflaged by ordinariness, all the more dangerous because he lacks the stagy stigmata of traditional movie criminals. This new type of bad guy turns up in *Mystic River, Capturing the Friedmans,* and *The Woodsman,* but nowhere with greater force than in *L.I.E.,* director Michael Cuesta's film about a fifteen-year-old boy stalked by a patriotic pillar of the community. Equally remarkable is *L.I.E.*'s depiction of the child victim as not helpless quarry but an agent of his own fate.

L.I.E. opens with fifteen-year-old Howie Blitzer (Paul Dano) balanced dangerously on a bridge railing above the Long Island Expressway (L.I.E.). In a voice-over he tells us that the road has killed many people, including his own mother. "I hope it doesn't get me," he continues, although he is clearly toying with the possibility of suicide. In the ensuing scenes Howie loses his best friend, fights kids who accuse him of "salami swiping"(masturbating other boys), is assaulted and apparently abandoned by his father, and is arrested for the burglaries he has been committing with friends. Moreover, he is stalked by a neighborhood ex-marine, Big John or B.J. (Brian Cox), a large, vulgar, and cunning predator with a gun collection in his basement as well as a bedroom for the motherless boys he "saves" from time to time.

In the key scene, B.J. rescues Howie from juvenile detention and brings him home, sending Scottie, his current teenage companion, to a motel for a few days. B.J., suddenly paternal, teaches Howie to shave—tenderly, repulsively, dangerously. They then hug, and Howie indicates he is sexually ready for what seems sure to come; indeed, he may even be a little bit curious. However, B.J.—touched by Howie's scared "racoon look" and realizing that the boy has just been devastated by news of his father's imprisonment—refrains for the nonce from molesting him, instead settling him for the night in a single bed. At breakfast the next morning, B.J. again throws himself into the role

Figure 8.2. *L.I.E.* (2001) portrays both the sexual predator (Brian Cox) and his intended victim (Paul Franklin Dano) as complex characters, coping with the ambiguities of daily life. Photo used by permission of Photofest.

of the good father, bustling about to cook breakfast and arrange for Howie to visit his dad in prison.

We know better than to trust B.J., who has heartlessly exiled Scottie to a motel and is drawing the net around his new prey. On the other hand, this revolting pederast has for a few hours given Howie the parenting he needs. Apparently even B.J., who earlier admitted to shame about his sexual compulsions, has a remnant of decency. Moreover, his dose of parenting puts Howie back on his feet, giving him the courage to confront his father and face the future. Scottie, displaced and abandoned, shoots B.J. while the latter cruises for boys along the L.I.E., an act that frees Howie from the sexual threat. The final scene returns us to the bridge above the expressway, where Howie still broods about the road's murderous potential but now concludes, in another voice-over, "I'm not going to let it get me."

The moral complexity of *L.I.E.*'s characters and plot emerges through contrast with *Sleepers* (1996), another movie centered on pederasty. In the latter, four boys convicted of a minor prank are sent to a juvenile home where guards sodomize and torture them over a period of months. The sodomites are one-dimensional bad guys, sadists, Nazi-like officers excited by cruelty. B.J., in contrast, is nuanced, driven by remorse as well as lust, a pedophile as well as a pederast, terrifying but not totally evil. In *Sleepers,* the main guard (Kevin Bacon) is easily recognizable as a bad guy: wiry, greasy-haired, pathological. B.J., on the other hand, looks like a favorite uncle—until you figure out what he is doing. In *Sleepers* the good guys win and the bad guys lose; in *L.I.E.* a monstrous bad guy does something generous, and instead of an uplifting hero we get a sad kid who survives sexual predation.

L.I.E. more closely resembles another recent film of moral ambiguity, *The Woodsman,* starring Kevin Bacon as Walter, a pedophile who has just been released after twelve years in prison for molesting little girls. Director Nicole Kassell's film is dedicated entirely to the development of Walter's character. (He is called a woodsman partly because he used to be a carpenter but mainly in recollection of the Little Red Riding Hood character who cuts open the wicked wolf and releases the girl whom the wolf had swallowed, intact. In this context, the woodsman is an ambiguous hero, a savior who nonetheless gets control of a little girl, just as Walter himself later does in a wooded park.) Walter, who wants desperately to go straight, endures daily struggles with his compulsion and with the fellow factory hands who try to mob him out of their workplace. Although he is helped by a new girlfriend, Walter leads a bleak existence, rejected by most of his family and loathed by a contemptuous parole officer. The film does not ask us to pity Walter but dispassionately follows his story, not to resolution but to a small, precarious victory at the end when he hugs the little girl on a park bench and then sends her home.

Recent films use the ordinary-guy image of the sex criminal to emphasize children's vulnerability and the difficulty of perceiving such offenses when they occur. Aileen Wuornos, we learn in *Monster,* was initially raped by a neighbor, and she seems to have been molested by her father as well. Arnold Friedman was a respected teacher and musician; one of the abductors in *Mystic River* wears a priest's ring. B.J., the hearty Vietnam vet of *L.I.E.,* is another respected community figure and pal of the juvenile police officers who, with painful irony, release Howie into his care. *The Woodsman* casts doubt on nearly everyone: When Walter sends the girl on the bench home to her father, it is to a father who jiggles her on his lap; in childhood, it seems, Walter himself sexually exploited his sister; and from his window he observes a man luring boys into his car. We can't tell where corruption lies, these films warn; and today's sex criminal may be yesterday's victim.

These films underscore the inability of communities to protect their children. *Mystic River*'s tight-knit neighborhood is in fact one of lost children and failed fathers. The parole officer of *Woodsman* may keep close tabs on Walter, but another man is preying on children just across the street, and ironically, Walter does not dare report him. Criminal justice officials in the Friedmans' upper-middle-class town probably implanted false memories in the children they questioned so relentlessly. Even the wealthy neighborhood in which Howie Blitzer lives, with its vast lawns and showcase houses, its school guidance counselors and juvenile court specialists, is impotent in the face of B.J.'s duplicity.

The Risks of Sexual Authenticity

In the Cut, Jane Campion's film about a not-so-young schoolteacher (Meg Ryan) searching for love and meaning, was panned by professional critics and run-of-the-mill viewers alike.[6] Audiences complained that it was nothing more than a "cheap erotic thriller," that Meg Ryan had shed her usual good-girl persona to become sluttish, and that her character should have taken so many risks in a high-crime environment. "Lackluster *Fatal Attraction*," one annoyed reviewer wrote, while another reported that "The only shock factor in this movie is getting the chance to see Meg Ryan naked, though I think most men still prefer Halle Berry." As these comments indicate, viewers looked for a traditional Hollywood category in which to slot *In the Cut,* and when they failed to find one, they were disappointed. Campion took this risk in making a film about sexual and emotional authenticity with a story line that keeps foraying into traditional genres (the love story, the serial killer film, the cop buddy action movie, pornography) and then pulling back to find its own groove. But the risk is also one of the film's virtues, for the difficulty of identifying one's own path is part of Campion's story.

That story concerns Frannie Avery, a high school teacher living in a crime-ridden section of New York's East Village, determined not to be intimidated by the city's violence, hoping to have a genuine erotic experience and to be true to her own ways of relating to students and the city. Dreamy and independent, Frannie pays little attention to her appearance (Ryan's unkempt hair drove some viewers wild) or conventional rules of behavior, instead allowing herself to be tugged along by her own values and sexuality. When a woman is killed and dismembered in her neighborhood, Frannie gets sexually involved with the cop who questions her, Malloy (Mark Ruffalo). But it seems possible that he is the killer. Other women are killed and "disarticulated," including her sister; and viewers, along with Frannie, begin to suspect a range of men: a student, Malloy, a former lover, an unidentified mugger. Frannie seems to put herself in dangerous situations— to dress provocatively, to hang out in unsafe places. In the background flickers the courtship of Frannie's parents, a frightful dream sequence in which the woman slips while ice-skating and the man skates over her legs, severing them. Eventually the killer comes after Frannie, but she manages to overcome him and returns at the end to Malloy.

In the Cut, then, is a film about a woman living with the constant threat of violence against women. It is also a sexually charged movie, with some of the most graphic (and—in a change from most movie sex—convincing) love scenes this side of pornography. At one point Frannie's sister muses unhappily that she always thinks about sex in terms of what men like instead of her own preferences; Campion has made a movie about sexual experience from a woman's point of view— unconcerned whether men might prefer Halle Berry to Meg Ryan. Her refusal to objectify Frannie's desires makes *In the Cut* a bold exploration of what sex would be like if women called the shots as well as of the dangers inherent in following one's own vision.

Like Frannie, viewers cannot be sure they perceive her world accurately. Who is dangerous, who a friend? Which settings are menacing, and which are merely part of the city scenery? Should one keep up one's guard, avoiding sleazy bars and unknown men, or pursue one's authenticity, sleeping with the window wide open and traversing deserted streets despite the risks? The two cop characters dramatize the problems of trust and perception. Malloy himself is an ambiguous figure—edgy, brutal, incoherent, oblivious to boundaries, unknowable. A scene in which he drives Frannie to a wooded reservoir makes not only Frannie but also viewers apprehensive. Equally disquieting is Malloy's buddy, with his endless sexist and racist profanity. Campion plays with the audience, thwarting our expectation that the buddy cop will merely echo the dominant officer, again forcing us into Frannie's viewpoint and the realization that we simply cannot tell where danger lies. In this context, the serial killer becomes a metaphor for living with risk.

Pushing the Boundaries: The Alternative
Tradition and the Future of Crime Films

Crime films, like all mediums of cultural expression, evolve over time. If we consider the alternative-tradition developments discussed in this chapter in light of the broader trajectory of crime films over the roughly eighty years since the first talkies, two trends emerge.

We find, first, a decentering of criminality, its gradual movement to the periphery of movie stories. For most of crime-film history, movies focused on specific offenses and their investigation, prosecution, and punishment. Moreover, they organized themselves around polarities: good and evil, hero and villain, normal and pathological. The definitions of the poles varied, but they determined what was shown and what was barred as extraneous; for example, because the purpose of *Scarface* (1932) is to pit a mobster against the forces of law and order, the movie shows nothing about Tony Camonte that is not relevant to his rise and fall. Critical crime films, in contrast, tend to decenter criminality, interweaving it with larger patterns of daily life.

An early sign of this trend appeared in Martin Scorsese's *Mean Streets* (1973), in which specific offenses are embedded in the mundane activities of small-time hustlers coping with relatives and girl-friends, visiting bars, trying to keep each other out of trouble, and wondering about the meaning of life. In more recent critical films, too, crime is often incidental to a bigger picture. *L.I.E.* concentrates on a kid's struggle to mature sexually, and the movie's crimes—pederasty, fraud, assault—are extrinsic to that struggle and less negative than Howie's emotional abandonment by his parents. *Capturing the Friedmans* concentrates on the making and destruction of a family, doing so through the home movies of the boys growing up, going to the beach with their parents, and celebrating birthdays; that there was a darker underside to this domesticity comes out only later, and unevenly. *In the Cut* depends utterly on our understanding that Frannie lives in a context that obscures distinctions between the threatening and benign. This embeddedness of crime in the wider fabric of daily life shows up again in *Boogie Nights* (1997) and *Happiness* (1998), movies that might not even be classified as crime films, so peripheral is criminality to their other concerns, even though both do depict serious offenses. That crime is marginalized in these recent movies reflects the loss of clear moral imperatives in modern society.

The second trend, one that is not so much revealed by this examination of recent critical crime films as underscored by it, is the movement toward genre dissolution. In fact, we have been observing a breakdown of traditional crime film genres throughout this book: the attenuation of the cop film, the virtual disappearance of the traditional courtroom drama, the ebbing of the prison film's vitality. This formal reconfiguration and transformation turns up especially frequently in films with a complex moral vision because many such films establish the ambiguous nature of their worlds by eschewing genre clarity. *Rashomon* interrupts a simple, almost mythic crime story to elaborate a panoply of narrative possibilities; *Breathless* turns the gangster saga into a text for existential revolution; and *The Conversation* stresses the importance of the traditional crime-film investigator and film itself as a means of communication.

Contemporary films of moral ambiguity do not always participate in this chipping away at genre orthodoxy. *Mystic River* is unmistakably a thriller and a mystery, and *Monster* is easily recognizable as a chronicle of a criminal career. But of the films discussed in this section, three not only refuse the traditional genre frameworks but also make that refusal part of their message. *L.I.E.* does not clearly belong to any genre: Is it a bildungsroman or coming of age film? a causes-of-delinquency movie? a film about failed fatherhood and abandonment? a crime drama? Because we don't know how to categorize it, we keep guessing at what is going on—which puts us in the position of the main character. Likewise, *In the Cut* does not clearly belong to a traditional genre (one of the reasons why viewers looking for a Hollywood standard got so frustrated) but rather has elements of the gothic thriller, the serial killer film, pornography, and the classic cop action movie. *Capturing the Friedmans* starts with unsophisticated home movies but ends up as one of the "new documentaries" identified by Linda Williams (see chapter 6, this volume), so completely upending the epistemological assumptions of conventional documentaries as to constitute almost an antidocumentary. Recent films of moral ambiguity, then, extend a trend that began decades ago toward the bending and blurring of genre boundaries.

Those who are pushing these boundaries tend to be independent directors, filmmakers who are relatively free of the committee decisions of megaproduction companies and less reliant on movie stars. Directors who work outside the studio system are better able to maintain their clarity of vision, create fresh characters, and ignore box office pressures—that is, to produce alternative-tradition crime films. True, Clint Eastwood is one of the world's best established directors, but he has his own company, Malpaso, which combined forces with Warner Bros. to produce *Mystic River*. And in any case, his very success gives Eastwood a high degree of autonomy in shaping his films. Similarly, Jane Campion often works with big-name producers while remaining famously true to her own vision and unusual directorial methods. *L.I.E.* and *Capturing the Friedmans* were their directors' first feature films, and *Monster* was director Patty Jenkins's first successful feature. The more independent the director, the more likely she or he is to produce an alternative-tradition film.

Alternative-tradition crime films are much less attractive than mainstream movies to those in search of escapist pleasures. Instead of Hollywood's explosions, car chases, and knife-wielding serial killers, critical crime films offer something very like the grind of daily life. In them, crime is something anyone can commit—not just a madman such as Max Cady but (as in *Happiness*) one's own father or the fat lady down the hall. But while their fidelity to the mundane makes it almost impossible for critical films to offer glamour and fantasy, it enables them to depict small, unnoticed—almost unobservable—acts of bravery that would get lost in action films: *L.I.E.*'s Howie signaling his sexual availability to B.J., for example, or *In the Cut*'s Frannie making herself stay calm when Malloy drives her to an isolated reservoir. The protagonists are more plausible and realistic than the characters of conventional movies. Whether or not they make money and garner kudos, critical movies will continue to appear because some directors will keep pushing the boundaries of what films can do, testing to see how much crime films can reveal about our selves and how accurately they mirror society.

Notes

1. A "caul" is the membrane that covers a fetus. Harry keeps himself covered up, physically and psychologically; he also operates at an infantile level with regard to others, as symbolized by his curling up in a fetal position while eavesdropping from a hotel room.
2. See also Tiso n.d. *Minority Report* (2002) has a similar message about the dangers and self-destructive nature of surveillance.
3. On the Kürten case, see Evans 1996: 591–610. On the social context, see Tatar 1995, esp. chap. 6, on "The Killer as Victim: Fritz Lang's *M*."

4. A similar Australian case, though not one involving charges of sexual abuse, provoked the Meryl Streep film *Cry in the Dark* (1988).
5. For useful background information, see Nathan 2000.
6. But some critics raved about *In the Cut;* see Press 2003 and Anderson 2003. For the comments of run-of-the-mill viewers cited here and later in this section, I relied on the Internet Movie Database (IMDB), s.v. *In the Cut,* section on "User Comments"; www.imdb.com.

Appendix

Crime Films Cited with Release Dates

10 Rillington Place (1971)
21 Grams (2003)
48 Hrs. (1982)
187 (1997)

Above the Law (1988)
Account Rendered (1932)
Accused, The (1988)
Aileen: Life and Death of a Serial Killer (2003)
Aileen Wuornos: The Selling of a Serial Killer (1992)
All the President's Men (1976)
American Buffalo (1995)
American History X (1998)
American Me (1992)
American Psycho (2000)
American Tragedy, An (1931)
Anatomy of a Murder (1959)
And Justice for All (1979)
Angels with Dirty Faces (1938)
As Tears Go By (1988)
Asphalt Jungle, The (1950)
Auto Focus (2002)

Bad Boys (1983)
Bad Day at Black Rock (1954)
Bad Lieutenant (1992)
Bad Seed, The (1956)
Badlands (1974)
Basic Instinct (1992)
Beverly Hills Cop (1984; sequels in 1987, 1994)
Beyond a Reasonable Doubt (1956)
Bicycle Thief, The (1948)
Big Heat, The (1953)
Big House, The (1930)
Big Sleep, The (1946)

Big Sleep, The (1978)
Birdman of Alcatraz (1962)
Black Marble, The (1979)
Black Widow (1987)
Blond Bait (1956)
Blood In, Blood Out (1993) (also known as *Bound by Honor*)
Blood Simple (1984)
Blow (2001)
Blow Out (1981)
Blowup (1966)
Blue Steel (1990)
Blue Velvet (1986)
Bob le flambeur (1955)
Body Double (1984)
Body of Evidence (1992)
Body Heat (1981)
Bone Collector, The (1999)
Bonnie and Clyde (1967)
Boogie Nights (1997)
Boondock Saints (1999)
Born to Kill (1947)
Boston Strangler, The (1968)
Bound (1996)
Boyz N the Hood (1991)
Breaker Morant (1980)
Breathless (1960)
Brokedown Palace (1999)
Brother's Keeper (1992)
Brubaker (1980)
Brute Force (1947)
Bullitt (1968)
By Whose Hand (1913)

Cabinet of Dr. Caligari, The (1919)
Caged Heat (1974)
Caine Mutiny, The (1954)
Call Northside 777 (1948)

Cape Fear (1962)
Cape Fear (2002)
Capturing the Friedmans (2003)
Casablanca (1942)
Casino (1995)
Catch Me If You Can (2002)
Cento passi, I (2000)
Chamber, The (1996)
China Syndrome, The (1979)
Chinatown (1974)
Citizen Kane (1941)
Cleopatra Jones (1973)
Clockwork Orange, A (1971)
Coffy (1973)
Collateral (2004)
Colors (1988)
Compulsion (1959)
Confessions of a Dangerous Mind
    (2002)
Conformist, The (1970)
Conversation, The (1974)
Coogan's Bluff (1968)
Cool Hand Luke (1967)
Cop (1988)
Cop Land (1997)
Cops (1922)
Copycat (1995)
Criminal Code, The (1931)
Cruising (1980)
Cry Freedom (1987)

Dalmer (2002)
Dead Man Walking (1995)
Dead Pool, The (1988)
Death and the Maiden (1994)
Death Wish (1974)
Deep Cover (1992)
Defiant Ones, The (1958)
Deliverance (1972)
Desperate Hours, The (1955)
Detour (1945)
Devil in a Blue Dress (1995)
Dial M for Murder (1954)
Die Hard (1988; 2 sequels)
Dirty Harry (1971)
Do the Right Thing (1989)
Doberman Gang, The (1972)

Dog Day Afternoon (1975)
Dolores Claiborne (1995)
Donnie Brasco (1997)
Double Indemnity (1944)
Double Jeopardy (1999)
Dr. Mabuse (1922)
Dracula (1931)
Dressed to Kill (1980)

Each Dawn I Die (1939)
Enemy of the State (1998)
Enforcer, The (1976)
Escape from Alcatraz (1979)
Escort, The (1993)
Excellent Cadavers (1999)
Execution Protocol, The (1993)
Executioner's Song, The (1982)
Eye of God (1997)

Falling Down (1993)
Falsely Accused (1907)
Fargo (1996)
Fatal Attraction (1987)
Felicia's Journey (1999)
Femme Nikita, La (1990)
Few Good Men, A (1992)
Fight Club (1999)
Firm, The (1993)
Fourteen Days in May (1988)
Frankenstein (1931)
Freaks (1932)
French Connection, The (1971)
Frenzy (1972)
Fresh (1994)
Fury (1936)
Fuzz (1972)

"G" Men (1935)
Gacy (2003)
Ghost Dog (1999)
Ghosts of Mississippi (1996)
Giovani Falcone (1993)
Godfather, The (1972)
Godfather, The, Part II (1974)
Godfather, The, Part III (1990)
Goodfellas (1990)
Great Train Robbery, The (1903)

Green Mile, The (1999)
Grifters, The (1990)
Gun Crazy (1949)

Hand that Rocks the Cradle, The
  (1992)
Hannibal (2001)
Happiness (1998)
Hard Eight (1996)
Hard Way, The (1991)
Henry: Portrait of a Serial Killer
  (1986)
High Sierra (1941)
Hot Rock, The (1972)
House of Games (1987)

I Am a Fugitive from a Chain Gang
  (1932)
I Want to Live! (1958)
In Cold Blood (1967)
In the Cut (2003)
In the Light of the Moon (2000)
In the Name of the Father (1993)
Informer, The (1935)
Inherit the Wind (1960)
Innocent Man, An (1989)
Insomnia (1997)
Insomnia (2002)
Internal Affairs (1990)
Italian Job, The (1969)
Italian Job, The (2003)
Italian Job, The, II (forthcoming
  2006)

Jackie Brown (1997)
Jagged Edge, (1985)
Jennifer Eight (1992)
Judgment at Nuremberg (1961)
Juror, The (1996)

Kalifornia (1993)
Kill Bill: Volume I (2003)
Kill Bill: Volume II (2004)
Key Largo (1958)
Kids (1995)
Killer, The (Die xue shuang xiong)
  (1989)

Killers, The (1946)
Killers, The (1964)
Killing, The (1956)
Killing Zoe (1994)
Kiss, The (1929)
Kiss of Death (1947)
Kiss of Death (1995)
Kiss Me Deadly (1955)
Kiss the Girls (1997)
Kiss of the Spider Woman (1985)
Knock on Any Door (1949)

L.A. Confidential (1997)
Lady from Shanghai, The (1947)
Lady Vanishes, The (1938)
Ladykillers, The (1955)
Last Castle, The (2001)
Last Dance, The (1996)
Last Detail, The (1973)
Last Mile, The (1932)
Last Seduction, The (1994)
Let 'Em Have It (1935)
Let Him Have It (1991)
Lethal Weapon (1987; 3 sequels)
Letter, The (1940)
L.I.E. (2001)
Life of David Gale, The (2003)
Limey, The (1999)
Little Caesar (1931)
Lock Up (1989)
Lodger, The (1927)
Long Goodbye, The (1973)
Lost Highway (1997)
Lost Weekend, The (1945)
Lullaby, The (1924)

M (1931)
Madame X (1966)
Madigan (1968)
Magnolia (1999)
Magnum Force (1973)
Maltese Falcon, The (1941)
Man on Fire (2004)
Man with the Golden Arm, The (1955)
Manchurian Candidate, The (1962)
Manhattan Melodrama (1934)
Manhunter (1986)

Manslaughter (1922)
Map of the World, A (1999)
Marathon Man (1976)
María Full of Grace (2004)
Marked Woman (1937)
Mata Hari (1931)
Mean Streets (1973)
Memento (2001)
Menace II Society (1993)
Midnight Express (1978)
Midnight Flower (1923)
Mildred Pierce (1945)
Miller's Crossing (1990)
Minority Report (2002)
Missing (1982)
Monster (2003)
Monster's Ball (2001)
Mrs. Soffel (1984)
Mulholland Drive (2001)
Murder in the First (1995)
Murder, My Sweet (1944)
Musketeers of Pig Alley, The (1912)
Mystic River (2003)

Naked Gun (1988; 2 sequels)
Nancy Drew, Reporter (1939)
Natural Born Killers (1994)
Negotiator, The (1998)
New Jack City (1991)
Night and the City (1950)
Night Falls on Manhattan (1997)
Night of the Hunter (1955)
No Way Out (1987)
Norma Rae (1979)
Normal Life (1996)
North by Northwest (1959)
Nosferatu (1922)
Nuts (1987)

Ocean's Eleven (1960)
Ocean's Eleven (2001)
Ocean's Twelve (2004)
Odds Against Tomorrow (1959)
Of Mice and Men (1939)
Of Mice and Men (1992)
Offence, The (1973)
Official Story, The (1985)

On the Yard (1979)
Once Upon a Time in America (1984)
One Flew Over the Cuckoo's Nest
   (1975)
One Good Cop (1991)
Onion Field, The (1979)
Open Doors (1990)
Out of the Past (1947)
Ox-Bow Incident, The (1943)

Pacific Heights (1990)
Papillon (1973)
Paradine Case, The (1947)
Paradise Lost: The Child Murders at
   Robin Hood Hills (1996)
Paradise Lost 2: Revelations (2000)
Passenger, The (1975)
Peeping Tom (1960)
Physical Evidence (1989)
Place in the Sun, A (1951)
Player, The (1992)
Pledge, The (2001)
Point of No Return (1993)
Police Academy (1984; 6 sequels)
Postman Always Rings Twice, The
   (1946)
Postman Always Rings Twice, The
   (1981)
Presumed Innocent (1990)
Primal Fear (1996)
Prince of the City (1981)
Prizzi's Honor (1985)
Psycho (1960)
Public Enemy (1931)
Pulp Fiction (1994)

Q & A (1990)

Raging Bull (1980)
Rainmaker, The (1997)
Rashomon (1950)
Rear Window (1954)
Rebecca (1940)
Rebel Without a Cause (1955)
Red Dragon (2002)
Regeneration (1915)
Reservoir Dogs (1992)

Resurrection (1999)
Reversal of Fortune (1990)
Rififi (1955)
Riot (1969)
Riot in Cellblock 11 (1954)
River's Edge (1987)
RoboCop (1987)
Rock, The (1996)
Romeo Is Bleeding (1993)
Rope (1948)
Run Lola Run (1998)
Runaway Jury (2003)

Scarface (1932)
Scarface (1983)
Scarlet Street (1945)
Sea of Love (1989)
Sergeant Rutledge (1961)
Serpico (1973)
Set It Off (1996)
Seven (1995)
Shadow of a Doubt (1943)
Shaft (1971)
Shaft in Africa (1973)
Shaft's Big Score (1972)
Shawshank Redemption, The (1994)
Shining, The (1980)
Shock Corridor (1963)
Shoot to Kill (1988)
Short Eyes (1979)
Show Them No Mercy (1935)
Silence of the Lambs (1991)
Silkwood (1983)
Simple Plan, A (1998)
Single White Female (1992)
Slammer Girls (1987)
Sleepers (1996)
Sling Blade (1996)
South Central (1992)
Spellbound (1946)
Spy Who Came in from the Cold, The (1965)
Stakeout (1987)
Star Chamber, The (1983)
State of Grace (1990)
Sting, The (1973)
Stolen Children, The (1992)

Story of Women, The (1988)
Straight Time (1978)
Stranger on the Third Floor (1940)
Strangers on a Train (1951)
Straw Dogs (1972)
Studio 54 (1998)
Sudden Fear (1952)
Sudden Impact (1983)
Summer of Sam (1999)
Sunrise (1927)
Sunset Boulevard (1950)
Suspect (1987)
Swoon (1991)

Talented Mr. Ripley, The (1999)
Taxi Driver (1976)
Ted Bundy (2002)
Ten to Midnight (1983)
Thelma and Louise (1991)
They Live By Night (1949)
They Made Me a Criminal (1939)
They Won't Believe Me (1947)
Thin Blue Line, The (1988)
Thin Man, The (1934; 5 sequels)
Thomas Crown Affair, The (1968)
Thomas Crown Affair, The (1999)
Through the Wire (1990)
Tightrope (1984)
Time to Kill, A (1996)
Titicut Follies (1967)
To Die For (1995)
To Kill a Mockingbird (1962)
To Live and Die in L.A. (1985)
Touch of Evil (1958)
Traffic (2000)
Trainspotting (1996)
Treasure of the Sierra Madre (1948)
Trial, The (1963)
Trial by Jury (1994)
Trial of Mary Dugan, The (1929)
True Believer (1989)
True Romance (1993)
Twelve Angry Men (1957)

Underworld (1927)
Unholy Three, The (1925)
Unknown, The (1927)

Untouchables, The (1987)
Unlawful Entry (1992)
Usual Suspects, The (1995)

Vanishing, The (1988)
Vanishing, The (1993)
Vertigo (1958)
Virgin Suicides, The (1999)

Weeds (1987)
Whipping Boss, The (1922)
Whispering Chorus, The (1918)
White Heat (1949)

Wild Bunch, The (1969)
Wild at Heart (1990)
Witness (1985)
Witness for the Prosecution (1957)
Woman's Resurrection, A (1915)
Woodsman, The (2004)
Wrong Man, The (1956)

You Can't Get Away with It (1936)
Young Mr. Lincoln (1939)
Young Philadelphians, The (1959)

Zabriskie Point (1970)

References

American Psychiatric Association. 2000. *Diagnostic and Statistical Manual for Mental Disorders*. 4th ed. Arlington, Va.: The Association.

Ames, Christopher. 1992. Restoring the Black Man's Lethal Weapon: Race and Sexuality in Contemporary Cop Films. *Journal of Popular Film and Television* 20(3): 52–61.

Anderson, Jeffrey M. 2003. A "Cut" above the Rest. *San Francisco Examiner*, 31 October. http://www.sfexaminer.com/article/index.cfm/i/103103a_inthecut.

Ansen, David. 1994. Raw Carnage or Revelation? (Review of *Natural Born Killers*.) *Newsweek*, 29 August: 54.

Archer, Margaret S. 2003. *Structure, Agency and the Internal Conversation*. Cambridge: Cambridge University Press.

Asimow, Michael. 1996. When Lawyers Were Heroes. *University of San Francisco Law Review* 30 (4):1131–38.

———. 2005. Popular Culture and the American Adversarial Ideology. In *Law and Popular Culture*, ed. Michael Freeman, 606–37. Oxford: Oxford University Press.

Asimow, Michael, and Shannon Mader. 2004. *Law and Popular Culture*. New York: Peter Lang.

Bailey, Frankie Y., and Donna Hale, eds. 1998. *Popular Culture, Crime, and Justice*. Belmont, Calif.: West/Wadsworth.

Bailey, Frankie Y., Joycelyn M. Pollock, and Sherry Schroeder. 1998. The Best Defense: Images of Female Attorneys in Popular Films. In *Popular Culture, Crime, and Justice*, ed. Frankie Bailey and Donna Hale, 180–95. Belmont, Calif.: West/Wadsworth.

Banks, Gordon. 1990. Kubrick's Psychopaths: Society and Human Nature in the Films of Stanley Kubrick. http://www.gordonbanks.com/gordon/pubs/kubricks.html (accessed Nov. 15, 2003).

Barnes, Harry Elmer, and Negley K. Teeters. 1944. *New Horizons in Criminology*. New York: Prentice-Hall.

Berets, Ralph. 1996. Changing Images of Justice in American Films. *Legal Studies Forum* 20: 473–80.

Bergman, Paul, and Michael Asimow. 1996. *Reel Justice: The Courtroom Goes to the Movies*. Kansas City, Mo.: Andrews and McMeel.

Black, David A. 1999. *Law in Film: Resonance and Representation*. Urbana: University of Illinois Press.

Bogdanovich, Peter. 1967. *Fritz Lang in America*. New York: Praeger.

Bordwell, David, and Kristin Thompson. 1997. *Film Art: An Introduction*. 5th ed. New York: McGraw-Hill.

Brown, Jeffrey A. 1993. Bullets, Buddies, and Bad Guys: The "Action-Cop" Genre. *Journal of Popular Film and Television* Summer vol. 21(2): 79–87; http://www .findarticles.com (accessed April 11, 2001).

Brown, Michelle. 2003. Penological Crisis in America: Finding Meaning in Imprisonment Post-Rehabilitation. Ph.D diss., Indiana University, Dept. of Criminal Justice and American Studies Program.

Callero, Peter L. 1994. From Role-Playing to Role-Using: Understanding Role as Resource. *Social Psychology Quarterly* 57 (3): 228–43.

Campbell, Russell. Forthcoming 2005. *Marked Women: Prostitutes and Prostitution in the Cinema.* Madison: University of Wisconsin Press.

Canby, Vincent. 1983. Al Pacino Stars in *Scarface. New York Times,* 9 December: C18.

Canfield, Rob. 1994. Orale, Joaquin: Arresting the Dissemination of Violence in *American Me. Journal of Popular Film and Television* 22 (2): 60–69.

Carey, Benedict. 2005. For the Worst of Us, the Diagnosis May Be "Evil." *The New York Times,* 8 Feb.: D1.

Cawelti, John G. 1992. (1979). *Chinatown* and Generic Transformation in Recent American Films. In *Film Theory and Criticism,* 4th ed., ed. Gerald Mast, Marshall Cohen, and Leo Braudy, 498–511. New York: Oxford University Press.

Chandler, Raymond. 1992 (1940). *Farewell, My Lovely.* New York: Vintage Books.

Chase, Anthony. 1986. Lawyers and Popular Culture: A Review of Mass Media Portrayals of American Attorneys. *American Bar Foundation Research Journal* 2: 281–300.

———. 2002. *Movies on Trial: The Legal System on the Silver Screen.* New York: The New Press.

Cheatwood, Derral. 1998. Prison Movies: Films about Adult, Male, Civilian Prisons: 1929–1995. In *Popular Culture, Crime, and Justice,* ed. Frankie Bailey and Donna Hale, 209–231. Belmont, Calif.: West/Wadsworth.

Clarens, Carlos. 1980. *Crime Movies: From Griffith to* The Godfather *and Beyond.* New York: W. W. Norton.

———. 1997. *Crime Movies: An Illustrated History of the Gangster Genre from D. W. Griffith to* Pulp Fiction. New York: Da Capo Press.

Clover, Carol J. 1992. *Men, Women, and Chainsaws.* Princeton: Princeton University Press.

———. 2000. Judging Audiences: The Case of the Movie Trial. In *Reinventing Film Studies,* ed. Christine Gedhill and Linda Williams, 244–64. New York: Oxford University Press.

Costello, Mark. 2004. Review of *Public Enemies: America's Greatest Crime Wave and the Birth of the FBI, 1933–34.New York Times Book Review* (August 1): 5.

Denvir, John, ed. 1996. *Legal Reelism: Movies as Legal Texts.* Urbana: University of Illinois Press.

DiMaggio, Paul. 1997. Culture and Cognition. *Annual Review of Sociology* 23: 263–87.

Doane, Mary Ann. 1991. *Femmes Fatales.* New York: Routledge.

Douglas, Susan J. 1999. The Devil Made Me Do It. *The Nation* 268 (13) (April 5): 50. Available from infotrac (Article A54403101) (accessed Dec. 19, 2003).

Douglass, Wayne J. 1981. The Criminal Psychopath as Hollywood Hero. *Journal of Popular Film and Television* 8 (4): 30–39.

Dow, David R. 2000. Fictional Documentaries and Truthful Fictions: The Death Penalty in Recent American Film. *Constitutional Commentary* 17: 511–53.

Doyle, Aaron. 2003. *Arresting Images: Crime and Policing in Front of the Television Camera*. Toronto: University of Toronto Press.

Du Bois, W. E. B. 1997 (1903). The Souls of Black Folk. As excerpted and reprinted in *Race, Class, and Gender in a Diverse Society*, ed. Diana Kendall, 48–53. Boston: Allyn and Bacon.

Dyer, Richard. 1997. *White*. New York: Routledge.

———. 2002. *The Matter of Images: Essays on Representation*, 2d ed. New York: Routledge.

Ellis, Jack C. 1979. *A History of Film*. Englewood Cliffs, N.J.: Prentice-Hall.

Evans, Richard J. 1996. *Rituals of Retribution: Capital Punishment in Germany, 1600–1987*. London: Penguin Books.

Everett, Anna. 1995–96. The Other Pleasures: The Narrative Function of Race in the Cinema. *Film Criticism* 1/2 (Fall/Winter): 26–38.

Fanon, Frantz. 1968. *The Wretched of the Earth*. New York: Grove Press.

Ferrell, Jeff, Keith Hayward, Wayne Morrison, and Mike Presdee, eds. 2004. *Cultural Criminology Unleashed*. London: Greenhouse Press.

Ferrell, Jeff, and C. R. Sanders, eds. 1995. *Cultural Criminology*. Boston: Northeastern University Press.

Freeman, Michael, ed. 2005a. *Law and Popular Culture*. Oxford: Oxford University Press.

———. 2005b. Law in Popular Culture. In *Law and Popular Culture*, ed. Michael Freeman, 1–18. Oxford: Oxford University Press.

Fuchs, Christian. 2002. *Bad Blood: An Illustrated Guide to Psycho Cinema*. New York: Creation Books.

Fuchs, Cynthia J. 1993. The Buddy Politic. In *Screening the Male*, ed. Steven Cohan and Ina Rae Hark, 194–210. New York: Routledge.

Gamson, William A., David Croteau, William Hoynes, and Theodore Sasson. 1992. Media Images and the Social Construction of Reality. *Annual Review of Sociology* 18: 373–93.

George, Nelson. 1994. *Blackface: Reflections on African-Americans and the Movies*. New York: Harper Perennial.

Gettleman, Jeffrey. 2002. When Just One Gun Is Enough. *New York Times*, 27 October: WK 3.

Gitlin, Todd. 1980. *The Whole World Is Watching: Mass Media in the Making and Unmaking of the New Left*. Berkeley: University of California Press.

Goldstein, Jeffrey H. ed. 1998. *Why We Watch: The Attraction of Violent Entertainment*. New York: Oxford University Press.

Gomery, Douglas. 1991. *Movie History: A Survey*. Belmont, Calif.: Wadsworth.

Greenfield, Steve, and Guy Osborn. 1999. Film, Law and the Delivery of Justice: The Case of *Judge Dredd* and the Disappearing Courtroom. *Journal of Criminal Justice and Popular Culture* 6 (2): 35–45.

Greenfield, Steve, Guy Osborn, and Peter Robson. 2001a. *Film and the Law*. London: Cavendish.

———. 2001b. Private Eyes and the Public Interest. In *Film and the Law*, ed. Steve Greenfield, Guy Osborn, and Peter Robson, 169–88. London: Cavendish.

Gussow, Mel. 1997. "Movie Fan Who Also Makes Them," *New York Times*, 8 March: NE 19.

Gutterman, Melvin. 2002. "Failure to Communicate": The Reel Prison Experience. *Southern Methodist University Law Review* 55: 1515–60.

Hale, Donna C. 1998. Keeping Women in Their Place: An Analysis of Policewomen in Videos, 1972–1996. In *Popular Culture, Crime, and Justice*, ed. Frankie Bailey and Donna Hale, 159–79. Belmont, Calif.: West/Wadsworth.

Hammett, Dashiell. 1972 (1929). *Red Harvest*. New York: Vintage Books.

Hannsberry, Karen Burroughs. 1998. *Femme Noir: The Bad Girls of Film*. Jefferson, N.C.: McFarland.

Harding, Roberta M. 2005. Reel Violence: Popular Culture and Concerns about Capital Punishment in Contemporary American Society. In *Law and Popular Culture*, ed. Michael Freeman, 358–74. Oxford: Oxford University Press.

Hardy, Phil, ed. 1997. *The BFI Companion to Crime*. Berkeley: University of California Press.

Hare, Robert D. 1993. *Without Conscience*. New York: Guilford Press.

———. 1994. Predators: The Disturbing World of the Psychopaths among Us. *Psychology Today* 27 (1): 54–62. http://web7.infortrac.galegroup.com (accessed October 29, 2002).

Hare, Robert D., Stephen D. Hart, and Timothy J. Harpur. 1991. Psychopathy and the *DSM-IV* Criteria for Antisocial Personality Disorder. *Journal of Abnormal Psychology* 100 (3): 391–98.

Hayward, Keith J., and Jock Young. 2004. Cultural Criminology: Some Notes on the Script. *Theoretical Criminology* 8 (3): 259–73.

Herman, Didi. 2003. "*Bad Girls* Changed My Life": Homonormativity in a Women's Prison Drama. *Critical Studies in Media Communication* 20 (2): 141–59.

———. 2005. "Juliet and Juliet Would Be More My Cup of Tea": Sexuality, Law, and Popular Culture. In *Law and Popular Culture*, ed. Michael Freeman, 470–88. Oxford: Oxford University Press.

hooks, bell. 1996. reel to real: race, sex, and class at the movies. New York: Routledge.

Jenkins, Philip. 1994. *Using Murder: The Social Construction of Serial Homicide*. New York: Aldine de Gruyter.

Kael, Pauline. 1991. *5001 Nights at the Movies*. New York: Henry Holt.

Kaplan, E. Ann. 1983. *Women and Film: Both Sides of the Camera*. New York: Methuen.

———, ed., 1998. *Women in Film Noir*. London: British Film Institute.

King, Neal. 1999. *Heroes in Hard Times: Cop Action Movies in the U.S.* Philadelphia: Temple University Press.

Koltnow, Barry. 1997. Brosnan's Rebirth: Equal Parts Bond and Belief. *New York Times*, 7 February: D8.

Kooistra, Paul. 1989. *Criminals as Heroes: Structure, Power, and Identity*. Bowling Green, Ohio: Bowling Green State University Popular Press.

Krutnik, Frank. 1991. *In a Lonely Street: Film Noir, Genre, Masculinity*. New York: Routledge.

Lane, Anthony. 1997. Untrue Blue. *New Yorker*, 18 August: 77–78.

Lawrence, Amy. 1999. "American Shame: *Rope,* James Stewart, and the Postwar Crisis in American Masculinity." In *Hitchcock's America,* ed. by Jonathan Freedman and Richard Millington. New York: Oxford University Press.

Lawrence, Jeanette A., and Jaan Valsiner. 2003. Making Personal Sense: An Account of Basic Internalization and Externalization Processes. *Theory and Psychology* 13 (6): 723–52.

Leitch, Thomas. 2002. *Crime Films: Genres in American Cinema.* Cambridge: Cambridge University Press.

Lewine, Edward. 1997. The Laureate of Police Corruption. *New York Times,* 8 June: CY4, 15.

Lombroso, Cesare. 2006 (forthcoming). *Criminal Man,* translated and with a new introduction by Mary Gibson and Nicole Hahn Rafter. Durham, N.C.: Duke University Press.

Lombroso, Cesare, and Guglielmo Ferrero. 2004. *Criminal Woman, the Prostitute, and the Normal Woman,* translated and with a new introduction by Nicole Hahn Rafter and Mary Gibson. Durham, N.C.: Duke University Press.

Lumet, Sidney. 1995. *Making Movies.* New York: Vintage/Random House.

Lyng, Stephen. 2004. Crime, Edgework and Corporeal Transaction. *Theoretical Criminology* 8 (3): 359–75.

Machura, Stefan, and Peter Robson, eds. 2001. *Law and Film.* Oxford, Eng.: Blackwell.

Maltby, Richard. 1995. *Hollywood Cinema.* Cambridge, Mass.: Blackwell.

Mason, Fran. 2003. *American Gangster Cinema: From* Little Caesar *to* Pulp Fiction. New York: Palgrave Macmillan.

Maxfield, James F. 1996. *The Fatal Woman: Sources of Male Anxiety in American Film Noir, 1941–1991.* Madison, N.J.: Farleigh Dickinson University Press.

McCabe, John. 1997. *Cagney.* New York: Knopf.

McCarty, John. 1993a. *Hollywood Gangland: The Movies' Love Affair with the Mob.* New York: St. Martin's Press.

———. 1993b. *Movie Psychos and Madmen: Film Psychopaths from Jekyll and Hyde to Hannibal Lecter.* New York: Citadel Press.

———. 2004. *Bullets over Hollywood: The American Gangster Picture from the Silents to* The Sopranos. Cambridge, Mass.: Da Capo Press.

McKenna, Andrew J. 1996. Public Execution. In *Legal Reelism: Movies as Legal Texts,* ed. John Denvir, 225–43. Urbana: University of Illinois Press.

Merton, Robert K. 1938. Social Structure and Anomie. *American Sociological Review* 3 (October): 672–82.

Miller, Carolyn Lisa. 1994. "What a Waste. Beautiful, Sexy Gal. Hell of a Lawyer": Film and the Female Attorney. *Columbia Journal of Gender and Law* 4: 203–32.

Mitchell, Edward. 1995. Apes and Essences: Some Sources of Significance in the American Gangster Film. In *Film Genre Reader 11,* ed. Barry Keith Grant, 203–12. Austin: University of Texas Press.

Morey, Anne. 1995. The Judge Called Me an Accessory. *Journal of Popular Film and Television* 23 (2): 80–88.

Morgan, David L., and Michael L. Schwalbe. 1990. Mind and Self in Society: Linking Social Structure and Social Cognition. *Social Psychology Quarterly* 53 (2): 148–64.

Munby, Jonathan. 1999. *Public Enemies, Public Heroes: Screening the Gangster from Little Caesar to Touch of Evil*. Chicago: University of Chicago Press.

Naremore, James. 1995–96. American Film Noir: The History of an Idea. *Film Quarterly* 49 (2): 12–25.

———. 1998. *More Than Night: Film Noir in its Contexts*. Berkeley: Universitiy of California Press.

Nathan, Debbie. 2000. Complex Persecution: A Long Island Family's Nightmare Struggle with Porn, Pedophilia, and Public Hysteria. *Village Voice*, Dec. 26. http://www.villagevoice.com/news/0321,nathan,44338,1.html.; accessed Feb. 22, 2005.

Neale, Steve. 1993. Masculinity as Spectacle: Reflections on Men and Mainstream Cinema. In *Screening the Male*, ed. Steven Cohan and Ina Rae Hark, 9–20. New York: Routledge.

Newman, Graeme. 1998. Popular Culture and Violence: Decoding the Violence of Popular Movies. In *Popular Culture, Crime, and Justice*, ed. Frankie Bailey and Donna Hale, 40–56. Belmont, Calif.: West/Wadsworth.

Osborn, Guy. 2001. Borders and Boundaries: Locating the Law in Film. In *Law and Film*, ed. Stefan Machura and Peter Robson, 164–76. Oxford, Eng.: Blackwell.

Packer, Herbert L. 1968. *The Limits of the Criminal Sanction*. Stanford, Calif.: Stanford University Press.

Parish, James Robert. 1991. *Prison Pictures from Hollywood*. Jefferson, N.C.: McFarland.

Parshall, Peter. 1991. *Die Hard* and the American Mythos. *Journal of Popular Film and Television* 18: 135–44.

Picart, Caroline Joan, and Cecil Greek. 2003. The Compulsion of Real/Reel Serial Killers and Vampires: Toward a Gothic Criminology. *Journal of Criminal Justice and Popular Culture* 10 (1): 39–68.

Polkinghorne, Donald E. 1988. *Narrative Knowing and the Human Sciences*. Albany: State University of New York Press.

Post, Robert C. 1987. On the Popular Image of the Lawyer: Reflections in a Dark Glass. *California Law Review* 75: 379–89.

Presdee, Mike. 2000. *Cultural Criminology and the Carnival of Crime*. London: Routledge.

President's Commission on Law Enforcement and Administration of Justice. 1967. *The Challenge of Crime in a Free Society*. Washington, D.C.: U.S. Government Printing Office.

Press, Joy. 2003. Making the Cut: Jame Campion's Feminist Film Noir Stirs up Pheromones and Occult Mystery in a Malevolent East Village. http://www.villagevoice.com/news/0343,press,48035,1.html (accessed Jan. 15, 2005).

Prince, Stephen. 1998. *Savage Cinema: Sam Peckinpah and the Rise of Ultraviolent Movies*. Austin: University of Texas Press.

Quart, Leonard, and Albert Auster. 1991. *American Film and Society since 1945*. 2d ed., rev. and expanded by L. Quart. Westport, Conn.: Praeger.

Querry, Ronald B. 1973. Prison Movies: An Annotated Filmography 1921–Present. *Journal of Popular Film* 2 (2): 181–97.

Rafter, Nicole. 2005. Badfellas. In *Law and Popular Culture*, ed. Michael Freeman. 339–57. Oxford: Oxford University Press.

Rapping, Elayne. 2003. *Law and Justice as Seen on TV*. New York: New York University Press.

Ray, Robert B. 1985. *A Certain Tendency of the Hollywood Cinema, 1930–1980*. Princeton: Princeton University Press.

Reid, Mark A. 1995. The Black Gangster Film. In *Film Genre Reader 11*, ed. Barry Keith Grant, 456–73. Austin: University of Texas Press.

Robson, Peter. 2005. Law and Film Studies: Autonomy and Theory. In *Law and Popular Culture*, ed. Michael Freeman, 21–46. Oxford: Oxford University Press.

Roffman, Peter, and Jim Purdy. 1981. *The Hollywood Social Problem Film: Madness, Despair, and Politics from the Depression to the Fifties*. Bloomington: Indiana University Press.

Rosenberg, Norman. 1996. Law Noir. In *Legal Reelism: Movies as Legal Texts*, ed. John Denvir, 280–302. Urbana: University of Illinois Press.

Russo, Vito. 1987. *The Celluloid Closet*. Rev. ed. New York: Harper and Row.

Ruth, David E. 1996. *Inventing the Public Enemy: The Gangster in American Culture, 1918–1934*. Chicago: University of Chicago Press.

Sandell, Jillian. 1996. Reinventing Masculinity: The Spectacle of Male Intimacy in the Films of John Woo. *Film Quarterly* 49 (4): 23–34.

Sasson, Theodore. 1995. *Crime Talk: How Citizens Construct a Social Problem*. New York: Aldine de Gruyter.

Schatz, Thomas. 1981. *Hollywood Genres*. New York: McGraw-Hill.

Schickel, Richard. 1996. *Clint Eastwood: A Biography*. New York: Vintage Books.

Selby, Spencer. 1984. *Dark City: The Film Noir*. Jefferson, N.C.: McFarland.

Shadoian, Jack. 1977. *Dreams and Deadends: The American Gangster/Crime Film*. Cambridge: MIT Press.

Shaw, Clifford. 1929. *Delinquency Areas*. Chicago: University of Chicago Press.

Shaw, Clifford, and H. D. McKay. 1931. *Social Factors in Juvenile Delinquency*. Washington, D.C.: U.S. Government Printing Office.

Siegel, Don. 1993. *A Siegel Film: An Autobiography*. Boston: Faber and Faber.

Silbey, Jessica. 2001. Patterns of Courtroom Justice. In *Law and Film*, ed. Stefan Machura and Peter Robson, 97–116. Oxford, Eng.: Blackwell.

Silbey, Susan S. 1998. Ideology, Power, and Justice. In *Justice and Power in Socio-legal Studies*, ed. Bryant G. Garth and Austin Sarat, 272–308. Evanston, Ill.: Northwestern University Press.

Simpson, Philip L. 2000 *Psycho Paths: Tracking the Serial Killer through Contemporary American Film and Fiction*. Carbondale: Southern Illinois University Press.

Spelman, Elizabeth V., and Martha Minow. 1992. Outlaw Women: An Essay on *Thelma and Louise. New England Law Review* 26: 1281–96.

Straubaar, Joseph, and Robert LaRose. 1996. *Communications Media in the Information Society*. Belmont, Calif.: Wadsworth.

Sumser, John. 1996. *Morality and Social Order in Television Crime Drama*. Jefferson, N.C.: McFarland.

Surette, Ray. 1995. Predator Criminals as Media Icons. In *Media, Process, and the Social Construction of Crime: Studies in Newsmaking Criminology*, ed. Gregg Barak, 131–58. New York: Garland.

———. 1998. *Media, Crime, and Criminal Justice*. Belmont, Calif.: Wadsworth.

Swidler, Ann. 1986. Culture in Action: Symbols and Strategies. *American Sociological Review* 51: 273–86.

Swidler, Ann, and Jorge Arditi. 1994. The New Sociology of Knowledge. *Annual Review of Sociology* 20: 305–29.

Sykes, Gresham M. 1958. *The Society of Captives*. Princeton: Princeton University Press.

Tatar, Maria. 1995. *Lustmord: Sexual Murder in Weimar Germany*. Princeton: Princeton University Press.

———. 1998. "Violent Delights" in Children's Literature. In *Why We Watch: The Attractions of Violent Entertainment*, ed. Jeffrey Goldstein, 69–87. New York: Oxford University Press.

Telotte, J. P. 1989. *Voices in the Dark: The Narrative Patterns of Film Noir*. Urbana: University of Illinois Press.

Thain, Gerald J. 2001. *Cape Fear*—Two Versions and Two Visions Separated by Thirty Years. In *Law and Film*, ed. Stephan Machura and Peter Robson, 40–46. Oxford: Oxford University Press.

Tiso, Giovanni. n.d. The Spectacle of Surveillance: Images of the Panopticon in Science-Fiction Cinema. www.homepages.paradise.net.nz/gtiso/filmessay (accessed Oct. 14, 2004).

Todd, Drew. 2005. Decadent Heroes: Dandyism and Masculinity in Art Deco Hollywood. *Journal of Popular Film and Television* 32 (4): 168–81.

Turner, Graeme. 1993. *Film as Social Practice*. 2d ed. New York: Routledge.

Tzanelli, Rodanthi, Majid Yar, and Martin O'Brien. 2005. Exploring Crime in the American Cinematic Imagination. *Theoretical Criminology* 9 (1): 97–117.

Warshow, Robert. 1974a. The Gangster as Tragic Hero. In Robert Warshow, *The Immediate Experience*, 127–33. Garden City, N.Y.: Doubleday.

———. 1974b. Movie Chronicle: The Westerner. In Robert Warshow, *The Immediate Experience*, 135–54. Garden City, N.Y.: Doubleday.

Welch, Michael, Melissa Fenwick, and Meredith Roberts. 1998. State Managers, Intellectuals, and the Media. *Justice Quarterly* 15 (2): 219–41.

Williams, Linda. 1993. Mirrors without Memories: Truth, History, and the New Documentary. *Film Quarterly* 46 (3): 9–21.

Willis, Sharon. 1993. Hardware and Hardbodies, What Do Women Want?: A Reading of *Thelma and Louise*. In *Film Theory Goes to the Movies*, ed. Jim Collins, Hilary Radner, and Ava Preacher Collins, 120–28. New York: Routledge.

———. 1997. *High Contrast: Race and Gender in Contemporary Hollywood Films*. Durham, N.C.: Duke University Press.

Wilson, Wayne. 1999. *The Psychopath in Film*. Lanham, N.Y.: University Press of America.

Wood, Robin. 1986. From Buddies to Lovers. In Robin Wood, *Hollywood from Vietnam to Reagan . . . and Beyond*, 222–44. New York: Columbia University Press.

————. 1989. "The Murderous Gays: Hitchcock's Homophobia." In *Hitchcock's Films Revisited*. New York: Columbia University Press.

————. 1992. Ideology, Genre, Auteur. In *Film Theory and Criticism: Introductory Readings*, 4th ed., ed. Gerald Mast, Marshall Cohen, and Leo Braudy, 475–85. New York: Oxford University Press.

Wright, Will. 1975. *Six Guns and Society*. Berkeley: University of California Press.

Index